OFFICE
POLITICS

by

Wilfrid Sheed

A Middle-Class Education

The Hack

Square's Progress

Office Politics

OFFICE POLITICS

A NOVEL BY

Wilfrid Sheed

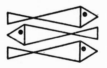

FARRAR, STRAUS AND GIROUX

NEW YORK

OFFICE
POLITICS

I

1

Behind the moldy green filing cabinets was a door marked
FIRE EXIT, with a red light over it. Nobody ever went out
that way, it would have been quite pointless.

George Wren peeped behind the cabinets, it was just a
thought, and froze. Gilbert Twining was standing under
the red light, incredibly, glancing at a book.

"Leaving, George?"

"Well, yes."

"How about a quick drink downstairs?"

"All right."

George couldn't think of any excuse for being behind the
files, there was nothing but hot dust back there, so he
walked to the fire door like a man in a dream and heaved it
open.

"You weren't really going out that way, were you?" asked Twining with that mild amusement of his.

"I was curious," said George. He gazed at the stone staircase. Twining had the damnedest effect on him. He felt like a schoolboy.

"Satisfied?" said Twining.

"I guess so. I hadn't been back here."

They headed toward the elevator. It was typical of the way things went around here that George could not begin to define this episode or say whether it meant anything; it was just one of those vague things that happened.

A few weeks ago, George Wren had been flattered when Mr. Twining asked him to come down for a drink. Tonight he supposed he had actually been contemplating escape (there was of course no question of just saying no). It was 4:55 and they wouldn't be out of the bar till seven at the earliest. Twice they had stayed until four the next morning. For a number of reasons, you couldn't leave until Twining gave the order.

"Let's sit in a booth, shall we?" said Twining, as they entered Sweeney's a couple of minutes later.

"Wife expecting guests."

"Yes of course, of course, we'll get you home." Empty, Englishman's gusto. George braced himself hopelessly against the red leather seat. Double martinis, oh my; put them on our bill, Harry. The bill would look like a supermarket tab by then. We'll get you home, oh sure. In an ambulance.

As they waited demurely for the first drink, George wondered which of Twining's two obsessions he was in for tonight. During the day Twining was a man of fairly wide interests; but over the martinis he tended to narrow sharply.

"I feel like a perfect fool, at my age," said Twining.

4

"Last Sunday I had a perfect opportunity, and I found my nerve had utterly deserted me. The poise of a schoolboy, you know. It usen't to be *quite* as bad as that."

"What happened on Sunday, then?"

It was a three-paragraph question, and George didn't really want any part of the answer. They had begun with the wrong obsession. Still, Twining's diction was a treat, you might learn something from that. At the end of each paragraph, George felt he should respond with a slight gesture, a nod or a click of the tongue, that was how they did it at the Racquet Club. He nibbled at his drink . . . "practically an open invitation," "mmm."

Smoothies at one end of the bar, drunks at the other under the television set. Class system a matter of instinct, we'll never get rid of it . . . that was the kind of thing George liked to talk about while he was drinking. But Twining had less panoramic notions. "She got fed up and went home." "Tchk." Shrug. Way of the world.

"I'm blessed if I know what to do next," said Twining.

"It's hard to say," said George.

"It seems quite clear at this point. I mean, either one does or one doesn't, but when the time comes . . ."

There were so many things he'd like to talk about with Twining. Anything but this, this conversation stank up the whole day. Retroactively. At times like this he felt that working for this man was one of the dreariest, most complicated things he had ever agreed to.

Looking at him across a barroom table, you would say that Gilbert Twining was the kind of Englishman who ought to be out posing for argyle socks or best paisley cardigans. He was terribly brown and weathered—campaigned under Kitchener, vice-consul in Rangoon, knocked about a bit. Settled down to "head up" (as you chaps call it) his own advertising agency now, or something amusing in the import-export line. He seemed to be absolutely invulnerable: light on his feet (this seemed important), self-possessed, absolutely effortless.

George had been in speechless awe for the first few days. Just the way Twining wore his clothes was enough for him. "Wren, come here a jiffy." Name of your tailor, barber, brown shoes, you say? Very well, brown shoes. George's mind floated further out. I don't care what you say—your British fighting man is the finest . . . What was Twining, anyway, forty-eight, fifty-three, had to be an odd year. Seasoned to perfection, ruggedly understanding face—might be only thirty-nine. ("You say it wasn't always like that?" asked George. O God, shut up, will you? . . . my good man?)

The first time Twining had asked George down for a drink, he had done it just right—masterfully attentive, understandingly amused when George began to slur a little: "Here, we'll pop you into a taxi; and charge it to expenses," a superb technician, to George's uncertain eye.

The second time was almost, but not quite, as good. George rationed himself to two martinis, and noticed that Twining got a little florid and stagy towards the end, a little more "old boy" than seemed necessary—but still, frightfully good. He wanted George to have that third drink, even to the point of pressing his elbow (he wasn't otherwise a toucher), and later he wanted quite desperately to pop George into that taxi again. He seemed to need to make his dominance official in these small ways. George was amused at that point, and not worried at all.

It wasn't till the third time that George received the understanding that these were to be regular meetings and that they were to follow a plan. Twining had lots of other associates, and certainly didn't need a drinking companion.

6

George bleakly took up the other question: no, Twining didn't seem to have sexual designs on him. His charm was too wintery and remote to lead anywhere but round and round itself.

George gave up and braced himself for a sequence of inscrutable, curiously dull, evenings. Then halfway through their fourth outing, Twining changed his tune and began talking the way he was talking tonight. The change had been startling, like a face changing in front of you, from young to old, well to ill. No doubt Twining had thought he was leading up to it carefully. By some private protocol, he had passed in midsentence from distance to closeness; closer than anything George had ever experienced, in Paterson, N.J., Ann Arbor, Michigan, or New York City, his principal settings up to now.

George was embarrassed because he didn't know how to conduct himself in this kind of conversation. Was he expected to confide back? Twining by the most graceful touches reminded him that he was still an employee with certain duties; but then, with exquisite tact, left the duties unspecified. George felt permanently harassed. He simply could not accept the possibility that Twining was the kind of man these discussions revealed. You couldn't get that face from living that kind of life. The distinction and self-possession could not be faked right into the cheekbones. It was either some grotesque modesty on Twining's part that made him abase himself—in itself a queer thought, but one you could just about live with—or it was an English put-on.

Now, if they'd started with Twining's *other* obsession tonight—that one at least had entertainment value. Of course it was nutty, so nutty that for a moment George had questioned its author's sanity, but you couldn't say that it wasn't interesting. It was worthy of Twining's regency style.

But the other theme, tonight's theme, was just hopeless

and humiliating. In brief: Twining had taken to looking out for some girl in the park, every Sunday, in an innocent way of course. ("I'm afraid it has been rather a habit of mine for some years") And now, to his dismay, the girl had shown signs of returning his interest. And Twining was in a terrible dither about it—married, you know, all quite desperate, and yet . . .

What could you possibly tell a man like that? George could find no point of contact with his own quite reasonable marriage, his own unneurotic Sundays . . .

The thing that made Twining's problems so desolate was that he didn't crack up and whine about them, didn't seem to feel that he was giving anything important away. He discussed his infantile behavior in a cool, man-of-the-world voice, and his manner lost none of its Foreign Office distinction. He might have been discussing the extraordinary difficulty of getting the natives to wear trousers to church.

"The best thing about this girl is her smashing appearance, and so the best thing one can do with her is simply to look at her. Yet there is an element of challenge, don't you think?" The reminiscences would become more specific. George would have to phone his wife. They weren't really expecting guests; but in any case there was no question of leaving.

Twining would keep him there until they were both a bit high, and George would be having to remind himself not to join in, not to exchange weaknesses and failures. Twining made it seem such a civilized, obvious thing to do. "Harry, I think we're about ready for another, aren't we?"

Two more double martinis—this would end with being popped into another cab. Oh, what the hell. Twining was worth studying, worth collecting. It was like talking about girls with Winston Churchill. (Make a note. Poem about a statue of Apollo, the plaster cracking and a funny old man peering out.) George picked up his glass, and sighted down the spiraling lemon peel. By the middle of this drink he would have entered Twining's world and it would all seem quite normal. Real life would not return until he got home and found a note in the bathroom in his wife's neat all-American handwriting, telling him to feed the baby or put out the cat. "And that's how it is, old boy."

The lemon peel formed an optical illusion, like a bed-spring. George studied it with care. The funny thing was, he admired the silly bastard, and wanted to keep it that way. At the moment, Twining wasn't making it any too easy for him. But George still dreamed that they would some day work through this undergrowth to a real intellectual companionship. Twining was the man for it, if anyone was.

2

Gilbert Twining did not, in fact, run an agency, but a small magazine called *The Outsider*. And George Wren had several reasons for wanting to admire him.

George had a collection of *Outsider*s next to his bed, dating back to its inception fifteen years earlier. His present mind and tastes had been largely formed by it: for the past seven years, Twining's stock of ideas—or rather, attitudes—had been hammered methodically one by one into his skull. Radicalism with responsibility, humanism without cranki-ness, everything paired off with its common-sense opposite; adding up to urbanity, lack of fluster, loyal, courteous, brushes teeth after every meal, it was sometimes hard to keep the image steady on a Thursday morning. Twining was basically anti-ideology, anti-slogan, so his position could only be expressed in examples, and George couldn't think of any examples. Anyhow, to snip short this skein of unraveling brain: getting a job there as number-four editor had excited him at first out of all proportion, and he had been warding off a letdown ever since.

9

His first surprise had been to find so august a journal being pasted together in such a woe-begone office. At one end there were the dusty filing cabinets, mimeograph machines, and other dimly understood paraphernalia, at the other were four tiny editorial offices, separated by duckboard partitions. Twining occupied the most fetid of these; George the second most fetid. There were no windows to speak of, to modify the darkness and grime; no street sounds to mingle with the steady pounding of the address machines. Yet from this setting emerged every second week a magazine almost as cool and amused as Twining himself.

George was late enough the next day for the Twining raised eyebrow: a beautiful piece of miniature engineering. The other two editors were at work in their warrens, sneering at dawn's early manuscripts. Miss Marplate, the human time clock who was in charge of accounting and such office discipline as there was, gave him a ferocious frown (that was the discipline) as he passed, and Philo Sonnabend asked politely his opinion on an ad he'd been working on unofficially. "A magazine of challenge," yeah, well. "An intelligent visitor in your home." Sonnabend hadn't really got the spirit, had he—but how could you tell him?

Now this was an extraordinary thing. Look at Philo, and look at Olga Marplate. A middle-aged man, in unsuccessful pinstripes (his teeth didn't fit either, but rattled like castanets in his loose-knit mouth), and a top-heavy frump in a basic black dress. Yet Twining thought that these two mediocrities were, well not plotting against him exactly, but *awfully stuffy in here, waiter loosen my collar* waiting for something.

That was his second obsession, the entertaining one, and he had gotten on to it around midnight last night. It wasn't

10

just those two, of course. Sonnabend could hardly have plotted his way to the washroom. But in combination with one of the two editors (some confusion in George's mind as to which), they were, well not plotting exactly, have 'nother drink, Georgie, but "They hate my insides, you see," Twining had explained. "Business people are always like that, you know. They imagine that they are solely responsible for a magazine's success. They begin to have editorial ideas. They send you memos. You ignore them and poof!"— George couldn't conjure up the rest right now; it gave him a headache.

What this success was that everyone was claiming credit for was hard to imagine. 21,000 subscribers (it used to be 27,000), a small, nagging deficit, a reputation that shrank a little every time a subscriber died. Yet, Twining was convinced, in his cool, General Kitchener way, that his position here was threatened: that Olga Marplate and the rest wanted to take over this grubby little office and the sway of 21,000 minds ("It doesn't bother me in the least, I find it rather touching," he said). A silly story, what George could remember of it; but he supposed that small offices hatched these out regularly, to pass the time.

It seemed especially bizarre today, what with a few inches of hangover behind his nose and ten semiliterate manuscripts piled on his desk. "Dear Sir, I have always wanted to write, people tell me I have a flair." "Does your magazine do stories on game birds?" This franchise wasn't worth fighting for, not on Thursday mornings anyway. Shabby unsolicited manuscripts concerning which he had to scribble shabby opinions (you could still see the thumbprints of the *New Thought* reader on the margins)—that was Thursday morning for you.

After two dreadful articles, he needed some water badly. He strolled over to the ravaged cooler and tried to coax a

Dixie-cup from its moorings. "Come here, you little bastard," he said.

"Don't let it see you're angry, George," said Fritz Tyler, who had lined up behind him.

"Damn thing's in crooked."

"Hey, George, how about some lunch today?"

"Yeah, O.K. Why not?"

"Around twelve?"

"Around twelve. Stupid little fink." He eased the cup out with the tip of his finger.

Office politics in a place like this really demonstrated the puniness of the human mind, he thought. With the world about to go up in smoke, as usual of course, people could still find time to worry about—but he didn't really believe they worried. It was paranoia raised to the level of a hobby on Twining's part, a delicious game, like looking at girls in the park. Extraordinary people, the English.

George went with Fritz to Luigi's, the Italian restaurant down the street, and for the first few minutes they complained about the unsolicited articles (all the editors had to read articles on Thursday morning, correct proof on Thursday afternoon, edit manuscripts on Monday, etc.—on such a small magazine there were no specialists; you learned the whole business quickly). Fritz said, "So. You've been here what? three months now? What do you think?"

After three months, George thought he had earned the right not to be asked this question one more time. So he just said, "It's O.K."

"You sound enthusiastic."

"Yeah, well I guess I am a little disappointed this morning. They didn't tell me about Thursdays. Or Tuesdays either. Wednesdays are O.K."

"Is it our greasy little play pit that doesn't appeal to you? Or the magazine that comes crawling out of it from time to time?"

George winced. On Thursdays, he was disgusted with language as such.

"Magazine's O.K. It doesn't impress you so much when you know how it's done. You know, like conjuring tricks."

Fritz nodded. Man called Fritz ought to be fat, but this one was quite thin. Well, there you are. Not only thin but dressy and unusually quick at eating Italian food. He was already halfway through his ravioli, and yet he didn't seem to hurry.

George didn't want to sound like a malcontent, until he knew whether he really was one. Vague dismay didn't quite qualify you. "If you look at the stuff that comes in, the magazine is pretty incredible at that, I guess. Ask me tomorrow," he said.

"And what do you think of the maestro?" asked Fritz.

"Mr. Twining?" The tables were on top of each other and the secretaries at the next one were watching him with large, Cleopatra eyes. "I think he's a fine editor. Don't you?"

"Oh yeah, no doubt about it. And such a distinguished man. Maybe he's not as good as he was. Which of us is? You go stale in this business. Everybody does. I'm even stale myself."

George had dismissed Twining's suspicions so completely that he was surprised to find them drifting into his mind. Fritz Tyler was a naturally sarcastic fellow, of course. He had been with the magazine for four years, and had developed an ironic style so that you never knew for certain what he was trying to tell you. The problem right now was keeping pace with his fantastic ravioli-eating. "You think Twining's lost his touch, then?"

Fritz said, "Oh no, no reason to think that. It's partly a summer thing. We've had a couple of dull issues, and it always begins to look like the end. Gilbert is basically a pro, so I guess he'll pull us out. If not—poof, as we French say."

He sounded like a lawyer who'd been paid to take a dive. George hadn't realized the magazine was in such bad shape.

The subject was dropped after that and George had a funny feeling that he had been watching the first syllable in a charade. He usually liked having lunch with Tyler, because Tyler made pretty good jokes and was born in Hoboken, etc.; but not today. He didn't want to be reminded of Twining's crazy suspicions, because it brought back the nightmarish taxi ride and the bitter taste of pillow. If Tyler didn't like Twining, that was his business.

When George got back to the office, Twining had some galleys ready for him that would keep him busy all afternoon. Book reviews that looked triter than they would in print. "This book should be required reading in every—" how had that gotten in? "Many perceptive insights." Yeah, yeah. (Don't we ever get any obtuse insights around here?) Article on Vietnam. What fun. He wondered whether Twining wanted another session that evening.

He squinted across from his cubicle to Twining's: a slit formed by two doorways provided a slim frame for the master. He looked professional all right in his grubby office, transcending it, wearing squalor like a badge. George really did want to admire the bastard—what was the use of anything if he didn't? He didn't want to hear about his girls in the park, or his cranky suspicions: those were just freaks, curiosities. The real thing was the professionalism that took this chaos and fashioned it into a magazine twice every month; a pretty good magazine.

Twining turned meditatively and caught George's eye for a moment. He smiled back superbly, not fatuously, not running for office, but with an undemanding charm that made you think, yes, I'll buy the socks, I'll drink the Schweppes, I'll even wear the goddamn eye patch.

Now for pete's sake don't spoil it, Commander Twining,

by talking a lot of crap down in the bar tonight. O.K. for once?

Twining might have sensed the request, for he didn't suggest a quick drink tonight, and George was allowed to go home on time to his wife and child in Queens.

3

Matilda Wren didn't want to hear about Twining. To her, though she never said it in so many words, *The Outsider* was just another little magazine: and he knew how people felt about little magazines—staggering through life in an endless dribble of opinion: "where Brecht fails is . . . overrated, underrated, the point is that he is *not,* precisely the opposite in fact . . ." She could hardly be expected to see the value of all this. He had given up a good job at C.B.S. to serve this broken-down opinion machine, to keep it at the same level (there was no question of improving it: it was too old and set in its ways for that), and he had assumed she would understand a move like that, based on principle. But she hadn't, he could tell. She resented the magazine, obscurely, subverbally. It prickled his mind uncomfortably every time he walked in the apartment. (Maybe that was one small reason he allowed himself to have that third drink with Twining.) After three years of marriage, he had to face the fact that his wife's opinions were often disappointing, not quite worthy of her. She had the look of one who knows more than she is saying, a cool, inward look, and when she did say something unbright he resisted the belief that that was all there was to it. She must be withholding something, an insight which she couldn't phrase. When a face was as pretty as that, you gave it the benefit.

Anyhow, whatever she felt about the magazine, she was

quite clear about Twining: she thought he sounded like some kind of nut.

"That man fascinates me," George said, after supper.

"As a pathological case, I suppose you mean."

"No, no, I shouldn't have mentioned that business, it isn't typical at all. Why do I always mention things like that?"

"I don't know. I *do* know that I sometimes feel as if you'd been working in a sewer all day. I don't mean the magazine of course, I mean . . ."

"Oh listen, that's plain hysterical. My God, all his perversions are perfectly normal, compared with, you know, some perversions." He rolled his napkin into a ball. "He talks about his trips to the park as if all the chaps do it, as if what else was a chap to do."

Matilda took his napkin away from him and carried it, between two fingers, to the garbage can. "I don't think you understand, dear," she said from the kitchen. "I don't mind about his trips to the park, he may be a perfectly normal, healthy English boy as you say, colder climate and all that, as you keep telling me. What I mind about is that he keeps you up all night talking about it. That doesn't seem right. Even for an Englishman."

George thought of the things he'd listened to over the years, boasts, confessions, owlish manifestoes. If you went into that line of perversion, there was no end to it. "You should hear what I tell *him*," he said. But Matilda didn't find this amusing, and began doing the dishes in rather worried silence. "Anyway, I'm glad you came home this evening," was all she said.

A furnished apartment in Queens was a bad place to sulk in: you were thrown too violently on your own resources. George went into their bedroom to look at his child (later on in the evening they would transfer the crib to the living room–dining room, so that the more trivial wails would not disturb them during the night).

"Hey man," he said to the baby, "how's it going?"

Peter Wren was just beginning to take shape. He was no longer last month's amorphous blob, but a boy you could talk to. "Office politics—aren't they a gas?" said George. "Aren't they ridiculous? Grown people—honest to God, Pete, you won't believe it. When your turn comes."

"Who're you talking to?" called Matilda.

"I'm talking to my son."

"Oh. I thought it was someone on the telephone." Her voice was unduly concerned, perhaps from fretting about different noises-off and evaluating them all day long. "Don't wake him up, will you?"

George sat a few more minutes in the half-dark, giving the crib a faint rock. The baby looked, and smelled, pretty healthy compared with, well, Twining. But perhaps that was an unfair comparison.

Healthy-smelling or not, the kid represented trouble. Soon George could hear Matty saying, "We need a bigger apartment for Peter . . . We need more money, for Peter . . . Peter doesn't see enough of his father." Working at the magazine was a sacrifice that would come in installments. He wished Matty understood why he was making it.

"Pretty demanding, aren't you?" said George. The baby looked suddenly stupid. "Babies are rotten materialists." He felt a slight uneasiness in his mind, because nothing was going absolutely right at the moment; his job wasn't quite right, and his wife was just the slightest bit off-center, half-a-note off, say, and the apartment they'd had to move into out here was of course an out-and-out disaster—but he got some comfort from sitting in here with the kid. It removed the ambiguous taste from his mouth and brought back a simpler flavor.

The next day Brian Fine, the other editor, suggested that they have a bite of lunch. The second time in two weeks. This was really too much—the boys were really trying to make him feel at home, weren't they?

He found himself thinking about Twining's conspiracy again, not because he believed it for a moment, but because of its sheer entertainment value. Perhaps thinking about it enough might make it come true some day. You would look for allies against it, and then begin to make your moves and countermoves, and pretty soon you'd have all the plot you wanted. Just out of boredom and mischief.

Now Brian Fine, he thought, was the one who should have been thin; but he was chubby and small. And here he was eating two and a half rolls with his martini, to keep himself that way, and driving them home with a plate of spaghetti. "How do you like *The Outsider,* George?" he said. "I mean, how do you *really* like it? You can be frank, you're among friends." Being amusing was part of a fat man's duties, and Brian fulfilled it with an almost physical effort.

The customers were bulging towards them from every side. One girl was almost in his lap, by George. This was a hell of a place for a confidential chat.

"To be quite frank, I find it perfectly spiffing, Brian old thing."

"Well that's wonderful, wonderful." One of the folk customs at the magazine was doing bad-English imitations and Fine picked up his cue with a hint of melancholy. "And the captain, what do you make of him?"

"A quite marvelous man. Peerless type."

"Seriously?"

"Oh absolutely." George had always found it difficult to be serious with fat people.

Fine concentrated on his spaghetti for a while and didn't speak again with any consequence until his cheesecake arrived; George concentrated on keeping the girl out of his lap, or at least being ready when she arrived. Fine frowned over the creamy goo. "Of course, Twining is certainly a first-class man. No doubt at all. But I sometimes feel that he takes on too much, if you know what I mean."

"I don't know what you mean. Too much what?"

"You must have noticed that *The Outsider* is basically a one-man show. We haven't had an editorial meeting in two months. The whole magazine expresses one man's personality. And however interesting that man may be—" He spread his hands.

He doesn't get a response out of me that easily, thought George. He'll have to work a hell of a lot harder than that.

Fine looked down at his gluey plate again and said, "Nobody knows what he's supposed to be doing. On other magazines people have definite assignments. And it isn't only editorial, it's the advertising, the, you should pardon the word, image. I mean, Philo Sonnabend is a nice guy, but he's never been given any responsibility, so he shrivels."

Keep trying.

"And the same thing with Olga. Who is by the way a *genuinely* nice kid—I'm awfully fond of Olga. But all the big decisions in her department are made by Mr. Twining; so how can she grow?"

"I'll have to think about it."

"Right now, those two are just sounding boards for Twining. Well, you know it's a weakness of great men to keep their subordinates from growing."

Wait a minute, you're supposed to be on *their* side. Don't

you understand the game? Olga and Philo and one editor against Twining and me and the office boy. George found that the game, as game, was getting a stronger grip on him. C.B.S. politics had been played on too large a field, so you couldn't see the players at the far end. This stadium was just the right size.

"Not that I don't appreciate some of the things Olga has done, and Philo too." George's unresponsiveness was making Brian twitter. "Loyal, good people both of them—but supposing something happens to Gilbert? The thing is built on sand. Gilbert goes, everything goes."

"Then we all have to go look for work."

"Yeah. And the nation loses a great magazine."

George was going to say, the nation'll probably get over it. But he felt this was *too* cocky. Also he was intrigued by his partner's sudden outcry of loyalty. Since George's arrival at the shop, Brian Fine had treated him mostly with a kind of brassy, saleman's humor that didn't really seem natural. Brian was a veteran of God knows how many years—he went back before Twining, to infinity: years of copy-editing, years of proofreading—and someone must have told him that humor helps.

So now to find out that he really cared desperately, well it made him a little more interesting, a little more of a man.

"*The Outsider* means a lot to me," said Brian. "There is no magazine quite like it."

I can think of only about three offhand—no, cheap again. I agree it's a good magazine. I haven't changed that much. On Fridays, it's a fine magazine. Brian leaned forward, looming up on George.

"Of course we owe an immense debt to Twining. We shan't—you should pardon the cliché—see his like again.

Which is precisely why I think he should start delegating a bit more. If we're not going to see his like—"

"Have you talked to him about any of this?"

"No, not in so many words." Fine was stirring his coffee now, around and around. "I find Twining a bit difficult to talk to these days. Withdrawn, you know. Always the gentleman, of course. But I have a feeling I annoy him in some way."

"Hmmm."

"So, how do you get on with him, George? I've seen you going into Sweeney's with him. He must listen to you, doesn't he?"

"No, I listen to him."

"You see, that's it, that's what worries me."

As they finished their coffee, Brian Fine reverted to his usual style, which was opaque and jocular. He kidded the waitress and even told George he needed a haircut. ("We're a long-haired magazine, but this is ridiculous.") He seemed to have no middle range, between banter and desperate sincerity.

The last time they had had lunch together, Brian had expressed a fear that George would get his hair caught in the machinery. Since he came from the Middle West, he also kidded George a lot about New Jersey, which meant that George had to kid him back about Iowa. Disappointing on a grown-up magazine. And yet George believed that Fine was rather a clever editor. *The Outsider* was probably like one of those old universities where the professors develop tics and private jokes. Fine had his own collection of tricks and imitations to pass the time. Being stupid was one of them.

George felt oppressed all afternoon. His little boy really did make more sense than these people. Brian Fine had apparently been trying to get him, George, to deliver a message to Twining, to ask him to delegate authority. What kind of relationship did people think he had with Twining? . . . Fritz Tyler's cubicle was diagonal to his and Brian Fine's was next door, so he felt their sly old bachelor presences all afternoon—they were both only in their thirties, but there was something musty about them on this hot afternoon. They had grown, like an old married couple, to think alike and talk alike, and he wondered how long you had to be here for that to happen to yourself.

He looked across at Old Perfection, who appeared to be cleaning his pipe. (His hands were just out of sight.) Twining had a kind of half smile that disappeared in certain lights and seemed quite broad in others. At the moment he appeared to be amused by something.

Matilda, who didn't trust English people anyway, seemed to think he was unclean. But honestly, there was no sign of it now. His face was strikingly open and pleasant. (It wasn't even *too* pleasant.) Matty would be surprised by it. Matty would like him. Why such a charming fellow was reduced to looking at girls in the park was just one of the oddities of the old university, like Brian Fine's jokes: it certainly wasn't serious.

At ten to five, George got up quietly and moved with half-unconscious stealth, away from the chink where Twining was framed, to the elevator. It was a rackety old elevator which always took several minutes to get itself up from the basement. George waited glumly, while the cables churned and grunted: by the time it had got to the sixth floor he knew that Twining was out of his office.

"How about a quick drink?" said Old Man Twining in that deep friendly voice of his. And George felt—well, it could be the truth in this crumby office—as if an insect had just dropped down the back of his neck.

II

$$\text{\reflectbox{C}O\reflectbox{S}O\reflectbox{S}O\reflectbox{S}O\reflectbox{S}OC}$$

1

George Wren was getting the glassy look, which meant that his memory was probably disconnected; he wouldn't know by tomorrow whether he had heard it or dreamed it, or had actually done it himself.

"You wouldn't believe," said Twining, "that a city like London could make a man, well, *burn* like that. I used to walk up and down those dingy little streets, unable to think, barely able to breathe. Have another whatisit, old boy?"

George shook his head stiffly.

"Yes, I used to stand on the platform at Chipping Wandsworth saying, today will be different, there's nothing to worry about today. Very peaceful little station, Chipping Wandsworth. Bird song, actual bird song, and an old porter limping up and down the platform. Country voices. Yet London would have its horny old hands on my throat even there.

"On the later trains the carriage was usually full of old ladies and, you know, knitting patterns. Safe enough, you would suppose. We used to stop at Molesworth and Fincham, more bird song and more limping porters I daresay and—are you asleep, old boy?"

George shook again and mimed brief alertness. "What happened after that?" Americans were so polite.

"Well, as I say, the place defeated me. By the time I got out of my carriage, London possessed me. It's rather hard to describe. I mean, while I was still on the train—have you ever been in an English railway carriage, by the way? No, how could you have? Well, it's all so frightfully middle class, I can't *describe* how middle class it is. Boardinghouses by the sea aren't in it with railway carriages. And the old ladies and the Daily Mail and the picture of Bournemouth, and yet it got in there somehow: the London thing. And one would be fairly burning with excitement and sick with depression—"

Gilbert Twining felt a little excited even with the memory. And yet his voice remained cool, he knew. His first wife used to say, "Gilbert never gets excited about anything." And she had seen him when he was drained and almost fainting from excitement.

"Well, anyway, George—George? Are you there?"

Young Wren was fast asleep. It was no good going on if he didn't hear it at all. (The listener didn't have to make sense of it, but he did have to hear it.)

Twining was disappointed. It was only five to twelve, and he hadn't begun to talk about the office. About Olga Marplate's latest insolence, and Philo Sonnabend's unending, half-witted duplicities. Between them, they had just concocted an advertisement that would have made the magazine appear simply asinine. It showed a dismal-looking man crouched in a doghouse, above the words "Don't be an outsider. Read the . . ." He winced at the whole concept.

"Oh, we've already sent it out," Philo had said, clicking his teeth cheerfully. "It's gone to *New Thought* in exchange for one of theirs."

"What do you mean, sent it out? Aren't you supposed to clear new ads with me, Sonnabend? Have we changed our policy on that?"

Philo looked stupider than one would have thought possible. "I cleared it with Olga."

"I cleared it with Mr. Fine," said Olga. "He thought it was perfectly—*you* know."

Well, he couldn't fire the whole staff. He might just fire one of them as a horrible example; but they knew he couldn't follow up and fire them all. The staff got tiny salaries as it was, and had very little to lose. His only hold on them was personal ascendancy; and that was something that he had to hoard like a miser.

If he had let himself get angry at Olga and it hadn't worked, his position would have been weaker by one rage. Strategy, strategy. By appearing to control his temper, and by using an irony somewhat beyond her powers of retaliation, he had shaken her slightly in spite of herself—and in spite of Fine's or Fritz Tyler's briefing. He had called up *New Thought,* in her presence, and canceled the ad. "Somebody here had a brainstorm," he explained over the phone. "You know how it is, please excuse." Olga Marplate, a few feet away, looked suitably shrunken.

But that was only one battle, and there would be others. Ideas opposed to his would be sneaked into the copy, phrases he detested, even—and this was almost too childish

25

to believe—little sneers at his country. He prowled the magazine for these things, wrenched them out viciously at the last minute, remained unruffled.

But how much personal ascendancy did one have? Carefully rationed, how long would it last?

He paid the bill and managed to wake George up just enough to get him out to a taxi. The answer was right there—to build a new staff around people to whom his dominance was fresh coin; people who were still impressed by the old tricks.

He restated George's address in Queens, rather more clearly than George could, and gave the boy an encouraging pat on the shoulder. Machiavellian, in the sense that all planning, all self-knowledge was Machiavellian. But he didn't really think of himself as a corrupt man. He loved the damn magazine and that was justification enough. *The Outsider* had saved his soul seven years ago when, at the charming bequest of Frank Tippett, the founder, he had left England, empty and spent and terrified, and come to New York for the first time. Like Lazarus from his tomb.

The risings and swellings of mediocre people, their banal dreams and shortsighted strategies, were not going to take his magazine and turn it into, say, another . . . he ran through four of five well-known names, shaking his head sadly at each of them.

He got his car out of the lot and swung it towards the F.D.R. Drive. The ritual of niggling your way through side streets, and then bursting suddenly onto a super highway, a great river of cream, was one of the excitements of this country. It opened the chest in a way that Chipping Wandsworth Station did, let's face it, not.

One felt awfully tired tonight. The burst of speed on the highway worked, like splashing cold water on one's face, for only a few minutes. Then things would get fuzzy with fatigue, and then unnaturally clear by bedtime, and another short sleepless night would take its place in the calendar.

Edgemont, N.Y., looked expensive even by moonlight. He left the car by the curb, and walked gently over the lawn, which was a dazzling shade of white. Wide, wide awake, of course. If he took a pill, it would clash with the booze, and give him three hours of horrible and destructive sleep. If he passed the pill up, he would at least be clearheaded till morning.

He opened the bottle and weighed the pill in his hand. What he really needed was a holiday, a three-month holiday. But there were at least two arguments against that. The main one was the picture he had of himself coming back and finding his name taken off the door: and Olga Marplate with her feet on the desk, telling him that some changes had been made around here—he put the pill back: insomnia was better than having that nightmare again.

His wife turned over with a grunt as he entered the bedroom, and her white nightgown swung peevishly out of the moonlight. Gray woman. Ugh, fundamentally.

Wide, wide awake. The eyes flew open as if they were on springs. Pulling the blind didn't help, pulling the curtain made it stuffy, back to bed to think it over. Very silly to stay out as late as this. Still, one had to rally one's forces, and George Wren was one of one's forces. Such a polite fellow, so much more mature than we used to be.

One wouldn't have dreamed of telling those things to anyone else. But George was so *ruddy* polite—Twining's eyes snapped open again like window blinds. What a lot of nonsense one talked.

Granted that sleep was out of the q, what was the best image? Punting? no, he'd done punting last night. The girl, no definitely not the girl. Or any other girl, for that matter.

Country scenes, Chipping Wandsworth, the light was much too bright, everything was outlined too sharply, the bird song sounded like a referee's whistle. Rugby game then, heel, heel, etc., come on chaps, *now*. His eyes opened slyly, and the scene dissolved into Westchester bedroom again.

The big thing was not to get angry about it. Anger only increased the throb in the temple and made consciousness that much more painful. Sleep wasn't absolutely essential, so long as you relaxed *thoroughly*.

He sat up sharply. Oh God, insomnia was a terrible disease, though. One night, all right; two nights, very well. But night after night after blooming night—he could almost cry with vexation. He stumbled out to the bathroom, and shook the damn pill onto his hand, and then another for good luck. His face in the mirror was pretty much its old self. He almost wished it would do *something*, show a little interest, a little concern—

Four o'clock, and he had to get up at seven. If he began arriving at *The Outsider* late, he was finished. Things would be sent out without his say-so. There would be a frost of mockery in the air, of "Yes, Mr. Twining, we've attended to that."

It wasn't possible to get any more tired—and yet, even in this condition, he was more than a match for them, wasn't he? Tell it to the medicine cabinet. If it came to brains, there was simply no contest, was there? He was always at least three moves ahead of them.

He was more relaxed now, knowing that the pills were already at work. The trouble was that one couldn't always tell what Americans were thinking. They were always so simple and sincere. Europeans were constantly being taken in by the cunning and cruelty underneath. Very well then, he knew all about that. He knew that American business was the most ruthless in the world—that was no excuse for standing out here in the bathroom talking to the mirror.

He shook his head. People might suppose that he was going starkers, but he wasn't really. Ajax, to take an excellent example, was bewitched and slew the sheep, mistaking them for enemies. His own case was different. Olga Marplate might look like a sheep, but she really *was* an enemy. He was tired, but he wasn't bewitched. Brain a trifle scrambled by gin, that was the worst you could say about it.

His eyes stayed shut this time, and he decided to look over the old house once more. The lawn behind it was its usual bleak, undulating self. You could walk over it, or you could just look at it. Those were your choices.

He was the last boy in the world still to have a private tutor, Mr. Walker, bleak if not undulating, and Mr. Walker played cricket with him for twenty minutes a day, saying things like "elbow up" and "nose down" as if cricket was a Christian responsibility, not a game at all—rather pleasant to remember now, though it hadn't been especially so at the time. Nose down, whatever that meant. Pock of ball on bat.

Apart from Mr. Walker there was nobody to play with and nothing much to do. The Twinings also had an old nanny called Renfrew who hung around vaguely, and probably hung around to this day if it came to that, even though there was nobody left to occupy her very mild attention. The Twinings talked about her as a rare find, a pearl beyond price: but Gilbert remembered her as quite useless: preoccupied and withdrawn. Her lips even in death would form the words "run along now"; and the look in her pale eyes, at once dead and fussy, would always make it a pleasure to do so.

With the pills inside him, this memory too seemed quite

nice. Nanny Renfrew suddenly had some of the charm of a stuffed bear. And the long empty walks over the endless lawn, under a spitting, midland sky were rather pleasant. The squelch of tennis shoes. (*Tennis* shoes?) The vaporous mist. Stillness. Miles away, the humming of a lawnmower: the gardener, too deaf to talk to of course, but an absolute jewel of a man, keeping the lawn spruce for Gilbert to wander over. Parfitt with his ears full of wax and red hair spilling out of his nose. Marvelous chap.

He took the path by the flower beds, his own ear cocked to the droning of the bees, and thought about girls—no, that came later. Gilbert Twining smiled without opening his eyes. The girls were another story.

The empty garden was paradise on two Seconal tablets. When he got to the very end of it, he heard again the mellow chime of a cricket bat. Two village boys with a bat bigger than both of them. "Can I play with you?" He surely hadn't liked cricket this much. They looked at him suspiciously—they weren't going to let him! Twining frowned and rolled onto his back again. Things often went suddenly wrong when he lay on his right side. (They *had* played with him, for a few minutes, uncomfortably: they had never played with a chap who kept his nose down before. He remembered it clearly.)

Now back through a lane of trees until he could see the house again, a gray Georgian box with long blank windows guarding dozens of empty rooms. Full of threadbare tapestry, no doubt. What year was this anyway? 1920-something, the most peaceful year that ever there was, almost oppressively peaceful by now. A lady with a huge floral hat bobbed out of the back door, looked around, didn't see him. Aunt Lily, oh dear—still, a very nice day and all that. Flowers, cricket: he backed towards the safety of the trees, but not in time. The door bashed open again, and out roared his cousin Charles: imitating an airplane (noisy coughing 1920's engine). Charles was followed by Sally, imitating a machine gun, and the oldest, Richard, simply being himself.

He turned to run, but they were across the lawn in about two strides, "Piggy, little fat face," Charlie zooming around in meaningless circles, Richard with his hands in his pockets. Nanny Renfrew's pale eyes would see nothing, for two awful weeks.

The sleeping pill had met the martinis in circuit, and his three hours of sleep had begun.

2

"I had a funny dream last night."

"Oh yes?" Polly Twining yawned. "So did I, as a matter of fact."

He could never tell her a dream without having to listen to one of hers. And hers were so pointless.

"Tell me yours first," she said.

"No, you go ahead." Get it over with, he thought.

Polly had dreamed about an old school friend she hadn't met in years, and they were walking through a park full of horses, a big park with a river in it, and a man came up and—details, duller than anything that ever happened to anyone in real life. Twining never remembered more than two or three images from his own dreams and these he had to hold on to tight.

"I was locked in the barn, and the horses were kicking down the door . . .

"Well, you know what *that* means?"

"Oh yes, I know what that means."

Polly wouldn't dare to have a dream without a few Freudian symbols in it. She was making it all up, to keep

31

him from telling his. He would have to leave in about ten minutes, dream untold.

"That's very interesting," he said, "and did the horses finally get in?"

"No, no, because the barn had turned into a battleship by then. And the horses were old school friends . . ."

"*I* dreamed about Cousin Richard."

"Oh yes." She looked suddenly bored. "Tell me about that."

"We were acting one of his plays, and of course I forgot my lines, and he was feeding them to me slowly, as if I were simple-minded. I was only the messenger boy, you must understand, with three very obvious lines. But in Richard's presence, I simply froze. Polly?"

"Yes, go ahead, I'm listening."

"I thought you were—

"I can do this, and listen." She was halfway out of the dining room with the two cereal bowls. It was all rather discouraging.

"Interesting boy, Richard," he said.

"He sounds as horrid as most small boys."

"No, that isn't quite true. He was horrid all right—but not like most small boys. He was, as you Americans would say, *creatively* horrid. Probably the only nonviolent bully I have ever met."

"Well," she hovered indecisively. "That's something, I guess."

"You see, I was by myself for the greater part of each year, so that I was quite unprepared—you know, to cope."

"Are you finished with this?"

"Eh? Oh, no, there are still a few drops in it."

She left the room, holding one butter knife. Hardly worth a separate trip, one would have supposed.

"Richard had *style*," he said. "Charlie had at best a certain rat-like confidence. Sally—"

"I've always thought," she said from the kitchen; the water went on, drowning the rest, so he finished it for her, "that your parents neglected you shamefully. Throwing you in with three older children and not supervising you. Of course the children were going to tease you." Twining grimaced. There must be more to Polly than he could see.

The water went off. It didn't take much water to wash two cereal bowls and a butter knife. "Long before anyone had ever heard of the word 'Establishment,'" he said loudly, "I knew all about it from Richard. The sneer, the elaborate patience—that's the face, you know, that I've been fighting all my life. That's part of what *The Outsider* stands for."

"That seems like an awful lot to put on one little boy. Surely there are more important reasons for being a liberal than that."

"I can't think of any, offhand."

"And after all, your own face . . ." More water for something, your own face is rather Establishment too, isn't it, dear, no native would dare to be rude to it—well of course, it wasn't just Richard's *face* that one minded, it was things like that play; and anyway, one *knew* that one wasn't like Richard, deep down. If Polly would just sit still for a minute, he could explain the whole thing.

He had developed, to be sure, a certain facial expression to counter Richard with, an expression not unlike Richard's own. "But you see, dear, the difference between *me* and . . ."

She came in again, wiping her hands. Probably hadn't heard a word . . . "I expect Richard was bullied by someone in his turn," she said briskly. "Some dreadful old nanny, and that's why *he* looked like that. And I further

33

expect that the nanny was bullied by someone and that's why *she*—" She didn't take his boyhood experiences seriously; she thought it was a kind of sickliness, to make them a basis for adult action.

All very well for someone with a bright monochrome background like hers—she had never gone shivering along dark corridors, shivering from Richard's coldness. If there was a better reason for belonging to the political left, it hadn't come his way yet.

He wanted to stay and establish a little ascendancy. But he could never polish off these arguments in the few minutes he had. Standing up, edging for the door, he said, "No doubt you can excuse Richard, *and* Richard's nanny— but you can't excuse the system that perpetuates them. Goodbye, dear—"

"But Richard grew up to be very nice, and uncomplicated, didn't he?" she said before he could move. "When we saw him last year, he was—I mean, he's really less complicated than you, isn't he?"

"I honestly must go."

"Yes, all right."

"I'd like to talk some more—"

She kissed him quickly on the cheek and went back to the kitchen. And he wondered for a wild moment whether the thing Richard had passed on to him, he hadn't passed on to her. It was at least an amusing theory.

The traffic was heavy this morning, some kind of breakdown in the far distance. He had lingered a bit too long over breakfast too, trying to erase the slight disappointment in him from his wife's voice. Of course, the day he could do that—

So he was going to be late after all. It was rather aggravating. He tapped his left foot and looked around.

There was a flash of gold hair in the next car. Rather ordinary when you looked at her closely, though. Whoops, she was looking *back* closely. And dammit—this was the point—he looked away.

Not a bit like Richard in that respect. Richard would have leered like Anthony Eden and bounded into the seat beside her. His picture of Richard would have. Come *on!* A curious reflex that, which made one look away. He glanced back at the girl, but she wouldn't cooperate any further. He had had his chance. A very silly game for a man of his years.

Things went more smoothly once he got past the ball of crumpled green steel that had caused the delay. Thirty-five minutes late or so wasn't too utterly degenerate. Should have left earlier, though. When Polly started talking about his complications, it was always ten minutes after he should have left. So silly to think that *talking* would help, with Polly.

"There we go." He turned off the drive and began the slow, stately city-wiggle toward *The Outsider* office.

He composed himself in the rackety elevator, which could hold 1,500 pounds and had been inspected by indecipherable, who obviously didn't ask much of elevators—he wished he could afford a new building, but it was rather too much of a gamble at present. Mrs. Wadsworth would give him the money in a twinkling, but then she would want to review the new plays as a reward. Wally Funk's reviews were bad enough, thanks all the same. Philo Sonnabend could earn the money by increasing the advertising: but it was bloody work, selling space, an inch at a time. At the moment, Sonnabend's efforts just about paid for his own salary.

Twining walked swiftly across the office, taking off his

hat, hooking his umbrella on the hatstand, looking as if he'd just come from somewhere. "Miss Marconi, come here a mo, will you?" "Mo" was good; Fran Marconi was his secretary, a big girl with bushy eyebrows. He hadn't wanted a good-looking secretary.

"I'd like you to take a few letters, Miss Marconi."

They had all looked up as he came in, but that was only natural. He couldn't afford to examine their faces closely: but in any case, they wouldn't be staring at him expressively. There might conceivably be a very slight chill in the air, Olga Marplate's glinting spectacles, Philo Sonnabend's jangling teeth.

He ripped open his own mail, while dictating to Miss Marconi. Invitation to lecture in San Francisco. Three hundred dollars and expenses. And a symposium at U.C.L.A. three days later. Very short notice on both of them—probably the same high-level fellow had canceled out of both. Might be a chance to get in a little equally high-level fund raising. Mrs. Fitzroy of Oakland was simply crazy about the magazine, although she had never quite got round to doing anything for it; Countess Sadowski of San Mateo was in similar case. Two wily old ladies, who liked to hang one from their watch chains. Well, why not hang a little? (And stretch it into a modest holiday at the same time.)

Brian Fine looked in and said, "I've been holding these proofs for your O.K., Mr. Twining."

"Very good, Brian." He reached for the proofs. They in fact did not need his O.K. And he had long ago asked Fine to call him Gilbert. In one short sentence, Brian had managed to get at him in two ways. Would that his editorials were half as efficient.

He felt a sudden, quite unreasonable alarm. If he went out to the West Coast, Fine would hold things that didn't need holding and Marplate would send out things that did need holding, and when he got back, they would blame it all on him; they would stand in his doorway holding bits of paper . . . He didn't know whether he could stand it.

He checked himself. It really was neurotic to feel that you couldn't leave the office for five minutes without someone sabotaging you. One was getting things madly out of proportion. Look at Fine, now, with his small eyes and rubber nose—really, Gilbert. What could Brian Fine do to one?

"Take a letter to these symposium people, here, the address is on this."

Fine was still standing there. The last time Twining had been out to the West Coast, abortively courting Mrs. Fitzroy and the countess, Brian Fine had made it abundantly clear that Twining had not only deserted his post, but had flopped as a charmer as well. "I hear that Mrs. Fitzroy just set up a chair at Berkeley," Brian had said pointedly. "I guess that's her good deed for the year."

"Tell them," Twining said, looking pleasantly at Fine, "that I should be delighted to take part in their thing. Standard acceptance letter, you know how it goes."

Fine shuffled out. Whisper, whisper with Mrs. Marplate. Fine was *such* a second-rate man.

"And the same to U.C.L.A."

God, he was tired. Only twelve o'clock. George Wren peeping in, hello George. It was nice to be hero-worshipped by somebody.

It was going to be hell getting through this afternoon. Everything should be off to the printers by tomorrow at the latest. Meanwhile Brian Fine would bring in little niggling things to trip him, slow him, send him sprawling over his deadline. Or perhaps Fine's game was to get him worked up, to make him lose his poise for a minute in front of the staff . . . Little did Fine know; much more likely to find me snoring. In front of the staff. Yards of galley proof, most soporific stuff in the world. Blue, yellow, violet strands. There were some pep pills in his desk which would see him through all right, but he was reluctant to add another voice to his nervous system. See how long he could last without them.

He went to the window, one of the two windows in the whole office, and looked out. Rows of jagged chimneys. (What curious sleight of hand made New York appear a modern city? It was ancient, older than he was.) "Lincoln Hotel" in dismal red paint on the side of the next building. Everything unnaturally sharp again. There was a painful haze over the East River. This city could blind you; one shouldn't look at it too long. But he loved it in his odd way, and was grateful to it. Even to be tired and nervous here was better than what one felt in the other places.

And here was Brian Fine again, an old New Yorker by now, full of city slyness and persistence. "Excuse me again, Mr. Twining, but Wally's theater column is still two inches long, and I wondered if you'd like to cut it a little more. It's a nice day, isn't it?"

"You can take out the third paragraph, Brian. Sight unseen. That's where Wally keeps his ideas."

Fine gave a slight smile, as if the cynicism of this was amusing in its way, but rather cheap too. "You know how Wally screams when his *ideas* are cut."

"Yes, I can take care of Wally's screams. There are no openings in the summer, Wally shouldn't be writing at all. What is it this time, the state of the drama?"

"He's in Stratford, Connecticut. I guess he needs the extra money."

"Oh, that. Cut the third paragraph anyway. 'The bard has been indifferently served,' that one."

"You're joking, aren't you, Mr. Twining?"

"Yes, I daresay. Here, give it to me, I'll find something. His obligations to dramatic art. Something."

One shouldn't make fun of one's own contributors. It was the kind of jest Americans never understood. And then again, Brian Fine could quite easily have cut the piece himself; he had been given use of the knife on Wally a long time ago. This was just his way of emphasizing that it was a one-man magazine when it wasn't at all.

There was something triumphant about the hunch of his fat shoulders as he went out. You may be hot stuff, Mr. Twining sir, but I'll get you, I'll get you. Twining did feel a flash of anger: the defense he had built against Cousin Richard and others would not be breached by this pip-squeak, he would never lose his temper in here, but he *was* awfully tired and hot, and Brian Fine was just a teeny bit too much this morning.

"Brian," he called.

"Yes, Mr. Twining."

"Tell Mrs. Marplate that the windows in here are getting disgracefully dirty."

A pause. "Yes, Mr. Twining."

And, for a moment or two at least, one did feel a little better.

III

1

"Lunch, Olga?"

"Love to."

"He says his windows are dirty."

"He's entitled to his opinion."

"I mean he told me to tell you."

"He told *you* to tell *me?*"

Olga Marplate shook her head unbelievingly. Brian Fine nodded grimly.

"He's going to the West Coast," Brian continued over lunch.

"What, again?"

"Yes, again."

"I hope he has better luck this time."

"I guess we could use the money, couldn't we?"

Olga Marplate grunted and made a gesture. A "Honey, are you kidding?" gesture.

"The trouble is," said Brian, "that I'm afraid the commander isn't as suave and English as he once was. And the rich widows are beginning to get on to it. I think he even gets his idioms wrong sometimes. He says 'mo' when he ought to say 'jiffy.' Anyway, I thought all that went out with the First World War."

"Search me, I'm from Bridgeport."

Brian Fine smiled painfully and dug into his spaghetti. He felt a little guilty because he had stolen most of his speech from Fritz Tyler anyway. Exploratory talks were all very well, but where did you go from there? He and Olga had long since felt each other out at this level and were able to talk irreverently about the commander. But what next?

"I hope he appreciates what you do for the magazine, Olga."

"Oh, I think he does. In his way."

"You mean everything short of actually mentioning it?"

Olga laughed shortly, and patted her hair with an awkward mechanical gesture. It was upswept at the back and tended to slither down. "You know how it is with editorial people," she said. "They think the business side is taken care of by pixies. I expect you're just the same."

"I certainly am not. You know that, Olga. I realize how much a magazine owes to the people who do the day-to-day accounting, the people who never miss a day and never take a bow . . ."

"Well," Olga lit a between-courses cigarette, and took a deep and thoughtful drag, "we know that it is ultimately editorial quality that sells the magazine. We can't sell a bad product, can we?"

41

That was rather good, thought Fine, seven types of ambiguity. For they sure as hell weren't selling *The Outsider* right now. He asked her what she wanted for dessert, cheesecake or what?

"I shouldn't, I gained three pounds last week."

"Just this once."

"I really shouldn't . . . it's going to be a strain on you people, isn't it, I mean Mr. Twining going away again?"

Brian shrugged ambiguously. "No, no, I wouldn't say so. Frank? Two cheesecakes, Frank." "Now, Brian—" "And two espressos." He patted her hand, and she said, "You're impossible." "No, it won't be a strain. We like the opportunity to make some decisions ourselves."

Olga's mind was sensuously slow: she lingered over an idea like someone lingering in a hot tub. "But you do have to clear them with him, don't you? I mean you and Fritz don't really make decisions, do you, even when he's away?"

"He has a veto, but it's usually too late, by the time we get his cables, to make any big changes. It's either do it our way, or leave these big holes." Well, it had happened like that once. When Twining had gone to Chicago three years ago.

"I never realized that."

"Editors and business people really should get together sometimes, don't you think? They live in different worlds. At *The Outsider* anyway."

"Oh, definitely."

The ground was well and truly prepared. Three lunches in the last month, all devoted to preparing the damn ground. Now he was probing for hopes and dreams. "You know, Olga," he experimented, "I love that magazine. If I sound off sometimes you know that that's the reason."

She was watching him with her fork in the air. What did *she* want? Gossip and sneers forever and ever?

"I think it's a great little magazine," he said, "and I think it makes a unique contribution. And I think it can go *on* making a unique contribution. But I'm just a little worried."

What did a woman of this kind expect from life? It was a great mystery to Brian.

She looked down at her plate for a moment, and then looked up again and said, "Worried about anything special?"

Phoomph! Well, there was plenty special—that snotty Englishman, amusing himself with the magazine, sneering at everyone else's efforts, rejecting their suggestions, making them seem comical—no, there was nothing special, my dear: nothing you could communicate without sounding like a whipped dog.

"We seem to be in a slight rut, a sort of Sargasso Sea," he said carefully. "Magazines go stale, they repeat themselves—well, I don't have to tell you."

"Yes, I know what you mean, in a way."

"All the departments are strait-jacketed. By tradition, custom, 'the magazine's character.' " He wondered how long it took a woman of this kind to get dressed in the morning. Hours, he supposed. This argued some quality of persistence.

She said, "And this character all comes from Mr. Twining, doesn't it?"

"That's it, that's absolutely it. The commander has been a great editor, and still is in many ways, I yield to no one on that—but one man, any one man—"

"Doesn't he listen to anyone else? To you or Fritz?"

That was an unexpected squeeze. "Oh, we get some things in there, you can be sure. But the dominating flavor is always the commander's."

43

"I see."

They drank their coffee and Brain asked for the bill. $7.45 seemed like a lot. What was that $1.50 for? **M** something. It was as illegible as a doctor's prescription.

"Here, I'll sign for it," said Olga.

"No, no, this was on me."

"The company won't notice a little amount like that."

"The hell it won't." He looked at her sharply. "Right?"

"Right, I guess."

The magazine had never had any money, so there was no special point in emphasizing that now; but he felt vaguely that anything that brought out the general desperateness of the situation served some purpose. He paid the bill crisply. "There we are."

He wasn't being paid enough himself and neither, he imagined, was Olga Marplate. That was so obvious that it didn't need stressing at all. These lunches, preparing the ground with her and Philo and George Wren, and even with Fritz, were just about cleaning him out. He couldn't manage one more until a week from Friday. He put his tattered wallet back on his hip. If he only knew what he was preparing the ground *for*—

Anyhow, anything he could do to harass that sneering, supercilious Englishman into a mistake would be done with pleasure. He really did love the magazine that Twining had perverted—and once upon a time he had even liked Twining too. But that was a long time ago. Before he had caught on to Twining. Before the public had caught on too.

Nobody read *The Outsider* now, nobody but a few dried-up dilettantes and chess-puzzle-fanciers. Twining's character had gotten through to the public all right; Brian wasn't the only one. Twining's pinstripe soul.

A beautiful little magazine, though, a gorgeous potential. If he could just get that dead man's hands off the steering wheel— A magazine that had once been endorsed by Adlai Stevenson and Madame Pandit Nehru shouldn't be allowed to end like that, as Fritz had recently put it.

He didn't like getting his jokes from Fritz, it was a bad habit. He smiled with effort at Olga Marplate and she stood up. Things were that much better between them. But she was still waiting for instructions that hadn't come through yet. God, she was unimaginative.

Maybe this trip to the West Coast would create an opening. If not, something else would arise. Brian Fine was, with good reason, a patient man. Whether Gilbert Twining was remained to be seen.

He felt a bit melodramatic and self-conscious as he escorted Olga past the dowdy shop windows between the restaurant and the office. (This must be the truss-center of the world.) He wasn't some sort of Iago-like plotter, just a man trying to help out a magazine. People were doing it all over town—in all those great morose buildings on both sides of the street, it was plot, plot, plot—cutting out tiny cancers like Twining, to keep the larger organisms alive. It was honestly nothing personal.

But trying to think of himself as a master surgeon didn't quite lift the after-dinner guilt. Playing up to Olga Marplate, whom he half despised, always took it out of him. What was he really doing? getting back at a man who had once laughed at him? There was some of that in it, let's face it. Brian Fine was not above personalities. He felt a slight dip of nerve as he entered the old building—if it really was a personal vendetta, it rather went against his conscience.

Brian deposited Olga Marplate, and shambled back toward his own cubicle. It was windowless, with peeling carbons on the walls. There was a memo on the pasteboard desk. "Have gone home. Wally cut, ditto Max's movies and your own editorial, which, I fear me, was 3 inches too long. Do make sure to tell Miss Marplate about the windows. They're lamentable."

"The son of a bitch," said Brian Fine.

2

Brian loosened his belt and felt like a man reprieved from the gallows. Whoof. $7.50 plus tip poorer, and where did he stand? Fritz strolled by with a smile that seemed to say, "I know who's been eating cheesecake." You couldn't tell about Fritz Tyler. He was sarcastic enough about the Leader, as meanly critical a man as you could want, but you couldn't be sure he was on your side either. Thin fellow with a bow tie. The war between the very fat and the very thin sometimes cut across party lines. "Must get back to my diet," thought Brian doggedly. His present size made him feel defenseless at times.

Which made George Wren the present balance of power. What about George then? He was a happy-go-lucky young fellow to all appearances; he hadn't got the worries and obsessions that come like hot rivets later in life. At present, he seemed to be understudying Fritz as office wise guy—but Fritz's malice at least gave him a point of view, whereas George was glib in a vacuum. No doubt a few years at *The Outsider* would take care of all that—narrow the focus, shrink his perspectives, give him that lived-in look. Meanwhile, Twining had the option on him, and right now it wasn't worth having. Kid was strictly a lightweight.

Which left one with Olga Marplate and Philo question-mark, a tattered little garrison if ever he saw one. Olga took herself so seriously now, she had swollen into a tiny person-age; she thought that she stood between *The Outsider* and extinction, and she bullied the secretaries like galley slaves. As for Philo, he seemed to agree with everything anyone said, so that while he was certainly on Brian's side, he was just as certainly on Twining's side too, and Fritz's side, and everyone else's side. Probably voted for both parties at every election.

Oh, forget the whole thing. It was just an idea. There isn't enough firepower in this place to start a war. People in this kind of business were notoriously low in vitality. He probably was himself.

Brian Fine looked at his truncated editorial, holy men's room, what had Twining wrought this time? Brian had worked for three days whittling three paragraphs on the race question, building carefully to a crescendo of outrage—and here Twining had gone and snipped off the crescendo: siphoned off the outrage. This couldn't be good editing, could it?

"Hey Fritz," he trotted out of his cubicle. "Look at this."

"What has his Grace done this time?"

"Look at this and tell me what you think. *Here* is what I wrote, and *here* is what he did with it."

Fritz took the two clippings and read them with a slight frown, nodding, rereading. Surprisingly methodical fellow, Fritz, considering his swift, lounge-lizard party manners. He was a puzzle that Brian would have to solve some day.

"Well, Brian old boy," he said finally, "I hate to say it."

"Really?"

"Yep. For once the old soandso has managed to improve something."

"But there's nothing left, not a goddamn trace."

"I don't agree with you, I think there's a nice little trace, a whiff. No dramatics, just that slight note of 'who made this mess?' that the Master aims at."

"Look, he told me there was plenty of space for this piece. What happened to the space all of a sudden?"

"The fairies stole it away. How the hell do I know what happened to the space? He's always doing it, to me too. It's an old-Etonian prank. Every thirty-second of May the Master of Revels takes a . . . ah, forget it. It's too hot."

Fritz Tyler seemed pretty surly this afternoon. Heaven knows what went on in his private life, but on Fridays he tended to be surly as a bear. He would have said the Gettysburg address was too damn long on a Friday.

Brian took his castrated editorial back to his cubicle and buried his thoughts about Twining in work. Reading galleys, measuring, clipping and pasting. The back part of the magazine had become temporarily his province, by the usual process of drift: plays, books, culture—not a bad assignment, Twining had told him, "once you got used to Max Klaus's aridity and Wally Funk's self-importance and all the pomposity, condescension and mincing exhibitionism in between . . ."

He was tempted to ask George Wren out for a drink, but he remembered his desolate wallet and decided to let it go. George was raspingly cheery on the way out. He and Fritz Tyler were laughing as they got on the elevator. Brian took the next one and kidded Miss Marconi about her hairdo and took the bus uptown.

The elevator in his building went purring up to the sixteenth floor, and the doors slid quietly apart, ejecting him onto the rug. Everything was muffled in this goddamn building except for his cat, which squalled in the doorway of 16H, greeting him wantonly and scratching maniacally at *The New York Times.*

His apartment was bare, except for a picture of his parents on the bed table and a fluctuating row of paperbacks. With parents like that, he was lucky to look as pretty as he did, he sometimes thought. In the icebox there sat a frozen pork chop and some frozen peas. Six cans of cat food for Herman. Three cans of beer for Brian. Two cans. One. He wiped his lips. Now let's see.

He turned one of the burners on. The flame appeared, silently. Peas, pork chop. Pork chop, peas. Way it goes. He stood back and watched. That was a hell of a thing Twining had done with his editorial. He knew most of the commander's tricks by now. He could just hear him saying, "Oh come now, Brian, does the race situation *really* shock us to the core? Again? And I see you've got the Judeo-Christian heritage in here—couldn't we try another heritage for a change?" Tight-assed bastard—of course phrases sounded silly if you said them like that. After a while, you couldn't say anything at all. You played everything below the level where mockery was possible. Bushwa. He jerked the burner to "off." What's the use of talking. *Do* something, or shut up. He put the chop on his plate and sat down at the kitchen table; he punched open his book on emerging Africa and read it sourly as he ate.

3

Fritz Tyler took a cab uptown. Mentally he tried to see himself in a white silk scarf and an opera hat. The right clothes would help enormously. "Excuse me while I slip into something comfy." Rustle, rustle. For this caper, anyway. The green velvet smoking jacket? or straight into the monogrammed pajamas? Fascinating swine.

As it was, he just changed his shirt and doused himself in Aqua Velva, and set out again.

He took another cab, three blocks over and twelve down, and arrived at Mrs. Wadsworth's place at six sharp. The doorman was gloating over the daily double at Belmont. The elevator man was happy because the Yankees had lost to Detroit that afternoon. Two wrinkled festive old men, who managed to make the building a little less formidable than usual.

Mrs. Wadsworth's maid opened the door. Swedish, no doubt—Harriet Wadsworth was hooked on Swedish maids. "Madam will be right with you," the girl said, in her Swedish way.

The living room was done in Park Avenue green. The chairs and sofa were covered in light green silk. On two of the olive walls, facing himself so to speak, hung the late Mr. Wadsworth, the founder of the feast. Fritz always felt dislocated at this stage of the evening. The old cultural-shock problem that volunteers to the Peace Corps experienced. He didn't really belong in this kind of room; the smoking jacket was a sham.

Of course, confidence was the secret weapon of a man like Twining. These English fellows went to Swiss finishing schools and took the tripos in self-satisfaction, poise and the thrill of being me. They were kept away from nasty experiences in alleyways, at least until they were ready for them. Fritz went to the sideboard to get a drink. Nobody felt at home everywhere. Twining wasn't bad at it—but he wasn't *that* good.

Harriet Wadsworth came in with a swish of more green silk. Fritz felt he ought to fling away his violin and crush her to him, but settled for a peck on her powdery left cheek. He knew her very well in a sense, but in another sense scarcely at all.

"You should have asked Winters to make you a drink," she said.

"I wouldn't trust him to," said Fritz. "Him and his white hair."

She smiled—Fritz's little jokes were perfectly acceptable; rather fun, in fact. He handed her a martini and tipped her glass with his. "You," he said.

They sat on the sofa and he told her he'd booked the table for seven, for an 8:40 curtain; and she said she'd been dying to see it, to see if it was as good the second time. There was no question of taking Mrs. Wadsworth to anything for the first time: that had already been taken care of.

H.E.W. on the matchboxes, H.E.W. on the cigarette box—he would never really understand these people. He was out of his league here. What kind of mind went to the trouble of putting its own initials on matchboxes? (Wonder how Twining would make out in *my* old neighborhood? We'd nail his whatzits to the floor, that much I know.)

They drank up, and she said the car was waiting. The Rolls, natch. (Couldn't he have started out with a medium-rich woman, and worked his way up? No choice, in this case: it was Harriet Wadsworth or nothing.)

The restaurant was the usual stuffy, thousand-dollars-a-square-foot place. The food was lousy, the helpings were scrawny, the décor was gross. If Mrs. Wadsworth had been even a little bit poorer, she would surely have protested at this insult to her money: as it was, she didn't notice a damn thing.

He was feeling tense tonight. "Gilbert's going out to the West Coast again," he said abruptly.

"Oh yes?"

"Yes."

"He's a dear," she said mechanically. "And such a good editor, don't you think?"

"Absolutely first-rate. A Napoleon among editors. We'll miss him when he goes to the coast."

She was so rich and vague and stupid that she wouldn't bother to find out that the trip was only going to last about five days. Meanwhile, the waiters were crawling round with those great heavy faces—getting angry helped him to keep his own equilibrium: but it also changed him slightly in a way that he didn't quite like. He felt he should watch this.

"Can't you manage without him?" she said after a moment.

"Well yes, we *could,* if he stayed away a bit longer we could probably manage perfectly fine. It's the quick-changing back and forth that's difficult."

"Oh yes, it must be."

She didn't know the first thing about it. Christ, she was stupid.

"Of course," he went on, "we'd have to strengthen the staff a little, Brian Fine is an excellent technician but well *you* know . . ."

"Yes?"

"I mean a man like Fine is an indispensable man in any organization; but he lacks, well what is it? Do you understand what I mean at all?"

"I think so."

Fritz winced. "But I really believe we could manage all right. George Wren—you know, the new fellow, you met him at the anniversary party (Doesn't ring a bell?) and again up at your place—well anyway, he's the new editor, and I think he's quite promising. When he gets over—"

"I think I remember him. Was he a small stout man?"

"No, that's Brian Fine. He's been with us for years."

"Oh yes, I'm always getting him mixed up with the man with the funny teeth."

They got to the theater twenty minutes late, as usual. Harriet didn't seem to sense the rage of the people underneath her, although Fritz felt it scorching his trouser legs. On the other hand, he had missed twenty minutes of what looked like a miserable play. Englishmen swearing never sounded convincing.

At the intermission, Harriet said, "I don't know why the English seem to handle this sort of theme so much better than we do."

"Hmmm."

"Americans are so adolescent . . . I wish I could review it for somebody."

"You do?"

"Simply adore to."

"Why don't you then?"

"Oh, Mr. Twining never lets me review anything. He says that Wally whatshisname would be offended."

"That's funny. He's allowed other people to substitute for Wally. In fact, between ourselves, I've heard him say that the more people we can get to substitute for Wally, the stronger our drama department will be."

"Really? Then I suppose he just doesn't like my stuff."

"Why don't you—no, forget it."

"What?"

"No, its impossible, forget it."

"What's impossible?"

"Well, I was going to suggest that you do a review and submit it formally to me while Gilbert's away—but it wouldn't work. Twining's much too foxy."

"Pity." She looked quite crushed, in her slightly unfocused way. Only a rich, spoiled nut would be taken in by an offer like that. She gazed sadly into her program, touched (Fritz hoped) by the goofy proposition, which hadn't cost him a damn thing. "He's quite right, you can't have a divided command," he said. Now think through the implications of that while I go the the men's room. Deep thinker.

The curtain went up on another stretch of shrill, me-working-class-Tarzan protest. He couldn't take the English class thing seriously, however hard he tried. Harriet Wadsworth, the fattest cat in the theater, loved every moment of it. That was one measure of its remoteness.

His knees were uncomfortable. Harriet Wadsworth's gleamed just an inch away. She wasn't so bad, wasn't even so stupid. At her prices, you didn't have to remember names and faces, didn't have to remember that Brian was the fat one and that Philo was the one with the teeth. He wouldn't himself—it was terror and cunning that jogged a man's memory. And she did seem to have a touching faith in *The Outsider,* enough to keep it more or less afloat. She had a poor mouth these days, and said that death taxes had cut the estate in half, but she still came across with the checks. And it occurred to him as he fidgeted through the last act that if she was allowed to do her crazy reviews, *The Outsider* would never want again.

On the way out, he caught a glimpse of himself in a full-length mirror. He looked as if he knew what he was doing, and that was something. He might have the occasional small lapse in confidence, when the chic became suffocating, but compared with, say, Brian Fine—

They climbed into the back of the Rolls-Royce. He really should have a silk scarf. Harriet Wadsworth wasn't so bad. She had rather a sweet, hopeful kind of face. At forty-five, she should be growing up any day now. It was a soft uncalculating face, absolutely guaranteed not to hurt anyone intentionally. He squeezed her hand, and was surprised to feel a crunch of white glove instead of skin.

Gilbert Twining could probably have sailed through the rest of the night without trying to like Harriet, without even trying to pity her. O.K.—that didn't necessarily make Twining a better man. There was such a thing as being *too* cool. Fritz had his own motives for making out with Mrs.

Wadsworth, and he admitted that they weren't all high-minded ones: but he wouldn't go on with it for another minute if he didn't like her as a human being. It was precisely this difference between himself and Twining that convinced him that Twining's liberalism was nothing but attitude; which in turn accounted for *The Outsider's* tinny ring these days.

—Tyler, however you slice it, you're still a bastard.

—O. K., but a bastard with a difference. A bastard with a heart.

IV

1

George Wren sat on the park bench, rocking the handle of the baby carriage and staring into space. He hadn't exactly been thrown out of the house, but he and Matty had had a painful conversation which had eventually sent him stalking through the door, wheeling Peter ahead of him.

"This is becoming ridiculous," she had said over breakfast. "You're a married man now, not a child."

"Look, I've got a headache."

"I'll bet you have."

"All right, you win the bet. Now let's drop it." She looked awfully pretty this morning, in her white blouse and pleated skirt, and he didn't want to fight with her. A fight could ruin the whole weekend. "I'm sorry," he said, "it was stupid of me."

"You don't have to do it, you know. He can't force you to have a drink with him. The worst he could do is to fire you—and being fired from *The Outsider* . . ."

"He wouldn't fire me."

"Then what *is* it? Has he got you hypnotized? Why do you *listen* to him?"

"I don't know . . . Look, I'll take Peter to the park, if you like."

It didn't help much, she was too smart to be fobbed off with a Boy Scout gesture. But at least it would keep him from feeding her anxiety any further. When Matty's anxiety reached a certain level, she switched reluctantly over to annoyance, and annoyance made her use more italics than he cared to hear. Then his own distaste had to be repaired, and before you knew it, another weekend was shot to hell.

The park was only a small, concrete playground. You could never forget it was concrete, because every now and then a child would fall off one of the appliances and start to scream. Great city, this. In spite of all the good advice it had received from *The Outsider* over the years.

He was the only father present, although this was a Saturday morning. The matrons skittered about in Bermuda shorts and fantastic-looking trousers. One of them even had curlers in her hair. Did women in other countries have these totally distinct phases—now I'm attractive, now I'm a totally dilapidated bag? Must ask Twining about it.

My God, Twining. What would *he* know? Sitting in a park, at this very moment probably, in heat for some two-bit girl. If I felt like that, thought George, I'd just go up and introduce myself, easiest thing in the world. There was a girl right here, up to her ankles in the sandbox—perhaps in the interest of science I should . . .

Well, that was enough of that. He was happy with Matilda. Very happy. Just this little difficulty at the moment, so easily taken care of, if he would just make the smallest effort. These evenings with Twining were really very foolish. There was no excuse for them.

His head was aching pretty badly. All the shady seats were taken; and anyway, he could hardly squeeze in among all those mothers. So there he was, stranded in the midday sun, listening to a compressed clatter and wail of children; the glare on his newspaper was too bright for comfortable reading; so he shut his eyes and at once Twining's voice came back, as if it had been there all the time.

"Fine, as I see it, is working to no plan at all. Couldn't if he wanted to. Tyler, now, is more interesting. Tyler . . ." George opened his eyes and the memory dissolved; Twining's voice was lost among the children's. Why was Tyler more interesting? He shut his eyes again, but the needle had moved on, and Twining was saying, "I'd like you to keep an eye on things while I'm away, George. Nothing official, mind you. But they may try putting things in the magazine or popping you home in a jiffy cab, old boy." . . . Twining never made any sense at that time of night.

Having come from a $13,000 job down to seven-five, he found it hard to believe that what was going on at *The Outsider* could be called a power struggle exactly. Of course, money was a ridiculous yardstick. The magazine's ideals were certainly worth fighting for. But he retained this silly superstition that you needed money for a power struggle.

Couldn't stand much more of this heat, it would be giving him hallucinations soon. What he really wanted was to lie down with Matilda and forget all this nonsense. But he supposed it was hopeless to think about that.

—So, look at it this way, even if Fine and Tyler and everyone else were massed in this insane conspiracy (to take over *The Outsider*'s debts and bad will), why should this worry a cool cat like Twining? He knew their motives and their limitations. Intellectually he could buy or sell them. So why—?

He wheeled Peter home, and since the street was empty, he said, "Was Aunt Sandra right when she said I was too young to marry?" out loud, to the baby. "Forget it. What's eating Twining?"

And the baby said, no it didn't really say, "Use your brains, Wren," think about Twining sitting in that other park, peeping at some two-bit girl, Twining on fire, tongue-tied, unable to bring the old charm to bear; you really think Twining is so hot? Really Wren.

But that was something he just couldn't believe. Twining had made it up. At worst, it was some crazy English thing about not talking to people you haven't been introduced to. It didn't mean he was a weak man in any sense known to George.

On a day like this you didn't attempt to unravel Twining's ingenious fantasies; you simply crawled into a hole and died.

"It seems very unimportant," he told Matilda hopefully.
"It does? Then why do you do it?"
"Curiosity, I guess. Burned-out hero worship. You know how I used to feel about *The Outsider,* still feel, in a way . . ."
"Yes, but that crazy Englishman . . ."
"English has nothing to do with it. Mr. Twining took over the original spirit without missing a beat. You know, he's a very compassionate man in lots of ways. But none of it seems important. I do agree with that."
"You know I don't mind if you stay out with your friends, dear, I've told you that."
"Oh, God yes."
"And I don't really want to nag you about anything at all. But when it comes to that, I don't know, that—"
"That what?"
"Nothing."

"No, go on, say it, you're getting a little closer every time."

"It's too hot."

Back to the park, men; the weekend was about to collapse in ruins. "I'll just say this quickly," he said: " (a) Mr. Twining is not a fag—"

"I never said he was."

"Yeah sure, and (b) it isn't Twining you're mad at anyway, it's the job. The cut I took to go to *The Outsider* really hurt, I know that better than anyone. As opposed to a little detail like saving my soul—"

"Oh George, you don't think you're saving your soul now do you?"

They stood looking at each other. In a two-room apartment, they couldn't both stalk out of the room at the same time. Besides, they still had a pretty good understanding at times. A very good understanding. This other thing was just a speck he hadn't quite blinked out of his eye yet. And it was so stiflingly hot.

For some unpredictable reason, he laughed. And then she laughed, uncertainly. And no more was said about it.

2

Polly Twining lay on one elbow, with her nightgown pouting around her thighs. "You can't blame it all on your cousin Richard. It just isn't fair," she said.

"Nothing I can do to little Richard's memory strikes me as being the least bit unfair. However—"

"I don't see how a man who calls himself a liberal can be so unforgiving."

"Oh, that's just silly, dear—you're a liberal too if it comes to that, everybody's a liberal. You can take any stupidity you like and say, there, that's a liberal for you. Word covers simply everything."

"Perhaps you're right." However gently he put things, his arguments always seemed to fluster her. In the old days she would have pressed forward anyway, in that solid American way, but this afternoon she just gave up. "Look, just this about Richard," he said quickly, "for the hundredth time, I hold nothing against him personally. He has grown up to be a big-hearted bore, a very uncomplicated chap, as you say; and no doubt all his more offensive characteristics were passed on to me in the process. I was foolish enough to suppose once upon a time that offensiveness had something to do with success . . ."

Polly pulled her nightgown over her knees. "If we're not going to . . . look, I have things to do."

"I'd like to talk."

"All right," she shut her eyes. "But please, not about your boyhood."

"All right. Though on second thought, what's wrong with my boyhood? I thought it was rather charming."

"Don't talk like that, *please*. Rahther charming." She made an effort. "It's all so totally bogus—your boyhood, I mean. As far as I can make out, your cousin came to visit you for two or three summers, you can't even remember which. Then at twelve or so, you left home, and didn't see him again for fifteen years or so. In between, your life was one continuous triumph."

"I wouldn't say that."

"No, I know you wouldn't. But it *was*." He sighed, because he knew very well what she was thinking. *Boasting is for wogs, isn't it Gilbert? Right-wing wogs. Come, Gilbert, admit that it* was *a triumph. Captain of this, captain of that—and what do you call those funny things? chief petty wrangler, honorable second tripod, winner of the Peckinpaugh . . .*

"Oh God." He knew that was how he must sound to her.

He got the same impression from old English films sometimes. Spare us from Anglophiles gone rancid.

"And you mean to tell me that two or three visits from one small boy, between the ages of eight and eleven, ruined your whole life."

"I never said they ruined my whole life. I only said that—oh, what's the use." Polly was beyond his reach. She would never take him seriously now. Why he went on trying to explain himself, to reascend, he honestly didn't know.

"I've changed my mind. I don't want to talk," he said.

She stood up with a sharp, slightly gawky movement. That damn nightgown didn't help. She might at least wear something attractive. He lit a cigarette and his tongue played around the smoke. She was too thin, why hadn't he noticed that in time? One continuous triumph. Ha, ha. The funny thing, though, was that she was right—up to a point.

Because, to his astonishment, the real world had proved rather easier than Richard had led him to believe. When he finally left home and went to boarding school, he found that there were very few Richards to impress, and a whole slew of unexpected, soft people who were on the look-out for leaders and culture heroes.

And Polly was right about the other thing too, he had modeled himself so closely on Richard by then (there were no other models to hand) that he found people responding to him in much the same way as he had responded to Richard: with a timid respect that neutralized whatever they really felt. He knew instinctively which boys liked him and which loathed him; and he knew that it didn't much matter which they did: his manner kept them out, like plate glass. Of course one blundered at first, through sheer incredulity, and made actual enemies; but by the time Twining reached University, he knew that his ascendancy was a fact of nature; and he knew it, still, today. Dozens of Brian Fines, half dozens of George Wrens, two or three Fritz Tylers—he had empirical foreknowledge of every last twerp in the office.

So why, as Polly said, was he angry at Cousin Richard, who had given him, by sheer fluke, this fairy-godmother gift, this Early Imperial style?

Well, that was the amusing part. Richard had taught him tricks, all right; the half smile, the controlled impatience (which incidentally Richard had since discarded himself, in favor of some more simple-minded mannerisms: based, no doubt, on some half-witted hero at his own school). He had passed on to Cousin Gilbert the Establishment face. But in the process he had also stepped on something in Gilbert and broken it.

This was what one tried to explain to Polly; and this was what she was constitutionally unable to accept. A straight, Freudian explanation would have been quite acceptable, but not this thing. It didn't interest her, it obviously struck her as an evasion. Why didn't he see a real psychiatrist? she asked—well, because he didn't need to; because he knew all about it. He had his little English children's story about Cousin Richard and the crowd at Pooh corner. He knew she didn't like it.

He stood up himself and removed his pajama tops. Lord, it was hot. He shouldn't have tried such things on a day like today. It only made everything worse for next time. He put on a pair of light summer slacks and a sports shirt with a handkerchief at the throat. He brushed his hair carefully and patted some talcum onto his cheeks, until he *looked*, at least, cool.

He went out to the hall and said, "Think I'll take a stroll."

Polly was fussing tensely in the kitchen. "All right," she said.

"Anything I can get you at the shops?"

"No, thanks."

"Well." He leaned through and kissed her on the neck and she didn't look round. "Cheerio, then."

After seven years in America, he couldn't remember whether cheerio was appropriate; it sounded faintly false, yet no other phrase had replaced it.

He walked lightly, hands in pockets, down Elm Street. The park was two blocks along Cedarhurst. And in the park, the girl.

The girl? After the recent unpleasantness, it would be ashes in the mouth. He hadn't seen her for two weeks now. Supposing she found some way to talk to him, and supposing one thing led to another— He started to cross Cedarhurst, with a view to continuing his walk, past the park and into the shopping center. But that was rather pointless too. The bars would be full of televised baseball; and it was awfully hot for plain walking.

He wavered a moment and then made the right turn. The girl would be there, in a white dress perhaps. The most beautiful girl he had ever seen. Her face was with him all week, gentle, tolerant. If she ever spoke, it would probably be with an awful secretary's bleat. The lovely eyes would go vacant and she would never look beautiful again. But just as things were at present, she was impossibly captivating.

He could see her from some hundred yards off. Her poodle had nested down by her feet. (The poodle seemed to be her excuse for visiting the park every Saturday and Sunday, but Twining was certain by now that she really came to see him.) He walked slowly towards her and she didn't look up: but patted the dog with one hand and turned the page with the other, as if to emphasize how many reasons she had for being preoccupied.

He sat on a bench not quite opposite and pulled the detective story from his own back pocket. She was almost as lovely as ever—nobody could be quite as lovely as his memory of her. He made a stab at reading, but the second time he looked up, she caught his eye and smiled, and he hadn't yet covered a page.

For once, he didn't look away. But he might as well have. For he knew he was giving her the stiffest little smile in return, the frostiest little acknowledgment. He wanted to be cordial, but by the time his features had decoded the order, she had looked away again.

Blast. It still wasn't too late, though. She was fooling with the dog, getting him ready to go. She was in easy hearing range; in fact, he could almost whisper to her on such a still day.

He sat there watching her in frozen silence. He could picture the conversation, that would be easy enough, patting the dog and calling him a splendid chap; but he could picture, above that, his wife, drained of all admiration, of all liking even; lying propped on one elbow in a pose of sour seductiveness; not saying anything, of course, but *in her mind* blaming his failure—or his brief, hysterical success—on Anglo-Saxon decadence. Polly had respected him so much once upon a time: to have killed that, and now to kill it again in another girl, was more than one could face on a hot afternoon.

Resistance flickered—perhaps with another girl—a girl less hard, less knowing than Polly—you never knew which kind of girl had which kind of effect until you . . . She looked at him once again, and of course it was at the worst possible moment. Since she wasn't smiling this time, his own prim acknowledgment must have looked even more foolish than before. She stood up and began steering the dog away. Twining put his head in his hands and felt the hot flush of his temples: that was it for this week. Tune in next Sunday for another indecisive episode.

The pleated white skirt flared and swayed out of sight at last, over a low rise, leaving one positively drained. This was one thing that Richard hadn't taught one to handle. Quite the contrary.

Still, it was too hot to get angry at Richard again. Dull fellow, basically. (I forgive you, Richard. *Quite* all right.)

He turned his thoughts to *The Outsider:* which always restored the tissues like a dip in cold water. He sometimes thought he had invented the place as a form of therapy. For his particular purposes, it was almost too good to be true.

3

On the Monday after going to press, *The Outsider* was at very low pressure. Olga Marplate spent Saturday mornings tidying ferociously, so that the place was neat as a morgue when the next week began. Since the building's only possible charm lay in raffish disorder, it was a grim place to file into after a Marplate weekend.

Olga had clipped out several ads for new office space which she presented to Twining in the form of a memo. We need, she said, daylight, more efficient use of space (no more wiggling between those packing cases), washrooms that actually work—the memo covered two sides and represented fifteen years of gathering grievance on Miss Marplate's part.

Twining was about to file it with Miss Marplate's other recommendations; but he decided on a slightly vicious whim to send for her instead. She came in looking cautious and medium-truculent, and he said, "I've read your memo, with the usual interest, Miss Marplate. Have you anything to add to it?"

"You know my position, Mr. Twining. I find this place extremely impractical."

"Have you been to see either of these places that you mention?"

"Yes, sir, both of them. On Saturday afternoon and again early this morning."

"I admire your keenness. What did you think?"

"Well," she said carefully, "they were both very distinct improvements on our present—"

"Won't you sit down, by the way?"

"Er, no, thank you—in the utilization of space, there was simply no comparison at all. And the atmosphere in each was much, well, cheerier."

"What was it, gun-metal partitions, men's locker-room sort of thing?"

"No, the partitions were a very nice olive in the one case; and in the other—"

"Long white corridors like a hospital, I suppose, marvelous public-address system, calling Miss Marplate, calling Miss Marplate—wanted in emergency accounting," he chivied.

"Please, Mr. Twining."

"And I can just see myself too, striding about in rubber gloves and a little white mask. Dr. Twining, wanted in surgery—nasty case of ruptured editorial."

"Thank you." She had turned already and was halfway through the door.

"I'm sorry, Miss Marplate, I didn't mean to tease—but you do see what I mean, don't you?" Just behind her, George Wren was obviously listening, and the ineffable Philo Sonnabend was probably listening too, with his smile for all occasions—Twining didn't want a public humiliation for Olga, at most only a small private one. It didn't do to overspend his ascendancy.

"I'm sure the places you saw had much to recommend them; and I'm sure that from a business standpoint this place must be truly exasperating. I've told Fred a hundred times not to put his packing cases right bang in the middle of the office. It creates the most frightful bottleneck."

"He's got to put them somewhere."

"Yes, well, there you are. But anyhow, quite apart from the sheer expense of one of these new places, they do generally turn out to be rather soulless, don't you think? The one you took me to last month—well, honestly, Miss Marplate, one would have needed roller skates and a megaphone . . ."

"You can sacrifice too much for quaintness." She had lowered her voice. She must know that a squawking match with Twining could only end in embarrassment. "To take just one thing, you can't even have a private conversation in this office. And of course what that does to employee morale . . ."

"Miss Marplate, the best magazines are all produced by chronic malcontents. Take away the note of hysteria and discomfort, and what have you got?"

"What have we got now?" she looked as if she was about to say, but Twining cut her off sharply.

"You've been here for, what, fifteen years, Miss Marplate? Ever since Frank Tippett started the magazine, in fact. Those must have been great days, a veritable golden age. Everything was new, everyone was young. You—"

"So, I can definitely tell them we're not interested in the new offices then?"

"That would be best."

Good Lord, why had he brought this on himself this

morning? Olga's memos arrived every week or so: it was her great dream, to have a business-oriented office, where the crud and filth of creativeness never had a chance to settle. Why not leave her with that? Why step on her little memos?

It must be some kind of Monday-morning death wish. He even felt a passing urge to tease Brian Fine. He was weary of fencing with these two seriously. How about saying to Brian: "So you want to have editorial conferences, do you? You want me to sit here listening to Fritz's jokes, and quivering to the miracles of group think, and generally rallying the team—oh, all the other magazines have them, you say? *That's* why you want them? Really Brian—"

Instead he picked up his layout dummy and began plotting the next issue. He would be out of town when it went to press, and he didn't want to leave too many loose ends for the lads to bollix around with. Time wasted frisking with Brian Fine would be paid for heavily.

He was getting a worse and worse feeling about the office. If they had been Englishmen, he would have known precisely where he stood. But Americans could be as inscrutable as a den of Chinamen. He remembered the omens whenever his cousins were plotting some fresh humiliation—a sense that they were sitting too quietly, or that their conversation was too neutral. There was something like that in the timbre of office noises, in the way they huddled together and went out to lunch together. He was actually almost afraid to leave. For five days, afraid . . . Perhaps he was taking all this too seriously, but the magazine meant so *bloody* much to him.

Then again, there was George Wren, who was trying to balance a ruler on his forehead. Him at any rate you could trust. The ruler dropped off and George caught it and bent lazily over his desk.

Must have one last good chat with George before leaving town.

George had had a pretty good weekend after all, and was bored, but not horrified, by the Monday bleakness. Putting together another copy of *The Outsider* seemed to be a new low in pointlessness; it was like wheeling an old gentleman down to the promenade for his afternoon airing. No one expected anything fresh and exciting from *The Outsider;* but a few were comforted to see the old fellow making his weekly appearances.

Did this happen to all magazines? He supposed it must. The editors clamored for new ideas, but always found something wrong with them, and were drawn magnetically to the old ones; and old subscribers woke up just long enough to deplore any change in layout, any modification of the puzzle page. George had been encouraged to come up with new ideas, but after five had been turned down in the first month, he had mercifully stopped having them. He thought like an *Outsider* editor himself now.

For instance, there was a very funny article on his desk right now—it made him laugh, it made some points—but automatically he had turned it down. Why? Fine and Tyler and everyone else were always saying, God the magazine needs humor. But the humor submissions never quite seemed to come off; Tyler or Fine would make a face over them. A face that said, you *see* why we can't take it, don't you? "Yes, it's quite funny," they would say, and George would feel like an idiot.

So George decided to save them the trouble and began turning the stuff down at source. Worse still, he was even beginning to see what they meant; he was getting the same mystical idea of what constituted a worthy *Outsider* article:

something intelligent, understated, tasteful. Everything else glared horribly on his desk.

Monday morning was no man's land between home atmosphere and office atmosphere. It coincided with a rhythmic idleness in the magazine's printing cycle, and he could still hear Matty saying, last night, comfortably, in bed, "Why do you go on with it then?" He imagined that he was back in bed with Matty, trying to answer that . . . "Believe in the possibilities of the magazine. No good? Oh, heard it before. O.K., how about this—always running into people who have just discovered it, and they're as excited by it as I used to be. *Where* do I keep running into these people? Well, at the Grimonds' there was somebody . . . and there must be others. I mean, it's only behind the scenes that you see how stale and tired everything really is. I was learning from *The Outsider* right up to the minute of going to work there." Am I boring you with this? Matty— wake up, damnit! Now then.

"I also feel I owe Mr. Twining something. For seven years, he was my teacher, my guide . . ." He looked in at Twining now: he was frowning slightly over the layout dummy. Why he bothered to frown was hard to say, since the magazine looked exactly the same every time around. Was this the fault of Twining or was it an institutional problem? could the magazine be reawakened by a kiss from a charming young editor? or was this whole train of thought just a comment on the weather?

Everyone said the summer issues could be written off in advance. And George had only been working here since the spring. Matilda's question had driven him into a more defensive position than the situation warranted.

Nobody asked him out to lunch today—the conspiracy had petered out or gone underground—so he had a sandwich at his desk, and prepared himself for a somnolent afternoon: thinking about Matty, perhaps, in some of her less controversial aspects.

The office droned through the afternoon in neutral gear. Miss Marplate's cemetery filled up slowly with wastepaper, cardboard, and huge, unwieldy crates. The rudimentary community that had formed itself by each Friday had as usual come unstitched over the weekend, and everyone in the place seemed to work in special isolation on Mondays. There was no public self, only the remains of private weekend selves. Besides, everyone was more or less waiting for Gilbert Twining to go away.

At ten to five, George Wren started for the elevator with real determination. Twining came out of his cubicle quite swiftly.

"Mr. Twining, I really must get home. My wife—"

Twining could not stand there arguing with him of course; it would have ended his domination forever. George counted on this, and was already pressing the button of the exasperatingly slow elevator.

"There are one or two things I'd like to discuss with you, if you have a mo."

"I'm sorry, Mr. Twining."

"Only take a mo," Twining said, as he reached for his hat, "here we are." The elevator arrived and he steered George into it by the shoulder blade.

Well, it wasn't precisely an order, it was something a little bit worse. An order was something you could disobey.

"Look, Mr. Twining."

"Yes, George?"

George realized that Brian Fine and Olga Marplate had followed them into the elevator and were listening closely. It was the damnedest impromptu happening. Twining had committed himself by getting into the elevator; if George refused the drink, the commander would lose some crazy kind of face, might even lose the whole colony. What was more, George could sense that Brian Fine definitely, and Marplate possibly, were silently beseeching him to refuse the drink. It was so goddamn silly, he wanted to bang all three heads together till the whole building rang with it.

"It'll have to be a very quick one."

"Oh quite, I have to get home myself."

The rest of the trip was taken in awkward, elevator silence.

4

"And you might keep an eye on our Mr. Tyler as well."

"Huh? Why Tyler?"

"You know, disciple and master sort of thing. Tyler used to imitate every move I made, you know. Now he's eager to move on to the next phase. Eating the parent."

Must be crazy, thought George, must be going off his chump. Thinks that people are eating him now.

Twining smiled at him in a knowing, tolerant sort of way. Probably thinks *I'm* imitating him, thought George with lazy truculence. Have I got some surprises for *this* baby.

"I'm not unappreciative of our Fritz, he has a certain amount of ability and I wouldn't care to lose him. But he mustn't get ideas beyond his capacity, must he?"

George shook his head. Sounded like that kind of question. George felt uncommonly relaxed and on top of things this evening.

"You may wonder why I talk to you in this way, George. But I have one or two excellent reasons. To begin with, protocol is rather a waste of time in a small office, isn't it? We have a certain maneuverability" . . . yak yak yak.

73

George had promised Matty he wouldn't stay out late tonight. What the hell was he doing here then? . . . "You and I have a certain understanding . . . size people up straightaway, and you . . . have also noticed a pronounced tendency over the past year or so . . ." George hated this lousy bar, with its cheap red seats and its imitation paneling. Probably made of cardboard, put a fist through it one of these days and find out. Drink up and get out of here. "So—if you happen to notice anything of the sort going into the magazine while I'm out on the coast, phone me collect, either at . . ." Anything of what sort? What was the dear chap talking about now? "Did you get that George? Here, I'll write it on this."

He jotted something down on a cocktail napkin and passed it over to George. Two telephone numbers. How about that.

"There, I don't expect anything in particular, but it's best to be on the safe side. *The Outsider* is rather unusual in its fundamental, what's the word, decentralization. I consider myself something of a constitutional monarch, you know. Harry, two more—but of course, one must . . ."

"No more for me."

"You're too late, I've already ordered them."

"Don't want any more."

"All right, you don't have to drink it. But wait until I've finished mine, will you?"

That sounded reasonable. George folded his hands over his stomach and virtually went to sleep just like that. The next thing he took in was "Imitation is a queer business. I had an older cousin—I may have mentioned him, boy called Richard. Dreadful little snob, everything I most detest. And yet . . ." George focused sharply on the colored lights dancing behind the bar. Drink up and get out of here. He picked up the new double martini and took a sip. Twining said, "And the funny thing was that my wife says we were *all* such, well not snobs exactly, but sneerers. My English friends and I would sit in a pub, or railway carriage, and sneer at everyone who came in. Make fun of them, you know. And we were *socialists.*"

"Well, why not?" said George suddenly.

"Eh? Why not?"

"Yes, why not? I mean I'm pretty far left myself, and yet I . . ."

"But my dear George—you don't know the first thing about sneering. You have to be an Englishman—or at least, so my wife tells me. She is, you know, a warm-blooded liberal, a different species altogether. And when she finally met one of my English friends she said, 'But he's just an intellectual Fascist, Gilbert. He seems to despise *everybody.*' And that chap was almost the *saint* of our group."

"I don't see what that has to do with anything. A rotten system has created a lot of rotten people. Socialists have every right to despise them, if they feel like it."

"Yes, but she says that if you don't really like people at all, what's the use of going on? Well, we have many merry arguments on the point which I won't bore you with now. Reform is all love, love, love with people like that, as you know. Tell me, how did we manage to get on to this subject?"

"I have no idea."

"Well, there it is. I suppose I was some sort of left-wing boy wonder when I met her. Just over from England, you know, brought in to take over *The Outsider,* no end of a chap. I'm afraid I've been rather a disappointment since then."

George took another belt of his martini. He was having

another spasm of wanting to leave. Twining leaned forward and said quickly, "About that other little matter. I'm afraid I don't seem to be getting anywhere at all."

"You don't?"

"No, that's the funny thing. You see my cousin Richard gave me all sorts of confidence with most things, but none at all with women. It's most curious—I couldn't have been more surprised when I first discovered it. I was in my second year at Cambridge . . ."

"Excuse me," George slid and clattered away from the table. "Got to go to the men's room."

He went out and read the inscriptions over the urinal and came back feeling cleaner. Four more swallows of that martini and he was free—no one was going to stop him, by God.

"Now about the magazine," said Twining. "I consider you my lieutenant from now on, do you understand? It's quite natural that there should be a power play among the others—it's almost a biological law. And perhaps, if any of them had sufficient stature—well, who knows? The fact is that they haven't. Perhaps, as an American, you view them differently? Tyler has been a great disappointment to me. Brian? Well, yes Brian. The others barely exist. They might have the strength to take over the magazine, but certainly not enough to run it decently."

"Tell me, Mr. Twining, does anybody else know the things you've told me about yourself? I mean the personal things."

Twining looked at him with a craftiness George hadn't noticed before. "You mean they might have less respect if they—a man who fails comparatively with women cuts rather a poor figure in this country, doesn't he? Is that what you mean? No, rest assured, I have never told another soul.

It was the sheerest impulse that led me to tell you. Since I picture you now as a sort of lieutenant . . ." Two more swallows and he really was free. George didn't want to be looped when he got home, so he didn't want to swig them down in one go; on the other hand, he felt he couldn't just leave them. So he settled himself for two or three long minutes more of Twining.

"You see, George, it's obvious that *you* believe in *The Outsider.* You gave up a very good job to come to it. And, of course, your letter to me was extremely eloquent. Quite a breath of fresh air after Brian Fine's editorials."

Then why do you cut *my* editorials to ribbons too, thought George. But relief was just a swallow away now, and he amused himself by singing the commercial in his own head, while Twining talked. Relief is just (dum-dum) . . .

"Brian, you see, hasn't the enterprise to go anywhere else. And anyway, he has a kind of infantile dependence on the magazine, which he mistakes for love. Fritz Tyler is too self-conscious, too artificial—you can't say what his feelings are about the magazine, because they are only imitations of feelings, second-hand reflections. Of course, that's his whole weakness, isn't it?"

Again, that terrible blackmailing trust in one, that sneaky Old World candor. George didn't want to hear Twining's opinions of his employees. It was even more indecent than his wretched little non-sex life.

He saw what Mrs. Twining meant about sneering. Yet subjecting Twining to his own kind of analysis, you had to admit that *he* loved the magazine. He could have gone on at any time to bigger and richer things—George had scarcely seen such professional ease and confidence any-where, even at Big Mother Network: you would pay him just to sit at a desk—and therefore he too must be staying with *The Outsider* out of love. Whatever that proved.

"But you," Twining came chiming in, with that extraordinary sensitiveness of his, "you *do* believe in *The Outsider*—isn't that so?"

George had half a mind to make a point. "Well, yes," he said, "of course. I think it does a lot of good."

"But?"

"But?"

"Yes—what's the reservation you were going to add to that?"

"Well, only that it seems funny to be having a power struggle over it. I mean it's a good little magazine—but really. On a cosmic scale—"

It took him a moment to register that Twining was annoyed by this. He had never seen it happen before, and it was only a very slight modulation anyway.

"Is that all the magazine means to you? You gave up a good job for that?"

"Well, yes, I mean no, of course I believe in the magazine . . ."

"I don't think you know what you believe, George. I think perhaps you've had a little too much to drink, and you want to say something that sounds important."

"No, I didn't, what I mean is, you've got to have sense of, you know, proportion . . ." He found himself stammering stupidly, so he stopped. Twining was putting him down, the way he put down Marplate and Fine; and George was just a little too high to do anything about it, right at the moment.

"We'll get you into a cab."

"No, I'll take the subway."

"Very well, old boy." Twining laughed. "As you wish."

George slapped his hat on. That British Foreign Office smile was just too damn much. He was shaken by a squall of tipsy rage: no wonder Twining had no friends. George was ready to join the nearest conspiracy himself.

He was careful not to trip on the way out.

V

1

The following Monday, Gilbert Twining flew to the West Coast.

There was a denser emptiness in the office, reinforcing the usual Monday emptiness. Olga Marplate quickly took the opportunity to activate her efficiency rules. The secretaries' lunch hours were timed and George Wren received an incredible memo about coming in late. ("An office cannot be run to suit the convenience of individuals.") These rules were always in potential effect; but Twining was so amused by them, and by Miss Marplate's ideas of efficiency in general, that nothing was ever done about them when he was around. George made an airplane out of his memo and sailed it out over Philo Sonnabend's desk; but this did not altogether relieve the bristling unpleasantness that Miss Marplate had set in motion.

Outside of his own vague appointment as alter ego and number-one snoop, George wasn't aware of any dispositions that Twining had made for his absence; he seemed to have left the editorial department on automatic pilot—which seemed reasonable enough. George asked Twining's secretary, Miss Marconi, what the system was when the commander went on holiday, and was told that as far as anyone knew, he had never been on holiday before. His business trips were shaved to a minimum length, so that while he was away reasonably often, he was never away for long. For the past three years at least, his hands had never been off the wheel for more than two days at a time.

Thus an unnatural dependency seemed to have grown up, and what would in a normal office have been a short and routine trip seemed to stretch interminably in front of them.

By midafternoon, George got a strange feeling that Brian Fine was creeping stealthily into the power vacuum. He seemed to be bustling about with an unusual air of importance, and conferring absurdly often with Marplate and Sonnabend. Sure enough, at 4:20 and with the end of the day almost in sight, Brian came sailing into George's cubicle with a long report on Nyasaland which needed editing.

"Christ, Brian, I never do that kind of stuff."

"I'm sorry, George, but you know we're shorthanded this week."

"Did Twining say anything about this?"

"No, he seems to have overlooked it. Oh, and I'm afraid it's kind of a rush—"

George took the manuscript, which seemed to be awfully long. Nyasaland. At 4:20 on a Monday afternoon, emerging Africa. "You will help us out, won't you, George?"

"Oh sure. Why not?"

Brian bustled out again. He passed Fritz Tyler in the

corridor, and Fritz turned and gave him a funny kind of smile. His version of the Twining smile: tweedy tolerance as interpreted by Fritz Tyler. This place is nothing but a bloody English finishing school, thought George.

Making all allowances for Nyasaland, and for the time of day, this seemed to be an awfully stuffy article. George slashed crosses through the first two pages of introductory matter, the author clearing his throat of statistics, and turned them over. To be greeted with, "Nyasaland has a population of . . . sea level . . . tablelands." He reached for the pencil again. It was like a *National Geographic* article, without even the prospect of brown bosoms to lighten the load.

He saw across the corridor that Twining's dummy was still on top of the desk. He decided to go over and take a squint at it. As he suspected, there was nothing about Nyasaland in there. Above the desk hung a long list of scheduled articles and Nyasaland wasn't there either.

He turned and saw Brian Fine watching him from the corridor. Nothing very sinister about that of course—in an office this size and shape somebody was always watching you. And Fine couldn't look sinister if he tried. Still: the fat stranger on the Orient Express, what are you doing in my suitcase, my stout friend? Humber aporogies, etc.

"I don't see this article in Twining's future," George said. "What's the story on it?"

"It just came in this morning. Nyasaland's been in the news—did you see the Sunday *Times?*"

"Yeah, but I didn't see anything about Nyasaland."

"Well, it was there. In the second section. Anyway, the gold-reserve story seemed to me expendable, did you read that one by any chance?"

"Yeah—it was expendable all right. But no more expendable than this piece of crap on Nyasacrapland."

"I happened to find that crap as you call it quite informative and interesting. Anyway, someone has to make these decisions."

George was about to question this—some decisions were best left unmade—but decided to let it go. Fine's little burst of brief authority didn't bother him. After fifteen years a man was entitled to his fling.

As George wandered back to his own cubicle, it occurred to him that this was probably the kind of thing that Twining wanted him to report on straightaway. Fine was really a crypto-Fascist, part of an international ring, trying to subvert the magazine with dull articles—Twining's paranoia would get a big boost out of hearing that.

He thought about it for a minute or two, and then he thought about Twining's Foreign Office smile and the insufferable way Twining had put him down the other night, and decided to hell with Twining.

At 5:30 Brian Fine looked in and said in a businesslike way, "How's it going, George?"

"Great guns, B.F. I think we can save some of it."

"Do the best you can. And don't stay too late, will you?"

Fine was every inch the city editor now, with his little rounded shoulders and sleeve garters. Maybe Fine was just what the magazine needed. Maybe it was time for a new act. But, oh my, these articles of his were going to take some getting used to.

George stayed in the office until past the rush hour, and then strolled to the subway in the comparative cool of the summer evening. He bought a big wheel of Dutch cheese, because Matty liked the stuff, and some herring in sour cream for himself. The city was mellow tonight, the recent fetid heat wave had moved out to sea, and he walked slowly with his package under his arm, looking around for a change, counting the spindly trees on the side streets, and reading the door numbers. He felt light, as if the air were of a finer quality tonight. For the moment he had the illusion that his life was exactly as he wanted it, and that he wouldn't change it for Ibn Saud's or anyone's.

The next day he was reamused to hear Brian Fine inviting Fritz Tyler to lunch. Tyler would be giving his small tweed smile. "Who's going to pay, Brian?" "This one is on me." "Good man." It sounded extraordinarily funny from the next cubicle.

2

"The summers are getting longer and longer," said Brian Fine.

"True," said Fritz Tyler.

"We could use some decent restaurants around here. I mean, I love Italian food, but . . ."

The minestrone bowls were almost gutted and they were still talking about restaurants and weather. Last night's cool snap had carried over. Brian shifted his burden of buttocks restlessly. "Look, Fritz, it occurred to me that you and I should have a talk while Twining's away."

"A talk about what?"

"Well, policy for one thing. Editorial policy."

Tyler laughed. "Twining's going to be gone for five days, old boy. There isn't much we can do about policy in five days."

"We can do something about the next issue at least."

"Yeah, well we're off to a great start with that article on Nyasaland."

"What do you mean? You okayed it."

"Of course, I'm that kind of fellow. I'll okay almost anything."

"Look Fritz, if you and I got together for a change . . ."

"Yes, old boy?"

"We could dictate things, we could have a voice. I think I know how you feel about Twining."

"You do? How do I feel about Twining?"

The waiter slithered the veal scallopini in front of Brian. Fritz had the chef's salad. It broke the conversation. Fritz and Brian both smiled at the waiter.

"Some people find Twining very arrogant," said Fritz. "I must say I've been lucky in that respect. He's never really given me the treatment."

Brian waved his hand casually and hit his water glass. "I've gotten hints of what you call the treatment—well, you've probably heard us going at it in that bandbox up there. But that part isn't important. It's just a routine. After all these years . . ."

"That's nice. I was just going to say that if I ever got a blast of hot air from the Master, I'd probably feel a lot more strongly about him. I suspect I'd hate his guts. So I'm glad to hear it's just a routine."

Brian mopped up the water with his napkin. He thought of his first encounter with Twining's routine. "My dear chap, this is wind. Wind in the, I fear, English sense." Like a whip cracked across the cheek. "Bombast again, I'm awfully afraid." "What precisely does this *mean* Brian?" "Brian, my dear *fellow*."

"I have nothing personal against Twining," said Brian. "I think he's nine parts bastard—well, who doesn't? But outside of that, it's mainly the magazine I worry about."

"That shows a nice spirit. Go through hell for the mag, eh?"

"Now come *on*, Fritz. Leave us not joke about this. Don't *you* think the magazine could stand improvement?"

"Oh sure. As you say—which of us couldn't?"

"That's all I'm saying then, that you and I should get together—"

"I thought it might be something personal. Didn't you like Mr. Twining once upon a time?"

That was a dirty question, because once upon a time everybody had liked Mr. Twining. His charm was almost irresistible, even for someone like Brian, who slightly resented his arrival. In fact he seemed to anticipate this resentment and to understand perfectly. Brian was the senior associate editor in those days and Twining used to go down to Sweeney's with him and listen respectfully to his opinions, and talk bawdy with him—Brian had never made such a warm friend in such a short time. It almost made him uncomfortable to have such a warm friend.

But then, maybe not so warm after all. Three months or so after Twining's coronation as editor in chief of the floundering *Outsider* ("We're getting Gilbert Twining from England." "Not *Gilbert Twining from England?*"), the commander called Brian into his cubicle and said, "Brian, old boy, I'd like to have a word with you about your editorials."

"What's on your mind, Gilbert?" Brian had called back. A pleasant spring evening, almost unbearably pleasant as he remembered it now.

After their sessions at Sweeney's, this interview couldn't be too painful: Brian strolled in, jaunty and grotesquely vulnerable, to have a word about his editorials. "Sit down a sec, Brian." Twining had his pipe in his mouth and a cluster of Brian's old editorials in his fist; and more on the desk. Brian was slightly alarmed at the size of the pile—Twining must have been ransacking the files all afternoon. Brian hadn't suspected him of such thoroughness.

"These won't do, you know," said Twining. The awful

little phrase. For the next two hours, Twining had gone through the damn editorials with him like examination papers, paragraph by paragraph, and every moment was painful. But Brian couldn't get past that first phrase. "These won't do, you know. Won't do, you know." Did he have to keep putting it like that? Won't do *what?* Brian forced his memory over the snag.

"You *do* see what I mean, Brian." Twining had remained impeccably friendly and polite throughout. Having ripped every bit of skin off his associate editor, having shredded his personality into blinders, he was more than willing to act as if nothing had happened; in fact he even suggested that they go down to Sweeney's for a quick drink. To talk about girls no doubt.

Twining's fingers, playing with the strips of paper: eight years of editorials—eight years' work, eight years of exaltation and righteous indignation, of sly thrusts and deadly parallels—all turning and twisting in Twining's Chippendale fingers. Twining created his own atmosphere. The cubicle was really a headmaster's study, with brown paneling and rows of leather bindings. Terribly English. In conclusion Brian would be asked to take down his trousers for a sharp smack with the riding crop. . . . "So," he said to Fritz abruptly, "didn't you like Mr. Twining yourself, once upon a time?"

Fritz smiled slightly and nodded, as if he had followed Brian's thoughts with approval. Perhaps he had some thoughts of his own.

"I remember," said Brian, "when you, too, were getting the Sweeney's treatment. Just like me, just like our young friend George."

"Yes, four wonderful years ago next week, as a matter of fact. Getting along with the chaps, one might call it, establishing a wonderful relationship with the men—I agree, Brian, I'm not crazy about Twining either. If that's what you've been trying to get me to say."

"All right then—why don't we get together and . . ."

"So, call him a poor man's Lawrence of Arabia and let it go at that. I'm just wondering, though—what kind of magazine do you suppose it would be in your hands and mine?"

"It would be different."

"Yes, true."

"It would leave the well-known Twining rut, it would have life."

"Life."

"Then why not . . ."

Fritz looked at him with a very knowing and irritating smile. Fritz couldn't quite conjure up leather bindings, but he could be a pretty big pain in his own right. Twining had hand-picked the whole staff on some principle of interlocking incompatibility.

"I'm sorry, I can't go along with you quite all the way, Brian. Twining, for all that he's an unparalleled pain in the ass, still turns out a creditable magazine. He's a professional. I'd have to be sure we had something better to offer. You and I, that is."

"Don't sell yourself short, buddy boy. We have experience at least. And you're a hell of an editor in your own right."

"Thanks, fella."

Brian hadn't meant to say "buddy boy" at all. Phrases like that were a sign of nervousness.

"And George Wren may yet turn into something."

"Yeah, he may."

"Well, we have to take the chance sometime. If we could just do one whole issue without him. Have a genuine editorial meeting, instead of a series of *fiats* from on high.

I'll kill the piece on Nyasaland if you like. I wasn't that crazy about it. It just happened to come in on Monday, and I thought—but there are several other pieces lying about that might do. Look, Fritz, this thing can't be done unless you and I work *together*."

"And do you want to be the one to face Twining when he comes back next week, to tell him what's happened?"

"Sure, I don't mind. I'm not scared of Twining."

"Brave boy. I'll leave that part up to you then."

"Does that mean that you agree? To experiment a little with the issue?"

That stinking smile again. Boy, after Twining goes, you're the next. Strawberry shortcake—just like Tyler to choose the most expensive thing on the menu. His childish way of getting at a guy. Really the only thing to be said for having this soandso as an ally was that he was kind of indispensable.

"I don't know, Brian. It seems like an ineffectual scheme to me. If we had a couple of issues to play with, it might be different—although even then, Twining would be a tricky man to beat. I have to doubt whether you and I are up to it. Remember, two slightly inferior issues and Twining is more powerful than ever."

"At least we could have a *meeting* . . . Have you got a better scheme then?"

"Supposing I wanted to nudge Twining out and someone else in—yes, I would definitely go about it differently."

After that, Tyler got impenetrably facetious and smiled his new smile and didn't offer to help even with the tip. Fine glumly pulled out a ten: he was sick of this greasy restaurant, why couldn't they afford a place with a little class? Tyler depressed him now, Tyler had always depressed him. He had never lost that slight edge of irritation with last year's boy wonder. He remembered his feelings of gloomy rage when Twining hired Fritz and gave him half of Brian's office and took the new boy down to Sweeney's. That clapboard partition had diminished Brian by half. He would never be Twining's number-one Kaffir again.

He made an effort to be civil. "Just tell me one thing, Fritz. Will you interfere with anything I might happen to do while Twining is away?"

Fritz laughed and said, "I can't very well stop you, can I? I have no authority over you."

So he supposed that was something.

3

Public appearances were always slightly overstimulating; one slipped into a kind of overdrive that was hard to climb down from. He sipped his drink slowly, waiting for the excitement to ease. He had shed his hosts half an hour ago, and all the twittering hangers-on and thrill-seekers had fallen away too, and he sat now in a dark bar, with nothing to feed his excitement, and much to deaden it.

It had been a more fretful day than he had planned on. Sipping iced tea on Countess Sadowski's back porch should have been all right. He had a clear view of the Pacific, between eucalyptus trees as graceful as candles: and he said that San Francicso was his favourite American city, and she said that *The Outsider* was her favorite magazine.

So far, so good. But than he suddenly got a wild notion, amounting almost to certainty, that not only was she not going to give him any money, but that she probably didn't have any money to give. Something in the way the garden was kept, something about the maid's uniform—it was impossible to pin down. Long experience at wooing hostesses had given him a nose for money, and he knew that there was very little about.

And here he was, trapped on her silly porch for the

afternoon. Sucking up to the rich was the least attractive part of his work anyhow: and when they weren't even rich . . .

He was bogged down in these meditations, wondering why he had ever expected a Russian countess (even a phony one) to have a social conscience, when a further irritant arrived: one of those small, fierce, brutally blunt Central Europeans, a baron something or other, who began to heckle him about the magazine: "It isn't so much the extra*ordinary* politics, etc., etc. (moth-eaten, right-wing aristocrat, type 2b—let it pass for once), but frankly I find it a bore."

"Perhaps if the politics were less extraordinary you would find it more interesting."

"Not at all, not at all. Left-wing publications *fasc*inate me—even yours did once upon a time, for at least three years. If one enjoys fantasy—"

Twining shut his eyes. Whether or not magazines got stale, readers certainly did. They should be ploughed under every few years and a new crop raised.

He wanted to say, have you any idea how hard it is to produce even a dull magazine; and how lucky you are that it is no worse than dull! With the best editors that poverty can buy, with no genuine correspondents—but only neurotic, wall-eyed dilettantes who like to travel, with home-grown writers whose *grammar* had to be corrected. (American education, oh dear!) . . .

My God, it was a triumph. Just take Brian Fine—he had been transformed from a sentimental windbag, a small-town orator with a tin ear, into a reasonably competent editor. One had lost his friendship along the way—that was a pity, a very big pity. One was new over here at the time, and had not gauged the national softness in these matters. Something to do with women schoolteachers perhaps? One had been incredibly excruciatingly gentle with Fine—you could hardly make any points at all, with less force—and Fine had gone stiff all over, very nearly burst into tears as well; and had nursed the grievance for seven long years since.

Take—while this preposterous little man was still talking, one might as well take everyone—Fritz Tyler. Fritz was the reverse of Fine in many ways, clever, self-critical, ironic. But how bad one was at judging Americans. Youthfulness had made Fritz look better, more generous, more promising than he really was. But Tyler's only real subject now was Tyler—Tyler the liberal, Tyler the intellectual. He had nothing original to say about anything else; nothing but interesting attitudes. God (the baron solaced him indirectly with the thought), what must it be like at a conservative magazine!

And now there was George Wren, his prose if not his brain rotted from working in television—Twining felt himself slipping back into the old English sneer that he had had to struggle so hard with; under the goad of the baron's heavier, less nuanced version, English sneering had a curious attractiveness. Like French cooking after German. George Wren was all right really, a bit malleable, a bit unformed: thinking it frightfully mature to say, as he had the other night, that the magazine wasn't really important—"on the cosmic scale"; not realizing yet that anything is important if you make it so; that ten people can be as important as ten million; that—

Well anyway, a dull magazine would be no small achievement, coming from that mob. And, peace to the baron, the amazing thing was that the magazine was much better than dull; it was, in Twining's opinion, outstandingly good. Perhaps it wasn't as malignantly clever as *The Watchman* in England had been—but then Americans didn't really appreciate that kind of thing. It made them nervous. The writing, God knows how, had style; there was—outside of Wally Funk's theater column, which was oddly enough considered one of the best in America—a minimum of posture and cant; it was possibly the most *civilized* magazine in the United States.

When the baron had finished talking (the chap had clearly brought his opinions straight down from Mount Sinai, such arrogance was almost more than one could bear), Twining told him all this. It wouldn't do any good and it always took a lot of energy, but this business about the magazine's being dull was more than he could take; he rose to it every time.

The baron continued yipping, because he was clearly a monstrously vain man, but he got a rabbity look under pressure. He had overextended himself, he didn't know his facts, proved to be, as one expected, a pathetic little diner-outer and loud mouth. Twining was depressed as well as keyed up when he left to go back into San Francisco. He despised bullying: when he disagreed with people he did so as affably as possible; and yet there it was again, that hurt, frightened look. How did one get anything through to these second-rate people? —And the countess enjoying the whole thing—although she hadn't paid to watch. (Give him Harriet Wadsworth any day, if one must do this sort of thing.)

After that came the lecture. And he found himself being very funny, a very good streak indeed, and the audience coughing and laughing in the brightly lit auditorium, and when he got down, the excitement was almost painful. The warm hum and the glitter as he marched up the aisle, quite intoxicating . . .

Never mind, it would go away in a moment. He glanced around the bar. He had long since given up noticing things or people as specifically American—yet the man two stools away looked American. Something to do with being in a strange city no doubt. One would rather have liked to talk to the man, but the big mouth and jaw didn't promise well: big buyer, slow deep voice, anecdotes—Twining was rather tired of talking to people in bars anyway. He was burning to talk, and at the same time tired of talking, if one knew what one meant.

It was rather difficult making friends with Americans of any kind. They drew back at the last moment. This fellow here—one could never be friends with him, not if one tried all night and half the next day. Just more and more anecdotes. Or take even George Wren: always a little stiff, always with the guard right up, even when the brain had gone to sleep. Queer.

. . . In England, of course, we all grumble and sneer together and are the best of friends. Well even if Polly was right about that, a sneer was better than no bond at all. And she wasn't right. Sneering (her word, not his, he had never thought of it as sneering) was an extra, one device among many for helping friends to enjoy each other: but it wasn't the basis of friendship. Polly didn't understand these things —what was the use of talking about it, even to oneself. Polly had never experienced friendship, hadn't the desperate need for it that we had; Polly was a healthy American girl with a simple nervous system. (And yet, a new duct of fever seemed to open in his forehead, Polly was right. He hated the sneering, in a way.)

He ordered another drink and looked beyond the big buyer. There was one other man at the bar—a recluse with a crushed hat. Forget about him. Kindest thing. Beyond that were some dimly lit pink booths and as far as he could make out there were two girls in one of them; by a curious arrangement of lighting, their legs were brightly floodlit but the rest of them was lost in night.

Their legs were crossed, and still as marble. Twining looked away quickly, but not before the idea had insinuated itself. Oh God, not that.

If he hadn't felt keyed up from the lecture, he would be all right; he would be all right anyway. He was old enough, knew how to handle it now. He remembered the old days, walking for miles along the Embankment, head down, exhausting himself, wearing it out. And then giving up after all and collapsing along the Charing Cross Road. Hating the cheapness and glitter, and flinging himself at it like a moth on a window.

That part of London made him almost physically ill; yet, furtive and eyes down, he went back to it; odi et amavi. There were lots of other men like himself, very calm and smooth to look at; city suits and club ties—flickering like ghosts in the corner of one's eye. They were brothers, but one never looked them full in the face.

And then home again, back to the half-witted silence of the country, to explain to Hilda why one was late again. Hilda was so much simpler than Polly: he associated her with the squeak of corduroys and the smell of dogs. She believed whatever was necessary. She told people, "Gilbert works so hard . . . Gilbert never gets excited." She still lived in Chipping Wandsworth, as far as he knew, with Wuffles the terrier (who must be a hundred by now), and her flaccid memories. (And drilled with the Women's Home Guard every third Saturday, no doubt, no doubt.)

He sipped his drink and tried to compose himself. Even the memory of Hilda jarred on him slightly: went off like a skyrocket in fact. The evenings in London had been a flight from this dull woman. Coming to New York had cured him of all that. Don't go back to it now. In New York he had felt clean for the first time in, oh, years; clean and free. It was all different there somehow. There was no magnet, as there was in every European city, that could jerk him downwards again. In fact, all that began to seem very silly and childish, and one almost began to wonder whether it had really happened at all.

He had even felt safe to marry again. His first wife's unresponsiveness had rather unnerved him. But Polly Silvers, the ardent young American for Democratic Action, who thought that he was a tremendous fellow almost by definition, because he had edited *The Watchman* in England and was about to edit *The Outsider* over here. Rapture! Surely it would be all right with Polly.

His second wife's gradual disillusionment was, he decided, a story for another occasion. One of the girls with the blacked-out tops had divined his interest, and was making a routine check. His own face shone in the bar lights: it looked a brownish red in the mirror across from him (one would have made a superb viceroy of India, he thought with feverish whimsy), and quite fantastically composed.

The girl had a wide, slack mouth and eyes dense in makeup. No doubt about her at all: she was the only kind of girl he could do anything with. She had never heard of *The Watchman*. Oh God, she looked so stupid and cheap. His hands were hot and the small of his back ached, but he said in a pleasant enough voice (a voice which sounded quite awfully English, in a strange city, and surprised the buyer two seats away), "May I buy you something, my dear?" And she sat down and ordered the warm tea or whatever it was, and called Twining "honey" and patted his knee and said he looked terrifically distinguished—all of which would have amused the staff at *The Outsider* no end, he thought wryly.

The thing that really frightened Twining, though, was

that the post-lecture excitement didn't go away, even now, in this hilarious abasement.

At this pressure one had to chose between the cheap pleasure or the most fantastic pain.

4

"You're much more relaxed," said Matilda Wren.

"And that's true," said George.

"Mr. Twining should go away more often."

"It isn't just that."

"Go away and stay away."

"All right."

He rolled over and looked at the clock. Twenty-five past eight. If he hurled himself into his clothes and went without breakfast, he would get to the office at 9:30, which was more or less "on time" for editors at *The Outsider*. He started to move, but found himself lightly pinioned by Matilda's arm. Being "on time" was all in the mind, wasn't it? He decided to stay put for the time being.

As it turned out, he didn't get to the office till quarter to eleven. Miss Marplate glared at him horribly as he came in, and very soon her secretary brought a fresh memo round to his desk. "Second time this week, intolerable, blah blah blah." Frustrated old hen. He showed the memo to Brian Fine, expecting jovial concurrence, but Brian said, "That's her job, you know, George. You should try to be on time. The rest of us are."

"Brian—it's me, your old buddy. You don't talk like that to your old buddy, do you, fella?"

"This place has become just too damn slack, old buddy—too damn old-buddy in fact. Miss Marplate is trying to turn it into an office."

George withdrew, scratching. Miss Marplate only had two more days to enforce her crazy rules. On Monday, chaos would resume, all the better for the rest. He decided, handsomely, to forget the memo.

But there remained all day a feeling of coldness, as if he had done something much worse than simply arriving late. Olga Marplate called him Mr. Wren—as in the sentence, "Will you be coming in at all this afternoon, Mr. Wren?" What was even more disturbing, Philo Sonnabend withheld his mechanical smile for the first time in months. His lips bulged grimly over his bridgework, until he looked like the most sinister character in the Hitchcock railway compartment.

Lucky I'm so relaxed, thought George. Otherwise Sonnabend's attitude could be pretty irritating. At these prices, you should be allowed to come in late now and then. (And just imagine the surrealist confusion in Philo's mouth if you gave it a tap with your fist.)

Brian Fine had placed an article on "Emerging Africa" on his desk. He thumbed through it and found the same ill-digested mixture of statistics and wheezing affirmation that had made the Nyasaland piece so hard to forget. Needless to say, it wasn't on Twining's schedules either.

"Mr. Fine, sir, sahib—what the hell is this one all about?'

"I thought it was time we paid a little attention to Africa. The future may be decided there."

"Yes, but I submit, my lord—a whole African issue!"

"Cut the comic irony, Wren. We've killed the Nyasaland piece, and we're using this one instead."

George salaamed and ducked out. Wonder what Fritz was making of this farce? He wandered into Fritz's cubicle to find out—and to put off working for a few minutes. But Fritz was playing it close to the chest today.

"Did you approve of this name-of-a-name article then?"

"Brian wants to do it, it's O.K. with me."

"Don't you think that this is one hell of a way to run a magazine?"

Fritz just shrugged and looked ever so slightly amused. The obvious message was, what the hell, Twining will be back on Monday. Relax.

So George relaxed, and cut emerging Africa from 4,000 words to 1,500, and went out to lunch. He was hungry, so he went to Luigi's even though he was by himself. Sonnabend, Marplate and Fine were three tables away, looking tremendously earnest and consequential. Fine had certainly become pompous during the last three and a half days, and now he was breathing it charismatically onto his companions. Miss Marplate had become quite a personage in her own right. Seven years ago—according to Twining—she had been a shy little creature, with dominion only over figures: but she had grown in confidence and swaggered now like a pigeon on a ledge, and made the editors sign for the petty cash, and billed them for any extra copies of the magazine they took home; and at the annual office parties, she asked the writers what they were working on now, and praised them judiciously, like a wise old football coach. Only Twining was out of range of her condescension; and with him away, she had come to a sudden magnificent flowering.

The three of them did look a bit conspiratorial at that. He fantasied through the spaghetti about this—wondering what position to take in the unlikely event that they really were conspiring. However annoying they had been to him personally, he couldn't get angry at them. Watching them huddled like that over their soup in solemn consultation, he half wished that they *could* put something over on Twining. Whatever it was that had made him come to *The Outsider* in the first place suggested that he should be on their side and not his.

In fact, the more he thought about Twining now, the more unequivocally he disapproved of him; his mind was solidifying on the point. George had been so charmed at first to have such a smooth fellow on his side that he had forgotten what he was about, had forgotten his own basic sympathies.

God knows, Fine and his group were not the underdogs of one's choice. They had been preshrunk out of sight by *lumpen* dreams, and by the whole machinery of, oh, city transport and self-service elevators and spayed cats and the whole squashing, squeezing life of the city. But they were the underdogs that came to hand. It was no use taking the right stance about Puerto Ricans and Angolans and missing sight of these, the victims of *this particular* situation.

And then who knows (he finished the spaghetti and ordered some cherry pie and ice cream)—maybe if they got a little power, they would straighten up from the embryo crouch, and see a little further. Maybe Miss Marplate would shed her pettiness and turn into a butterfly; maybe Brian Fine would abandon this cautious conventional African crap and really begin to swing; maybe Philo Sonna-bend would get his teeth fixed. At any rate, he believed in giving them the chance.

After a strict calendar hour, the three of them stood up sharply. A concession to Miss Marplate's rules, no doubt. They had to pass him on the way out, as he was lighting a lazy cigarette between courses. Olga glared at him again and, so help him, she looked at her watch and pretended to give it a small wind—Attagirl, Miss Marplate, he thought; you do it your way. He felt, as they waddled soberly past, averaging out at about five foot six, an affection bordering on tears.

When he got back, he found another article from Brian on his desk, to mock his fraternal sentiments. It was a solemn analysis of beat poetry, and it did give him the germ of an idea.

For George wrote poetry himself (mostly for a broadsheet called *Awake V*), but had never dared show it to Old Supercilious. How about taking this opportunity—now that everyone was sneaking junk into the magazine—to help himself to a larger audience? (*Awake V* had seventy-three subscribers.) —It was just a thought. *The Outsider* used poetry now and then, to fill in the corners.

At any rate, it wouldn't do any harm to feel out Brian Fine. George took his three latest poems out of the drawer and carried them diffidently around to Brian's office.

"What is it, Wren?" Brian said briskly.

"I have some poems here."

"By you?"

"Yes."

"For the *magazine?*"

"Yes."

Fine put down his cigar and reached out. The cigar smelled wretched. Brian read slowly, turning the first one over as if he expected to find something on the back. He put it down and grunted. The cigar smelled wretched and he was losing his hair. He put down the second one with either a grunt or a sigh, depending on which you were listening for. His cigar smelled wretched, he was losing his hair and there were discs of sweat as big as the great outdoors in his armpits. All that could be overlooked, however, if he liked the poetry.

"Well?"

Brian Fine jostled the three sheets together and handed them back.

"What do you think, Brian? Tell me, man."

"I'm sorry, George."

"No good?"

"No good for *The Outsider*."

O.K. I was just asking. George had been turned down by better editors than Fine. It had nothing to do with the quality of the poetry.

Still, Fine didn't have to look so magisterial about it. Being a top editor didn't add any special luster to his opinion: it was just an opinion.

"You write poetry, Brian?" he asked.

"I'm an editor, not a writer."

Coupling that with Olga Marplate's icy frown when he passed her on the way out reminded him that it would be uphill work indeed, rooting for these particular underdogs. He put the poems away and picked up the new manuscript. "The integrity of Allen Ginsberg's vision," it began. Here, let me shut my eyes and prognosticate. Ginsberg has ploughed a lonely furrow. Right? A conspiracy would be a nice change from this kind of thing, but Fine barely made the weight; he lacked leadership potential, he was a schnook.

He thought once more of writing to Twining, but Fine was too pathetic to scab on. And Twining was still Twining.

He put the poems back, where no one would see them. A poet must cultivate cunning and patience. Ginsberg wasn't the only one who could plough a lonely furrow. The seventy-three readers of *Awake V* would spread the word eventually.

5

Fritz Tyler polished off his editorial on federal aid to education and checked it through with Brian Fine. It was nice to know that it wasn't going to be cut and renuanced by the master. Fritz had become adept at anticipating

Twining's foibles, but every now and then his stuff came under the knife, and it was still quite a painful sensation.

Brian measured the piece carefully, but could hardly presume to judge the contents. Fine and Tyler were equals on the masthead and therefore in life.

There was an amusing aura of make-believe about Brian Fine as he bent over his measurements. After so many years of rather passive efficiency, he had managed to plunge himself into a political role at last: action and power, the things he talked of so knowledgeably in his editorials, were in his own hands. Or so he thought.

It was a comment on Fine—told you all you needed to know about him in fact—that he thought that one issue made a difference. In real life, Twining would be back on Monday, would raise an eyebrow and Brian Fine would topple over like a doll with a round base. As a political quasi-expert, Fine should know by now what happened to small risings and half-assed juntas.

It would be instructive to see how Twining handled the matter. With his great-man perspectives, he would see that one number buried in the middle of August was not worth a fuss. It was barely even a pseudo-event. And since Twining never allowed his enemies to accumulate, he would not chew them all out at once, but would focus his irony on this mistake and that mistake—all by bad chance, Brian Fine's. Next Monday would be one long purple blood-bath.

Fritz felt sorry for Brian, but not terribly sorry. Fine was like a child begging to be punished. He had been goading Twining for months now, itching for a test of strength. He had even been inserting things into his copy, and into other people's, that were obvious attempts at commander-baiting. Now he was making his big move.

"O.K., Fritz, we'll run it third. Thanks." Brian gave him a bracing smile. Very funny. Fritz sauntered back to his

cubicle. Fine's glory chart must be near its peak this afternoon. His whole lifetime had been a preparation for this.
On Monday it was back to GO. But he would have lived for
a few days.

Fritz's own strategy was radically different. Agreed that
the Twining situation had become impossible, a frontal
assault on the magazine's copy was not the way to dislodge
him. That was only to fight the commander with his own
weapons.

It was possible that Brian's floundering attempts to make
trouble might produce an unintended blessing or two. By
sheer, indefatigable, leech-like persistence, Brian might
wind up getting under the commander's skin. He had the
makings of a pretty maddening fellow.

But, in any case, it made no difference to Fritz's own
plans. At five sharp, he left the office and grabbed a taxi. A
pencil-thin mustache was one way of doing it, he thought.
Or hair parted down the middle.

He felt more at ease at Harriet Wadsworth's than on
previous occasions. For instance, he was amused, rather
than alarmed, when the butler changed the plates *before*
they had eaten anything; and the finger bowls hardly
bothered him at all. Harriet had had to learn these tricks
herself, once upon a time. He had recently discovered that
she hadn't been *born* rich and stupid, and this discovery
had made a tremendous difference.

. . . Boy, you'd never guess it, though. For sheer, insolent vagueness he had never met anyone to touch her.
"Who's Brian Fine again?" she asked in the middle of one
conversation. "Oh yes. That one." And you didn't want to
discuss anything more general with her, because you knew
she was going to say, "Where's Albania?" or "What's
hegemony?"

Yet it might be a mistake to treat her like a child. She

didn't know anything, and didn't intend to learn anything, which in Fritz's circles spelled "stupid." But, on the other hand, her sex life seemed to be a model of planned drift, and she probably understood how money worked. You couldn't call that stupid, could you? (And she could serve herself without getting food down her front, too.)

"I don't understand the first thing about politics," she said. "My friends are surprised that I should have anything to do with a radical paper."

Fritz had a feeling that the Swedish maid was lurking behind the silk screen waiting to take away his plate and bring him a whole new set, if he laid down his fork for a moment. Harriet had already finished her own small supply of food, and he felt that he ought to gobble his—gracefully of course. He was a fast enough eater in his own set, but this was the big leagues. These endless tactical problems made conversation difficult, so he just nodded, for the time being.

"The thing is that Mr. Twining is so persuasive. He says that my conservative friends are the real radicals. I can't tell you what he means by that, but he makes it all seem quite clear at the time."

"He's a very good talker."

"Yes, he's a dear. And such a good editor, don't you think?"

Fritz nodded again, listlessly. "Yes, of course. It's a sort of cliché by now, isn't it? Twining's brilliance, I mean. It must be a millstone for him."

"I really couldn't say how it affects him, I haven't seen Mr. Twining in such a long time. He's on the West Coast now, you say?"

"Yes, trying to raise money, I suppose."

Harriet Wadsworth would get that one all right. She was the magazine's backer-in-chief, owner of one third of its largely worthless shares, and would hardly take kindly to interlopers.

"That's quite a good idea," she said. "It's so difficult to raise enough from one source these days."

"He wasn't very successful the last time he went out there."

"No? That's a pity."

She changed the subject rather abruptly, to one of her old stand-bys—the state of the drama. It was in the doldrums, she said. Thank God for the British. "I wish I could express myself better. There are so many things I'd like to say."

"I'm afraid we're stuck with Wally Funk," said Fritz. "Otherwise you could say them for us maybe." (Thank God for Wally, he added to himself.) Wally had actually been quite a good critic in his day, with enough native intensity to last about two years—after which most critics should be shot anyway. Since then, he had inflated ridiculously; his columns began coming in longer and heavier, and his jokes got smugger and flatter. He held court at parties these days, and he couldn't answer a simple question without wheezing out great lumps of irony like a cat spitting up fur. He wore velvet waistcoats and made a fuss about his food; he was halfway to wearing a cape on opening nights.

Still, he was better than Harriet. He was one of the magazine's assets, maintaining a number of very vague admirers, who didn't know that writers change from minute to minute and that no talent is safe forever; also, who didn't know what went on behind the scenes at *The Outsider,* where Wally's stock was somewhat lower. Twining cut many of his worst excesses, and Wally wailed and banged his cane each time. But he seemed to know, with the ferret-like cunning of the burnt-out writer, that it was Twining's editing that kept him respectable. His tenure at the magazine made his baroque social life possible. So he allowed himself to be humiliated again and again. He flounced about the office in bogus outrage, and gave an impression of getting his own way, but Fritz knew that Twining's cuts always stood. (To be technically accurate, the preliminary cuts on Wally were frequently done by Brian Fine these days: but the curious thing was that Brian's editing was now quite similar to Twining's and you often couldn't tell which of them had done what.)

That was *The Outsider*'s drama department. It was typical of the whole magazine—a round-about emanation of Twining himself. Twining had a weakness for corrupt, played-out writers whom he could manipulate like that. Wally was one of his masterpieces.

What made him relevant here was that Wally was also the only thing that stood between Harriet Wadsworth and the dream of a lifetime. She was daffy enough, and sated enough with reasonable pleasures, to pine for *The Outsider*'s drama column. Her soft face came into slightly sharper focus as she talked about it now—although her voice remained languid, and her words averagely goofy.

After dinner, the butler and Swedish maid said good night rather obtrusively and went out together. Fritz was somewhat preoccupied, and he put his arms around Harriet right away and said, "Darling" in a way that, he realized a moment too late, might have struck her as a bit mechanical.

She drew back, and said, "No, darling, please."

He looked at her more closely and said, "I'm sorry. That was clumsy." And began again, kissing her with a magnified gentleness.

"No," she veered off in the same slightly indecisive way, "I don't feel like it. Right now."

She sat there tilted against him, at an angle which suggested to Fritz that she wasn't serious, that she wanted to be coaxed. A tiresome development. She brushed his hand away from her shoulder, watching him closely all the time, like a greedy child. What did *that* mean? Her childish eyes contained some simple message. He tried to remember what that expression had meant when he was a little boy.

That she wanted something. That she wanted something for something. That she wanted him to say something or promise something. And that then she would make love— very much so.

He kept his arm awkwardly around her and tried to think. Harriet held to her own pose of semicompromise, hardly breathing. You never had far to look for farce, in real life. Her pale eyes brimmed with slyness and promise. Fritz's fingers hardened on the fleshy shoulder. Oh no—it couldn't be. Her mind, her world picture couldn't be so tiny that she was holding out for *that*.

"Have you guessed?" her expression seemed to say. She was incredibly desirable now in her childish greed, and Fritz was in rich turmoil, his coolness a memory. But there were limits. He couldn't face Twining, simply couldn't, if he ran a theater review by Harriet Wadsworth.

For a moment he held on blindly, riveted by desire and an outraged sense of fitness. He had never seen such wantonness in any social circle and he hated to see it go to waste. Of course, he told himself desperately, one could rewrite the damn thing—she would be too stupid to notice it; or, alternatively, one could promise it and then say that Twining had stepped in at the last minute . . .

The tableau seemed to last forever. He wondered if this had ever happened to Twining: Harriet whispering into the captain's ear, "Gilbert, darling, I'm mad about the theater." "Come to bed and we'll talk about it . . ." God, rich people were fantastic. He must just let go somehow and call it an evening.

Gilbert had never run one of her pieces, whatever the provocation. So now she was working her way down through the staff. Fritz had always been faintly puzzled at the way she had taken up with *him*. She had invited him to the theater, she had invited him home, she had more or less invited—and all for a few stupid inches of print with her name under it. Next year she would try Brian Fine and George Wren. And possibly even Philo Sonnabend.

If he still stood for anything, he ought to be disgusted: and he was, in a way. But as he straightened up, it occurred to him that he was in no position for an adolescent burst of principle. Four years of editorial writing had trained him to see the whole picture. And he reminded himself that he was using Harriet Wadsworth just as much as she was using him—for a higher cause, as you might say.

And, as he mulled over his next move there on the green sofa, his disgust and guilt were further dispersed by a question that amused him slightly:

If she was so batty about the theater—batty enough to seduce the whole *Outsider* editorial staff in slow rotation— why did she always get to the theater twenty minutes late?

6

By the next afternoon, the bulk of Brian Fine's issue had straggled off to the printer. George Wren was curious and managed to sneak a look at most of it, including the parts that didn't concern him at all. There was no doubt about it—Fine had been up to something after all. He had ignored Twining's dummy completely.

Yet George was even more surprised to find that Fine's maneuvers added up in total effect to an average summer issue. The piece on Africa that he had edited himself read by now like an eerily typical *Outsider* piece. Ditto the articles that Fritz and Brian had worked over. Except for a slightly florid editorial on the importance of Africa, there was nothing to distinguish this number from the lower twenty-five percent of Twining's output.

Whether Brian had lost his nerve, or whether a week was too short for his purpose—whatever it was, the gesture had failed. He had played things much too safe. Even the florid editorial was pretty cautious, when you came right down to it. Brian must have been holding himself back out of habit when he wrote it: as if Twining's irony had become built into his skull, a terrible adjusting mechanism.

George felt a little disappointed. Maybe the magazine could be changed only by new people after all; maybe even he, George Wren, boy editor, was beyond it by now. The routine had so conditioned their collective reflexes that they could only produce the one kind of magazine forever and ever.

George was also depressed by the prospect of Twining's return on Monday. He could just hear himself saying, "I don't feel like a drink this evening, Mr. Twining." "You don't? Not just a quick one?" It made him nervous to think about it. Matty had been so much more her old self in Twining's absence, as if he had actually been a guest in their house whom she had finally managed to get rid of. She even seemed to talk more freely, and make jokes. Still, he would probably have the damn drink. And after that, "George, why didn't you tell me what Brian was doing? George, I asked you to be my lieutenant, George . . ."

The best solution might be simply to resign. Go back to C.B.S. and write his symphony at night. Or sculpt the Spirit of Progress out of soup cans. He yawned. There was a certain lassitude about the office today, as if everyone had suddenly realized for the first time that Twining really would be back on Monday and that nothing really had changed. Brian Fine continued to bustle bravely, but he must be feeling like an idiot by now. George could just hear the conversation: "We wanted to see if we could do an issue entirely on our own, Mr. Twining." "Well, now you know, don't you, Brian? Now you know."

Even Fritz looked rather withdrawn and thoughtful. And Olga Marplate and Philo Sonnabend, who had been so full of power-elite swagger earlier in the week, seemed to have shrunken out of sight by now. (Who, me? I wasn't a Nazi.) Why had Twining been nervous about leaving this group for a few days? He could go away for a year, and it wouldn't make any difference. They each carried his point of view, like rats carrying a plague. George felt almost frightened of seeing him again: it was like confronting a rather more powerful and coherent version of oneself.

Wren, you're talking a lot of crap. And to yourself yet. He yawned again. Nervousness and apathy were playing alternate numbers this afternoon. He strolled into Fritz's office and said, "How do you like the issue?"

Fritz smiled and shrugged. "Dull."

"How will Twining like the issue?"

"I think he'll be amused. 'If you chaps wanted a dull issue, why didn't you use my dummy?' "

"What are you going to do? Blame it all on Brian?"

"Why not? If it comes up. He acted as if he'd been left in charge, didn't he?"

"Well yes, but."

"No 'but' about it. If Twining had put me in charge, I would have done him a magazine. But he didn't trust me enough. Or—he might have put *you* in charge, although that might have made things uncomfortable for you, as a junior. But maybe the truth is that he couldn't bring himself to put anyone in charge. He's a funny fellow."

"So, why should he put anyone in charge? He was only gone for five days and he left an outline."

"Yeah. Well, you see what happened." Fritz kept filing his nails, as if the whole thing was beneath him in any case. George didn't much care for this plan of his of throwing Brian to Twining . . . There wasn't a hell of a lot of human warmth in this office, was there? Not this afternoon anyway.

"How's tricks, Philo?"

"Tricks?"

"Yeah. Hey, Olga, when are we going to move out of this mineshaft?"

"I have no idea."

The old elevator suddenly clanked open. "It's Twining," George said to Olga, just to make her jump. But it was only a boy from Western Union with a telegram. Olga took it and ripped off the yellow skin. The messenger boy stood there watching her. She must have read it two or three times before she took it in to Brian. He relayed it to Fritz, and finally someone showed it to George.

It said: "Gilbert Twining found unconscious in hotel bedroom. Heart attack. Sadowski."

VI

1

Miss Marconi burst into tears. The secretaries and the people in the shipping room took a simpler view of Twining than those close to the throne: he was a kind and easygoing employer, and for the older ones at least an orthodox "great man." He maintained a very courteous interest in their doings, and took the trouble to remember the names of babies, the state of parents' health and even the dates of birthdays.

There was therefore an atmosphere of tragedy in the office which came as rather a shock to George. He had come to suppose that everyone in the place had designs of some kind: and the unambiguous grief of the invisible people in the back took him off balance.

Miss Marplate bowed her head, looking more embarrassed than anything else. Brian Fine spent half an hour on the telephone, so there was no chance to calibrate his first twitch. He came out and whispered something to Fritz, who opened his mouth in un-Fritzlike surprise, and then nodded solemnly. They started to walk out together and Brian stopped and said to Miss Marplate, "They might as well go home," and whispered something else to her. Olga made the announcement, "We don't know whether Mr. Twining's condition is critical," and Miss Marconi gave a deep sob. George thought it would be nice to be able to react like that. He felt cheap now, because his own first thought had been, now Brian really has his chance—if he wants it; now he can really cut loose—if he has the nerve.

Brian and Fritz walked out, looking, for the first time since George had known them, more or less like friends. They were followed by a line of sorrowing girls and by Fred the mail boy and Wilbur from Cornell, the summer assistant, and George saw them clamped together like a funeral party in the elevator.

"How old is Mr. Twining?" he asked Miss Marplate. "He's too young to be having heart attacks, isn't he?"

"I don't know. I should say fifty-something. Wouldn't you, Philo?"

"I always thought he was around thirty-five."

"Oh, no, he couldn't be thirty-five."

George took the elevator by himself. Everyone seemed very gentle, Olga and Philo and everyone. Thirty-five or fifty-something. Quite a spread. He was glad he wouldn't have to face the commander on Monday, anyway. Did Brian really want the responsibility? What about Fritz? Would John's other wife marry the doctor? He felt confused about the whole thing.

"Well, I'm *not* really sorry. Why should I be?" Matilda said when he got home.

114

"I don't know why you should be."

"I don't see any point in being hypocritical."

"O.K. How's the baby?"

"Do you see any point in being hypocritical?"

"No, not much point."

"All right then." Matilda was usually very gentle, but in this instance she had steeled herself, and seemed to distrust even the most conventional concern. The funny thing was that that *was* all he felt—though she apparently suspected something deeper. He was certainly concerned that a man who might have been thirty-five should have had a heart attack; and he was concerned because things in general had become very confused; but as to Twining himself—all he felt was a tremendous relief from an indefinable pressure.

Brian Fine had hoped to spend Friday evening with Fritz. But after twenty fairly satisfactory minutes at Sweeney's, Fritz appeared to change his mind about something, gave a little nod and stood up and went to the phone booth. A few minutes later he left. It was as if the period of mourning was over, and with it the solidarity. So Brian went to the movies, but pulled out halfway through, and spent the rest of the night in various bars.

The next morning, suffering from an immensely complicated hangover, he called Philo Sonnabend and arranged to have dinner at his place. He decided to kill the time between at the Central Park Zoo.

It was a limited zoo, but he had always found it pleasantly relaxing. There were some unpretentious monkeys and a couple of seals, who were cut-ups in their way. The children plopped things into the water and the seals galumphed after them—Brian stood and watched for the best part of an hour. He had become a city man by the usual bending and hardening process, but part of his heart still yearned for something simpler; and the zoo was what you settled for in cases like that.

You never knew when your chance was going to come in life, did you? Seven years ago he thought he had missed the brass ring for good: but now it seemed to be whizzing by again. Grab it this time, or resign yourself to the gray life of a gentleman spinster . . . Once upon a time, he had taken a different view of success. He had imagined that you gathered a little more each time you went around the board. That was how it had been for his first eight years at *The Outsider*—a steady, lulling process, from copy-editor to opinion-maker, from, socially, someone who just works at *The Outsider* to quasi-celebrity, to second-grade lion.

When Frank Tippett, the founding father, resigned, Brian had mixed hopes of being made editor in chief himself. He realized that he hadn't accumulated quite enough chips yet; but he began to see also that fate was not quite so symmetrical as he had supposed, and that he might have to wait a long time for another opening. Twining's appointment gave him a distinctly clammy feeling. But Twining, when he finally turned up, struck him as an impermanent sort of fellow—too much flash and charm to stay in one place. And Twining affected in those days a beguiling helplessness—"I'm a new chap, just getting my land legs, I'll need all the advice I can get"—which helped to seduce Brian into thinking he wouldn't last long. In their nightly conferences at Sweeney's, Twining gave the impression that he wouldn't dare move an inch without Brian's guidance. Perhaps he had been hired as window dressing. Anyway, by the time Twining moved on to his next boy-genius assignment, Brian would have gathered enough credits, enough unanswerable experience, to be the only possible successor.

So he supposed. But then something peculiar happened.

He stopped moving. His hair began to thin, and his waist to bulge, but he couldn't move a step. During the course of that one miserable afternoon in Twining's office, he had changed from a young man who was moving silkily toward a very reasonable ambition into a middle-aged man who was getting nowhere at all. Twining showed him, the afternoon he criticized his editorials, what a fat lonely man of thirty-seven looked like from the outside—a man with no real experience and no real future, a dealer in windy metaphors and flabby thinking. "I've been here *longer* than you," he wanted to say. "You can't talk like that to a man of my age."

Before that, thirty-seven had been a good vantage point, just the right place to be; now, suddenly, all the hope was squeezed out of it. His self-respect was strewn across Twining's desk in those yellowing mounds of paper. He was too old to start compiling new self-respect; too old to change his act. To have been looked at like that, to have been talked to like that—he left Twining's office relatively old and broken.

Oh, of course it didn't all happen in one afternoon (writing editorials made a man chronically judicious). He didn't want to get fixated, to keep repeating that cruel memory, as if nothing else had ever happened to him.

Growing old comes in spasms. For three years Brian remained thirty-seven, before suddenly moving on again. Being thirty-seven began to mean good things again, like coming to terms with oneself, having no foolish illusions, knowing one's limits—thirty-seven wasn't so bad at all. For three years he was still Twining's top assistant, a reliable professional, a damn-good journalist (someone had actually used that phrase and it had stuck in his mind, to taunt him later). He knew how to face hard facts. The stomach, the baldness, the being a bachelor—these were the hard facts he had in mind. He knew they wouldn't go away tomorrow. But he could live with them. (And to compensate, a lot of odd people recognized his name at parties in those days.)

Then his old colleague Fred Pringle retired and a bright bumptious fellow called Fritz Tyler was installed in his office and Brian moved into a new phase. This was forty—*extreme* old age. He had thought he could face facts before, but nothing as painful as this. Fritz was a bright young activist, a marcher and sitter with a light step and honest-to-God experience. Brian, white and sluggish from years in that terrible office, bumbled up to him like a mole the first day he arrived. "Fritz will help you out with *some* of your tasks, Brian. We'll sit him in here for the moment." Fritz had sized him up quickly and had never shown the slightest interest in him since.

It made him uneasy to have any stranger sitting at Pringle's desk. And Fritz treated him like a rather ineffectual old man left over from some not very interesting regime. He asked Brian questions about type sizes and line spaces, but took anything more serious round to Twining. Brian began to feel like an old clerk on a high stool. He wanted Twining to say, just once, "Ask Brian. He knows about this"; he wanted someone to pay him a little attention. But Twining seemed to play up to Fritz.

The worst pain was to find out how much he resented being left out. After work, Twining and Fritz would go down to Sweeney's, and Brian waited vainly for some word of invitation, until finally one day he invited himself and talked too much and felt irrationally younger than Fritz and more callow. He remembered capering before the two older men, begging for their attention, drinking, slurring—a terrible evening never to be repeated. At times like this, Brian felt that he was acting somehow *Jewishly*. People thought that Fine was a Jewish name, and this made him feel Jewish—but not real-Jewish, parody-Jewish. His father had been a desperate anti-Semite, presumably also because of his name, and he had done terrible Jewish imitations around the house, wheedling and strutting, and carrying on—at first occasionally and later as a matter of course, so that in a way they were his own style and no one else's. Brian had picked up some of these mannerisms, and was afraid ever after that they would slip out and reveal him as the Jew that he wasn't. Thus the name Fine had affected his character after all.

After that, all the facts that he had been facing the last few years began to come unraveled one by one. His fatness and his baldness were enough to make a man cry. His professionalism was a joke. All day he had to listen to Fritz's phone calls—in those days, Fritz had a lot of hot contacts, a lot of leads, where were they now? Fritz was an old man now, too.

Brian had become just an old office creature, very good at correcting French accents and regularizing British spellings. But no phone calls, no contacts. At thirty-seven he had resigned himself to just missing the top. Now he saw that he should have set his sights even lower. He felt *physically* incapable of ever commanding people like Fritz, even if fate gave him the opportunity. And all the time Twining was reinforcing his humility with periodic ironies, corrections, "really—Brian's."

The last good thing that had happened to him was Fritz's demotion from teacher's pet; but his elation over this was tinged with melancholy, because in effect it pushed him down even further: and besides, he recognized it as a loser's elation . . .

His next birthday was the hiring of George Wren. Another bright young man, another insult from Twining—but this time he reacted differently. He was ancient by now, forty-four, and harder to hurt. Wren could not put him down the way Fritz had. He had developed an old man's cunning, and he knew how to handle brash young men.

He gazed into the dank, seal-infested waters. If he ever killed himself, God forbid, it would certainly be by drowning. He wasn't old at all, of course. Futility could easily be mistaken for age. And maturity, it was well known, included a quota of absolutely crushing defeats. For seven years, his forward motion had been stopped by that bastard; Twining had mesmerized him into helplessness.

And now suddenly it was coming round again, the brass ring, gleaming as bright as ever, and he was, however he had got there, in his prime. Success, he now knew for sure, was not something you won by attrition, but something that you must be ready to grab for at any time. It might come on the first day or the five-thousandth. His present feeling that this was the worst possible time—that last month or next year would have found him better prepared—was a sure sign that it was almost in reach.

He must form a plan. It was no longer enough simply to harass Twining and wait for something to turn up. In a sense, he had won that part. His harassment had helped to wear out the boy genius. A thousand small worries prodding at Twining's rib cage. Collapse. Triumph. Whoever heard of a fop with staying power?

It did occur to him briefly in passing, as he stared glassy-eyed at the flobbering seals, that these were rather harsh thoughts to have about a man who had recently suffered a heart attack. It made him uncomfortable to pitch things at this level: but you couldn't entirely extricate personality from principle here. Twining's sneering manner (which no doubt he couldn't help) was precisely the trouble with *The Outsider*. Brian was not the only man to have been crippled by it. God, no. Wally Funk was much worse. Wally had been one of the magazine's real assets in the old days. "Yes, yes. Well you see, what happened to poor Wally is this—the chap has lost confidence in his mandarin methods, and a mandarin without confidence . . ." An imaginary Twining threw poor Wally to the seals.

Well, that was the kind of thing that had happened too often. The magazine was full of people who had been inhibited by Twining and had then, through some macabre process, somehow turned *into* Twining, writing like Twining and thinking like Twining. The result pleased nobody except, presumably, Twining.

Brian turned away from the seals and one of them appeared to give a small wave. The children around him found them irresistibly funny. Yet watch them for long enough and they became pathetic and then monstrous—monstrous, a Twining word: the seals are absolutely monstrous this season. Twining was like a cancer of the lip. The surgery would have to be partly on oneself. . . . Last week was play-acting, this week was the real thing. It was a weak miserable existence he had slipped into; and he felt himself tempted to cling to it now as a man clings to a bad dream rather than face the birth agonies of waking. But he knew he really wanted to be awake. Five o'clock, if he hurried, he would have time to get home and have a quick drink before heading for Philo's and the first chapter.

Philo at home was a fresh creation. To take only one thing, he wore a green velvet waistcoat at home.

Under the encouragement of a gentle wife (who had funny-looking teeth, too), he assumed a certain definition: call it a modified dandyism. Between them they gave Brian a surprisingly exotic meal, and Philo crowned it with balloons of Five-Star Brandy, thoughtfully poured, swirled and sniffed.

Brian began to relax and bask, for the first time since the telegram. It was with people of the middle range, people like Sonnabend in fact, that a man like Twining was at his weakest. He could be gracious with office girls, and foxy with associates: but a man like Philo, with a stubborn private self, he was likely to overlook altogether. And this was where Brian accorded himself the edge.

For he knew that it was possible for a man to be slow and not very efficient, to have bad breath and an unfortunate style, and still to have real value. Arrogant people like Twining missed this, and always left the Sonnabend flank unprotected.

But he must stop thinking of everything in terms of Twining. Brian gave his balloon a swirl. He must develop his own style. Not just a counter-Twining style. Monomania could ruin everything.

"The doctor says he won't be back at work for *at least* three months. So it's up to us now, Philo."

"You can count on me, Brian."

"Thanks. I'll need all the help I can get. In fact, I'm wondering if we shouldn't take on a new editor as well. What do you think, Philo?"

"Well, it mightn't be a bad idea."

"Fritz can be counted on, of course, to do what he always does. He's competent at any rate."

"This is probably speaking out of turn, Brian, I don't like to express opinions about personalities—but Fritz has always seemed a little bit phony to me. I shouldn't have said that, I guess."

"No, that's good—I want to hear your opinions. Tell me, what do you think of George Wren then?"

"Well, if you promise it won't go any further . . ."

"Of course."

"Well, I think he's insolent and cruel. I think he's a pocket edition of Mr. Twining. What do *you* think, Brian?"

"I think that's very interesting." Brian's cheeks were warm with brandy.

They were still sitting at the dining-room table. Jane Sonnabend had a curious steadfast quality, giving an incessant impression of standing by her husband, even when there was no danger. And Philo seemed to take on an air of toothy defiance. "I know I'm not expected to have opinions, I'm good old Philo, you know, Mr. Twining practically hangs his coat over me when he comes in and George Wren regards me as a joke."

"Yes, he's a very sarcastic fellow. I think he picks it up from Fritz."

"I shouldn't be saying these things, they're just opinions."

"No, no, go on." Nobody else at *The Outsider* suspected Philo of even having opinions. That great little group of liberals, Twining, Tyler and Wren treated him the way Marie Antoinette treated her servants. (If he had been a colored man, or a war orphan, they might have taken him more seriously.)

Brian was astonished by the bitterness that had apparently been festering in Sonnabend. The inefficient smile they saw every day probably wasn't meant to be a smile at all, but a snarl: that was how inefficient he was . . .

"George is young," said Brian. "He makes fun of me too. It isn't important."

"People have feelings—he's old enough to know that. Anyway, it's just a personal thing, I wouldn't make a production out of it, of course."

"So what do you think about George Wren professionally?"

"Well, I suppose he's clever."

"In a sophomoric sort of way, you mean?"

"I didn't say that. I'm not an expert at these distinctions. But I do think—in line with what we were saying at lunch the other day—that he is definitely Mr. Twining's man. And that if you want to give the magazine the new lease on life that you were talking about, you'd better forget about George Wren."

"You really believe that, eh?"

"Definitely. What do you think, Jane?"

"Well," said Jane, "I've never met the young man, but from what you say—"

They left the table and surged over to the sofa. It was a tight fit but they were happy to be together. The table on Brian's right was covered with miniature elephants made of glass, china, porcelain. On the mantelpiece stood a row of gaudy German beer mugs. Philo had interests, all right. Mark him well. Prick him and he bleeds. Insult him and he remembers. In England you might be able to dismiss half the population as beneath consideration—but not here, baby.

"I expect you have some advertising ideas, haven't you, Philo, that the commander has squashed."

"Well, he hasn't exactly squashed them. He gives me a very free hand with the department—"

"Yes, he goes on about that all the time, giving people free hands. But somehow—"

"You're right, somehow something goes wrong every time. He makes me feel like an idiot."

"Dear Mr. Twining."

"Philo has some wonderful ideas," Jane put in.

"I'll bet he has."

Brian shut his eyes. He could see nothing but teeth. Whether or not Philo is any good, let us at least do him the honor of finding out, shall we? This peculiar kind of living death, in which a man ostensibly runs a department, at the cost of constant humiliation—he opened his eyes. He had worn a groove of rage with Twining that it was all too easy to slip into. That wasn't the point now.

"On Monday morning," he said, "bring me all the ideas you have, never mind if they're lousy. Creativeness involves risk; we've got to start swinging a little more loosely. Intellectual constipation—you'll excuse the expression, Jane—is going out of style at *The Outsider*."

They laughed, a little nervously he thought, but excitedly too. A small dream had been ignited in Sonnabend. Brian swigged his brandy and asked for another one; Philo got it for him with an eagerness which was in itself, and apart from all other considerations, a gratifying and encouraging thing.

2

George went to the office on Monday full of good will for the new regime. He was on time too, and expected a small round of applause for that: but Olga Marplate and Philo Sonnabend had gone back to being icy. They looked as if they had sat up all night together talking about him. —O.K., just catch me being on time again, you ungrateful bums.

Brian had dumped some more junk on his desk—back of the book stuff that Brian usually did himself. George was about to go around and bleat for a few minutes, but Philo Sonnabend beat him to Brian's cubicle. So he began mechanically penciling through the stuff—Wally Funk was lusher than hell this week—while trying not to be distracted too much by the voices in Brian's cubicle.

Philo was in there a long time, and after a while George just gave up and listened. His attention span was down to about three seconds these days. Cigarettes were killing his brain cells by the thousands, that was the trouble. Soon he wouldn't have any left at all. He could picture them going out one by one like the lights in a big city.

Philo seemed to be mumbling optimistically about something. You mightn't suppose that a mumble could be optimistic, thought George, but in fact it probably happened all the time. He balanced the ruler on his palm and wondered what a man like Sonnabend could possibly have to be optimistic about.

"Yes, I understand that, Philo." Brian's voice was quite crisp today; his sinuses must have taken a turn for the better. "But I'm afraid these just won't do."

George laughed and dropped the ruler. Philo Sonnabend had probably been showing Brian some poetry and had just received the imperial stroke in the back of the neck. You shouldn't judge a man by his teeth—and yet, in another sense, what better?

He slipped into Brian's office as Philo was slipping out. Little office dramas made a bright splash in a dull life. Philo looked miserable, and his grin was suddenly made of crumbling plaster. Brian's eyes looked small—well, that could mean anything. Cocaine, fear, anything.

"Hey, Brian."

"Yes, George?"

"What's the idea of dumping your garbage over my partition? Funk's festering lilies are your problem, not mine."

"Some changes are being instituted this week, George, in Mr. Twining's absence. I thought you might be glad to have a new assignment." Brian's humorous manner had dropped away, as if it had never existed. There would be no more joking about New Jersey.

"Yeah, well, you might have asked me first. Now you've gone and hurt my feelings."

"I'm sorry about that."

"Is that all it means to you, Brian baby? I've always thought of you as a buddy, Brian, not a schoolmarm. What's the matter, don't we relate any more?"

"Look, George, I'm aware of your various devices for killing time around the office. This kind of conversation is one of the most annoying."

"Well, that's true, that's true." George began to forage restlessly on Brian's desk. He came upon an enormous scissors and a glue pot and a big, thick ruler. Brian was a gnome making toys for Santa Claus. A little glue, snip snip, whistle while you work. George picked up the ruler and made a graceful thrust at Brian's chest: *"En garde,* you Saracen dog."

Brian looked up, as if he had never seen George before; his face was hard and almost powerful, in a nervous kind of way. "That's enough, George. If you can't behave like a grown-up . . ."

"What then?"

"We'll just have to see."

George didn't know why he felt so frivolous today. A wild elation over Twining's absence, over having old Brian to tease—he knew he was being childish, and that he ought to stop. But he couldn't resist at least one more wild one.

"Hey, Brian, I bet I know why you've given me the back of the book to take care of. It's so you can have the front to yourself, right?"

Brian looked at him with ever diminishing pupils. He was not particularly good at repartee, but it was clear that George was doing himself no good here. He started to leave, but his steps only waltzed him around to the other side of the desk. There was something about riding fat people . . .

"You have a five-part serial on Borneo that you're just itching to run in the front; you have a thrilling geological survey of the northern Sudan; and a report on homosexuality along the Zambesi."

"George . . ."

"O.K., I'm leaving, sir. But before I go, I just want to ask you one question. What have you got Fritz doing? The puzzle page?"

He ducked out and thought, what the hell was the point of that? He wanted to help Brian with the magazine, not rattle him with a lot of hysterical jokes. He returned remorsefully to his cubicle and set to work clipping Wally Funk's blooms. "I find it harder and harder to take the American stage with any kind of seriousness." Christ, that's too bad, Wally. "It has become a rank waste of a civilized man's time." George had never seen a Funk column in a state of nature before: it was pretty heady stuff.

As the morning went on, George tried to sober up little by little. Luckily, Brian was a good sport with a thick skin. The type who never minded being kidded, so long as he knew he was loved. The love play of elephants, so George had heard, would kill an ordinary man, and that was how it was with Brian.

He went back to Brian's cubicle, looking and talking extra-seriously. "I've cut about five sentences off Wally. How do you suppose he'll feel about that? I've heard him arguing with Mr. Twining."

"Let's see what you've done."

George handed over the typescript. Brian went through it twice, rubbing out George's pencil marks the second time round. "Here, I'll do it," he said.

"What is this, Brian? What are you doing to me?"

"Leave it here, I'll fix it," said Brian.

"No explanation, no unforgettable lesson from wise-old editor?"

"I haven't the time, George."

Brian kept right on working with his head down, there was obviously no arguing with him at this point. George wandered out, not sure what to do next. He wanted to cooperate and give Brian a chance, but Brian to this point was resisting cooperation pretty effectively.

"Hey, Philo, how's it going?"

"All right."

"How's the little Balinese mistress. O.K.?"

There was something exceptionally baleful about Philo this morning. George had the feeling he was going to burst into tears. But with a face like that, who could tell? A distracting woman had just gotten off the elevator and was walking toward them. Blond, Viking, good seat on a horse he bet. "Hello, Mrs. Wadsworth"—Philo was briefly galvanized.

"Hello there," she said. She smiled at George, and George prepared himself to move forward smoothly. But Fritz Tyler was out of his cubicle in a flash. "Hello, Harriet," he said. "You know George Wren, don't you, and Philo . . ."

Brian Fine had come to the door of *his* cubicle and was standing there indecisively. He caught Mrs. Wadsworth's eye and gave her a funny little wave. "Hello there," she said.

Mrs. Wadsworth drifted handsomely through the office clutter to Fritz's den. You would suppose that a fur-lined broad like that would be slightly sickened by the dinge, but she didn't seem to notice it at all. Fritz swept her on in, and then, rarest of gestures at *The Outsider,* shut his door behind her. "Have you had any news about poor Mr. Twining" clunk. Brian stood in his doorway a moment longer biting a finger; then he seemed to wake from a doze, and withdrew.

Twenty minutes later, Fritz opened his door again.

George, half sick with facetious boredom, managed to get out in time to watch them leave. Brian was watching too, obviously ready to drop everything and join them for lunch. "See you, Brian," said Fritz. Mrs. Wadsworth gave him the vaguest of smiles. Brian nodded.

"Can I do something for you, George?" he asked, noticing Wren craning behind them.

"Don't mind me. I'm just browsing."

"See anything you like?" mumbled Brian, in his old vein.

Fritz was promenading Mrs. Wadsworth back to the elevator. George had a feeling that Fritz was putting on a show of some kind—establishing an alibi, maybe. Mrs. Wadsworth was one of the magazine's backers, and everyone smiled at her warmly on the way out, including George, who was carried away by mob sentiment, and the anonymous folk in the shipping section, and she smiled back, and afterwards people turned to each other and thought what the hell are *you* smiling about. It was like a royal visit.

Brian had to settle for lunch with Olga. Which left only Philo to dance with, and George decided no, not today. He ordered a sandwich and a container of coffee and sat by his cruddy, abortive window looking down at the street. Olga and Brian looked preposterous from this position, bobbing along the sidewalk toward Luigi's. It was impossible to take anything seriously today. After a few minutes, it began to rain. They'll all get wet, he thought somberly.

Everyone bobbing along to Luigi's year after year, the comic pathos of everyone else's life. Ho-hum. He stretched, and a thought occurred: Hey, I wonder what Brian does with Funk's stuff? Well, now was the time to find out—he swung his feet off the desk and tiptoed around in his socks. My God, that couldn't be it, could it? On top of the desk, a manuscript sprawled lifeless. It was covered in hideous red gashes, like Caesar's body. George hesitated to touch it. Brian must have gone berserk—George could picture him up to his elbows in blood, his eyes reduced to pinpoints, "Take that . . . and that, you you manuscript . . ."

George had never seen anything like it. He almost wanted to add a wound himself. So this was how Brian got his kicks.

But this was really no joke. Wally had been a hero of his once upon a time. No doubt he had become a bit slovenly since then, his tongue wagged; George had heard him arguing with Twining over minor cuts. (George assumed they were minor cuts.) And Mr. Twining had even turned Wally's gaudier effects into a gentle office joke. But he didn't deserve *this*.

A leading critic, maybe our best—you don't treat him like this.

Philo called out to tell him that the wind had changed and to shut his window. He did as he was told and soon it became very stuffy and the grime smeared on the window-pane. God, what a dump. Wally Funk's wounds gushed fountains in the next room. There must be dirtier ways to make a living, he supposed.

Brian and Olga came back from lunch looking damp and harassed. George went up to Brian and said, "That's a bloody mess you've made in there."

"What do you mean, bloody mess? Put your shoes on, for godsakes."

"Funk's theater piece."

"I don't want you looking among my papers, George. Even for laughs. All right, since you bring up Funk, that's about the way Mr. Twining cuts him too. If you don't like it, take it up with Twining."

"I can't very well do that, can I? Shit, Brian, I thought we were on our own now."

Brian started to say something and then changed his mind. That slight indecisiveness of his was what made him vulnerable, and ultimately lovable. He's annoyed with me, and therefore he doesn't want to agree with me; at the same time, he doesn't want to admit that Twining's ghost calls the shots. And of course, on top of that, he's wet and uncomfortable.

Twining would have reconciled these elements into a dazzling riposte; but Brian just blinked, and said, "I'll take another look at it."

So O.K., he lacked any talent for leadership. But mightn't it be better to work for a man like that than for a man who marched his army confidently into the sea? George was really shocked by the extent to which Fine, standing proxy for Twining, had cauterized Wally Funk's essay. That kind of editing was inhuman, arrogant beyond Fine's native capacity. He thought of what Twining had done to some of his own editorials, and decided that he had the makings of a nice little grievance.

George resolved during the lank course of the afternoon to try to stop riding Brian on Tuesdays and Thursdays at least, and to encourage this very mediocre man to swing a little on his own. If the magazine could be eased out of Twining's corsets and allowed to get a bit sloppy, well that might be just what was needed to make it the magazine he thought he remembered.

Some day, who knows, it might even run some of George Wren's poetry.

3

"The funny thing about that," said Fritz, "is that when he first got there he used to say, 'You American chaps edit far too much, you know.' That's what Brian tells me he said, anyway. Brian was the first settler and he remembers these things. He says that Twining didn't want to touch anything at first."

"He seems to have gotten over that."

"It began with grammar and usage. He discovered that 'you Americans' use the most extraordinary phrases. Things like effectivity, and interpersonal relationships, honestly chaps. He had the whole office tittering over jargon—very embarrassing by the way, to titter over something and then find it in your own copy. It was all a huge joke of course, but a public-school-prefect kind of joke. 'You can't have meant this, Brian. Could the printer have made *another* mistake?' "

"Nice fellow."

"Well, it did tighten up the magazine."

Fritz was genial today, and George was eager to pick his brains. Brian was still treating him like a leper, but Fritz had just as mysteriously taken him up, and had even bypassed the inevitable Luigi's in favor of a restaurant where the main courses averaged out at about $4.95. George was gorging himself on oysters and Fritz was saying, "Twining gradually developed this notion that no American could write decent English. All our phrases began to make him jump after a while. He even stopped finding our language 'extraordinarily vigorous.' "

"Tough apples."

"It was discouraging for Brian. I think he used to care about his prose. Until Twining showed him that he was barely literate."

The wine waiter came along with some claret that Fritz had ordered with some show of scholarship. Fritz sniffed and gave a brief nod. He seemed to be simply terrific with wine waiters.

Was this how things were going to be at *The Outsider*

from now on? Even while Twining's body was still warm, Olga Marplate had started repainting the office. (In fact, George was glad to be away from the stink.) And here was Fritz talking about good years and good bins. "There's no need for the place to be so damn tatty and second-rate," he said. "A lifetime of Luigi's and you begin to look like Luigi's." George, his palate ravished with slithering bluepoints, concurred with this.

"So—now that he's discovered that it's perfectly O.K. to overedit in this country, he weighs in like perfect billy-ho, is that what you're trying to tell me, Fritz?"

"That's about it—though there again, I think he's right a lot of the time. Wally Funk, for instance, is a terrible writer when you come right down to it."

"I hadn't noticed."

"Americans have no ear. Ask Twining."

The next course was Chateaubriand avec this and that. George hadn't eaten so well since leaving C.B.S. He had already asked Fritz where the money was coming from, and he wasn't going to ask him again. Fritz had said that it was all on the magazine—an incredible statement, which George was entirely prepared to accept.

Fritz's attitude about Twining was funny: the message might be translated thus: yes, he needs replacing, but not by just *anybody*.

"How do you think Brian is going to make out, as pro tem editor?"

"How do you think?" asked Fritz. "You know Brian—do you think he has what it takes?"

George shrugged. "Grow in the job," he mumbled, his mouth already deliciously full again.

"Yeah, well I hope so. I'm going to give him all the help I can, of course. But you know Brian—he's been under Twining for a long time, his bones are set."

"All right, then—what happens if he can't make it?"

Fritz smiled. "That leaves me and you, doesn't it? You're the only man with any real ability in the place. Don't be modest, God knows the competition isn't all that fierce."

Don't try to Twining me now, thought George. Don't make me your lieutenant. Just buy me some more of this wonderful food.

"No, it isn't the editing I mind with Twining so much. O.K., he misses some of the values in American speech—but it's a well-written magazine. Overediting is the price you pay."

If any two of us could agree about anything, thought George, we might get somewhere. However, magazines aren't everything, either. The waiter was lighting up a crepe suzette at the next table. A sexy blue flame burst to life over it like a morning-glory. Why does everyone go on about the damn magazine all the time?

"My complaint is basically political," Fritz said. "I look on Twining as a peculiarly English problem, a tame left-winger, a dilettante radical. Nothing has done more to emasculate the labor movement than these housebroken smoothies from the very best schools—the sort of people who request to have their names removed from the Social Register, without success."

"Well, you're pretty smooth yourself," said George. "Ordering wine like that."

Fritz laughed. He wasn't like Brian, he could take a joke. He was a fine fellow. God, I'm immature, thought George. Pass the peas, will you?

"I don't object to his being a dandy," said Fritz. "I don't believe that a socialist has to be a puritan."

"So I see."

"But there's something a bit decadent about Twining. By the way, I hear he's off the critical list."

"So it's O.K. to knock him, right?"

"You're full of fun today, George. You must have been hungry. Yeah, Twining will play the violin again, I believe. But he won't be editing magazines for a while—six months, a year, maybe never. The magazine must have been a great strain, the doctor says."

"He never showed it, I'll say that."

George ordered the crepe suzette, because he wanted to watch the flame dancing across it. It was all right with him if Twining never came back at all, as long as they could keep on going to this restaurant every day. The waiter was a fat, jolly fellow who enjoyed playing with his fire machine. "Yah, gentlemen," he said, flicking at it with his cigarette lighter.

"Don't you feel there's something a bit off-center about Twining?" Fritz went on. "Why is he left-wing at all? I had a tough childhood, and I expect you did—but not Twining. Twining's never been hungry in his damn life. O.K. —I admit, that's not necessary, you don't have to experience poverty in person, look at Roosevelt, look at Kennedy. But you have to have been in a situation which you couldn't control, where you were begging for mercy. Otherwise you're talking about something different when you're talking about poverty."

"And how do you know that Twining has never been in a situation like that?"

"Are you kidding, George? You can spot those untouched babies anywhere. It's a kind of, what's the word, virginity that upper-class people have. They've never had to compromise, or fake, they've never needed to use a mean thought or a cheap smile, they've never opened their psychic legs to anyone. It's the only real test of who's in and who isn't. To give you an example of someone who isn't in—and, boy, it took me a long time to find out—you know our patron

Harriet Wadsworth? Well, she hasn't got it. She acts stupid and vague, and smooth and unviolated, but she's been had, she's been *had*."

"How do you know her so well?"

"Oh, we're old friends. But to get back to Twining—that boy is still a hundred percent intacta. The flawless finish, George, the deep-dish self-confidence, you just didn't pick those things up in my neighborhood. You have to be raised under glass.

"Then of course, you can take up socialism as an amusing hobby if you like—and sell it out, if you like . . ."

"I think you're oversimplifying, Fritz." George wasn't completely sure what he meant by that. The crepe suzette, like so many things in life (he was stuck in the philosophical phase), was not quite as good as it looked. He had a notion that Fritz was genuinely worked up about this matter, but what really concerned him was why a man who ate ravioli so quickly should eat fancy food so slowly. *That* was a question for you.

"Oversimplifying, George? Do you know anybody who has had things his way as much as the commander has? The only child of rich parents, followed by instant success at school, all the prizes in real life, have I left out anything?"

"Think you're oversimplifying."

"Has *any*one ever denied him anything? With that manner? It's a self-perpetuating thing, you know—he gets what he wants because of the manner, and he has the manner because he gets what he wants."

"How do you know so much about his past life, then? I mean, maybe a failure or two sneaked past without you spotting it. In the nursery or some place."

"He used to take me down to Sweeney's every evening, George—you're not the only one, by the way. He got bored with me eventually, you haven't reached that stage yet, but you will. But as long as he wanted me to drink with him, I *did* drink with him, I *did* drink with him. As you probably know, it would be violating a law of nature to say no to Twining.

"So that's how I know about his Eminence, George. The hard way. The beautifully controlled boredom when he'd got all he could out of me. You'll be amazed at how mediocre, how *limited* he can make you feel, if you let him. The manner—the goddamned manner.

"However, I didn't mean to go into all that. I only meant to say, what can a man of that kind know about the rest of us? And how dare he tell underprivileged people what to think about life? It's a fucking insult, George, a blasphemy.

"Anyway, there's no point getting mad at him, he doesn't know any better, the man is incurably innocent. None of it would matter if he didn't happen to edit a potentially valuable magazine. This gives our society a dead cell where we ought to have a live one."

George agreed with this pretty much. His tendency to heckle was thwarted by the fact that he had more or less reached these same conclusions himself, in a fuzzy sort of way. He was getting mentally sloppy and his head was full of quite contradictory tendencies. Might do something about that after lunch.

Fritz ordered some espresso coffee and said, "Well, I've talked a lot, probably too much, but I feel that you and I may have to work together for the next few months, and we might as well be candid with each other. Maybe when the commander recovers, he will want to pursue his successful career in some other direction. Or maybe he will want to devote himself exclusively to seduction. In any case . . ."

"Seduction?"

"Yes—a man with his style, what a pity to waste it on a

small magazine, don't you think. If women find him even half as irresistible as we do . . ."

George laughed. Of course, that was the hole in Tyler's thesis. Twining had been as helpless as anybody, Twining had been in situations he couldn't control with a check or an infectious smile.

"I hate to contradict a good theory," he said, "a potentially *great* theory. But in the interests of historical truth—I don't believe Twining *does* make out very well with women."

That had a pleasant effect on Fritz. He looked incredulous. Wonder if he's going to order brandy, no, that would be asking too much. George stretched comfortably in the nice empty restaurant. This was living, make no mistake . . . Now *don't* contradict me, Fritz—this is something I know about.

Fritz said, "Well, that will come as a nice surprise to his wife."

"What do you mean, his wife?"

"His wife Polly. It was Polly Twining who got me the job at *The Outsider,* you know. An old friend. We were in college together. I was her idea of a young radical genius— before she met the master, of course. *Zut,* how I wander. I talked to her over the weekend. It seems that there was a girl in the room with Gilbert when he had the heart attack. It seems that the dear fellow was raising funds and whoopee at the same time, and it was too much for the old ticker."

4

George's first reaction was rather hysterical amusement, and he and Fritz made some jokes about Twining, and he felt quite hearty and locker-room about the whole thing.

But later in the afternoon a profound depression took over. He felt as if he had recently walked into the wrong room and seen something he wasn't supposed to see. He felt personally humiliated.

"Here, George, look this over, will you?" It was Twining —no it was Brian Fine, puffing on a pipe for heavensakes.

What the hell did he, George, care how Twining got his heart attack? He turned his mind to the piece of iridescent crap that Fine had handed him. It already carried a light sheen of soot. God, this was a filthy place.

By four o'clock he had a feeling that he was Twining and that someone else, who was also Twining, had walked in on him, by mistake. There had ensued a huge explosion of mutual embarrassment and contempt: "What the devil do you think you're doing . . . meaning of this . . . explanation." There were grains of soot on George's wrists, and the back of his collar was brown and dank, he could tell without looking. What a dirty, filthy place this was, to be sure.

He left at five, and the subway home was a writhing screamer, twisting and whining all the way home. He could imagine pores bursting open on all sides and great festers of sweat streaming over fat cruddy flesh; if you stopped to think about the dirt in this city, you could go out of your mind. At home there would be a layer of nameless junk— hair, fluff, coal dust—in the bathtub. Even the avocado plant would look gray and dingy. (You never knew how wretched city life could be until you tried growing plants.)

The apartment building was just one off-pink monster out of five, you could wander into the wrong one and not discover your mistake for days. Wherever you went you would meet the same mild, unaccented, Eastern-seaboard people, who got their opinions in a cellophane bag: the same thin, nervous wife. . . .

Matilda was in a good mood this evening. George had been very lighthearted when he left for work and she had put the bookmark in that. She said she had bought some herrings for dinner, and that Peter had stood up against the side of a chair, a lot of aimless crap that only emphasized the pettiness of his life. He hated to waste Matilda's good spirits, so he stalled by taking a bath.

He swished out the sludge and got in the tub. He was still feeling a little heavy from lunch. He hit the water, with a dull clunk. His slightly distended stomach recoiled from the hot water. In ten years he would look like Brian Fine. Brian Fine was the third stage of an editor's life cycle. The first stage was going to Sweeney's with the commander; feeling that you were on your way; basking. The second stage was being dropped by the commander. Profound humiliation here, the commander making it quite clear that he has spotted your outer limits (no appeal against this verdict, of course). Compensations: fopping around like Fritz, experimenting with irony, bow ties, wine waiters. The third stage was Brian Fine. Fat, desperate, beyond humiliation, beyond irony. George looked at his small, sedentary pot—he already carried the third stage in his womb. But then Fine would some day hurl off his grubby cocoon and step glowing into the fourth stage.

The fourth stage was the commander himself, as elegant as a butterfly: heart pounding and splintering over some broad, an amused smile on his face—God, it wasn't funny, it was terrible. George stood up with a spastic splash. Matty would accuse him of flooding the bathroom.

"You're very glum this evening," she said over dinner. "Is anything wrong, dear?"

"I ate too much lunch."

"Well, that's nice. Did somebody take you?"

"Yeah, Fritz Tyler."

Matty liked to talk, all right, so long as someone else started it. If George didn't speak first, nothing happened.

He sensed Matty's good mood slipping away, under his silence, but he couldn't do anything about it, even though he knew it might be gone for some time: he tried to lighten his heart, but it lay like a rock.

"Fritz told me something that bothered me a little."

"Oh? What was that?"

"He told me that Mr. Twining had a girl in the room with him when he had the heart attack."

"Well, good for him," she said, tentatively—this wasn't her usual style of comment, and it made an awkwardness. "I mean, that's the healthiest thing I've heard about Mr. Twining to date."

"It's, I don't know, disappointing."

"Why? After what he used to tell you about himself. Aren't you hungry tonight?"

"No, I had a big lunch."

"Oh, Georgie, don't tell me that you're feeling bad just because of Mr. Twining. You're a big boy now. The world is full of things like that."

"Don't do the worldly bit, Matty. It's a disappointing thing, for a man of Mr. Twining's distinction. That's all. I used to admire him."

"Oh, you sound like a boy of twelve. What has Mr. Twining's distinction got to do with anything?"

The unfocused anxiety was coming back. The sparkle, the easy intelligence of the past week seemed to fade. It was a stupid development, so easily avoided—it would make him boil back at her, until they wound up in a screaming snarl.

"I don't want to talk about it."

"Well then—why are you so grumpy?"

"Look, I've been in a good mood for days, isn't that enough for you? Men have moods too, you know."

"I think it's perfectly ridiculous. Mr. Twining isn't your

daddy, you know. This isn't some primal scene you've stumbled upon . . ."

"Oh, for godsake, five-and-dime psychology yet." He left the table and stormed the few feet into the next room, where Peter slept smugly.

"It isn't that you feel sorry for him is it?" she called after him. There were no words for how much he hated her when she used that voice. It meant that she totally misunderstood the situation. It meant that she had given in to some awful, cheap, popular interpretation of human affairs. He wanted to stuff the words back in her mouth like cotton candy. But he said, "No, thanks. I'm just a little disgusted, that's all. It's a dirty thing."

He had to do his bristling quietly, because of the baby. The baby was clean anyway, the cleanest thing in New York. It was accustomed to sleeping in the light and under the blare of television. So another small argument wouldn't hurt. But George didn't want it to waken to what Matty called a primal scene—the sight of its parents fighting like cave men.

"I think there's something unhealthy . . ."

"Ssh."

There was something unhealthy all right. His dismay over Twining was out of all proportion, he realized. This Rover-boy loyalty to the magazine, and to Twining—he, George, *was* childish. He was a clown. Everybody knew it.

. . . Never mind, 3,000 more meals at Luigi's and I'll be dead. By then my little boy will be stale as an old cigar and middle-aged; my wife will be a shrill old woman in a red wig. Spending my Social Security like a drunken sailor. A picture of her ex-husband will sit gathering its own special thin dust on the piano. She'll think she once liked him—me.

George would be extinguished, there would be no more

George. Fantastic. And then thirty years later there would be no more Matilda either—and then no more Peter. The whole thing would have been a waste of time. Worse than a waste of time. Yes, Peter dead, nonexistent, was worse than a waste of time.

He wanted to talk to Matty about it, but they were well and truly cut off by now. She was reading a book, and frowning over it, although it had a funny jacket on. George's own death was a joke—but Peter's death was a tragedy. Peter old and dried-out and boring was a tragedy. And George was the only one who saw it.

The first time he had ever felt the fear of death, at the age of eleven or so, George had gone to his father about it. And his father had reacted as if he had been waiting for the question all his life. He removed his pipe and began talking about the whole universe, about swirling gases and collapsed super-giants, etc. It was such a surprising reaction. In a sense, the whole human race was a waste of time, said Mr. Wren, it grew and withered like one tiny man, and turned into blue gas, and away we go again. George had been curiously soothed by this mystic inflation of the problem, and by his father's enthusiasm. It was the best talk they had ever had together. But the thought of Peter dying lay heavy tonight. A baby was something that spilled over with promise. It shouldn't be allowed to turn into gas. Something should be done about it.

Matilda gave him a look, anxious but not altogether sympathetic—as if he was running a fever, but could stop if he wanted to. He got up and decided to take a walk. A need to look at the sky. Matilda asked him if he was all right.

He wanted to say something reassuring, but he couldn't think of anything. The pink buildings outside had a certain brooding power in the dark. Like the walls of a medieval town. There was really nowhere else to walk, the playground was locked by now, so he walked around the buildings along the narrow cement walks, saying "hello" to the doormen and the people going in and out.

The feeling of death embraced him and Peter and Twining, like Laocoön and the snakes. He felt utterly desolate, utterly abandoned. The theme of childishness had played different variations all day—a funny child this morning, a greedy child at lunch, and now a frightened child. Twining in his undershorts, the final humiliation. How could he have done it to us, to the magazine?

The dirty bastard, he thought, the dirty corrupt bastard. He won't get any sympathy from me.

Put away the things of a child, for Christsake, George; no, I won't be so vulnerable again. (Won't be so much fun, either, but I won't be so vulnerable.) "Hello, Charlie." "Evening, sir." He bowed to the doorman. Talk to Matty about it. Like a child. To hell with that. He started walking around the buildings again instead.

VII

The damn smell of paint was everywhere. You kept having to walk around bits of petrified newspaper, and around surly men in white suits and what looked like paper hats. And then having to leave your cubicle while they did your ceiling. He should never have agreed, this first nervous week, to have the place painted.

Brian paced restlessly outside his cubicle. He didn't want to commandeer someone else's desk, and nobody was volunteering to lend him one. Fritz worked expressionlessly, cooperating mechanically: "Hey Brian, sit down, you make me nervous, boy." "I can't, they're painting my office." "Oh, don't bother then." George Wren seemed to be working hard for a change. He hadn't said anything cheap or silly yet this morning. Give him time, though.

Just beyond the editorial enclave sat Philo Sonnabend, still true-blue, although obviously remorseful about the fate of his advertising ideas. Christ, they were awful. Brian had wished to hell he could use them, transmute them; but he could just see Twining sitting up in some hospital bed, laughing his gut out, if Philo's ads turned up in *The Outsider*.

Anyway, you couldn't run an office on sentimentality. You had to have people's respect before you worried about their friendship. Philo was professional enough to see that. Brian had asked him out to lunch and, goddamn painters—they wanted to paint *between* the cubicles. The whole place was going to be an Olga Marplate paradise in cream and turquoise. It was the one thing she wanted, so why not let her have it? Twining underrated the value of these small concessions. Olga's loyalty was purchased forever by a few pots of paint. Twining was a fool in those ways.

Brian looked over at Olga. Lots of human value there. Not such a good businesswoman as he had hoped, but excellent values. If you got the full mileage out of people like Olga and Philo, you could have a pretty damn great little staff. Twining, on the other hand—Olga caught his eye and beckoned him over.

"Mr. Fine?" she said, "could I have a word?" She thought it was better for office discipline to call people "Mr." and "Miss," even old friends like Brian.

"Yes, Olga. What can I do for you?"

"Haven't you got a desk, Mr. Fine? Would you like mine?"

"No, that's O.K."

"I was just wondering, Mr. Fine, if you'd care to have a little supper at my place tomorrow night. That is, if you're not, you know—"

"Well—" It was silly to hesitate, but that would make

the third time this month, and while of course it was silly to think of Olga in that sense, the most amazing misunderstandings were possible. Brian remembered, oh years ago, when Bernice Fitzwilliam in the Accounting Department had invited him to dinner, oh twice, and had well, sat next to him and shown him photographs and breathed on his hands, and she was almost as old as Olga. These women living by themselves had a very hard time, and it wasn't fair to give them ideas.

"There are some business things I'd like to talk about, and I thought—over a leisurely dinner."

"Yes, well, all right," he said, in a tone of: just this once. On business.

The new issue was shaping up pretty well. He had had to withstand a barrage of preposterous suggestions from George Wren at the beginning of the week. George apparently wanted to turn *The Outsider* into a humor magazine. Satire, satire, satire—that was all these young bastards ever thought about. There was nothing left to satirize anyway, except all the other satire.

George wanted something funny about the H-bomb. And he wanted something funny about the race question. And he wanted something funny about mental health. Next week he would be wanting something funny about cancer. Great little generation.

Brian believed that he had a well-balanced issue. A very interesting article on farm surpluses. An analysis of Action Painting. A thing on French foreign policy. Symmetry, balance. They had had a noncommital editorial conference about it; Fritz and George tacitly yielding to his leadership, at least for the time being, but the working out of the arrangement was not yet satisfactory. It was a pretty sad little conference. The other two contributed almost nothing. He felt uncomfortable doing so much of the talking, and he ended it abruptly with most of the decisions unmade.

The sensible leadership-type thing to do now was to relax completely between issues, empty his mind and unfasten his nerves; but a slight edge of tension carried over. He was used to small-scale worrying, had woken up with a fresh worry every morning for years—had he violated his diet again, had he drunk too much last night and said something foolish, had he, *you* know, and worries about worrying: but this was different.

Those pimple-sized worries had always dispersed over breakfast; but this was an all-day sucker. No doubt you got used to it after a while, and stuffed it all into the one ulcer and let that do the worrying for you. But at the moment a light tension was diffused through his whole system, now in the arms, now in the groin, and when he got home at night he even found that his feet were hot, from worrying.

"What is it, Philo?"

"Would you like my desk, Mr. Fine?"

"No, that's all right."

Philo teetered, and then blurted, "I've reworked some of the ads. I agree that they weren't any good, they were just rough, you remember I told you that."

He leaned forward and his breath smelled of failure. It was like trying to shake off a drunk. Brian's impulse was to push him blindly away. But he said, "O.K. I'll look at them. But don't be disappointed, will you, if . . ."

"No, no, that's all right."

Brian knew they were going to be hopeless. He had kidded himself, in a gush of populism, that Philo had talent. But Philo had neither eye nor ear. His layouts were drab, off-center and, for all their ugliness, not even especially noticeable; his lyrics were stiff and totally uncon-

149

nected with the spoken language. Brian looked at them without bothering to focus, groping instead for the firm, kindly phrase that would keep this from ever happening again.

"I think you're too ambitious, Philo. With a magazine like *The Outsider* you just want to tell people what's in it. The man-of-distinction image, you know, this fellow you've got here—where did you get him by the way?"

"He's my brother-in-law. I took the picture myself."

"I see, well it's a very nice picture." Brian gazed at the florid mountebank—thank God he'd asked who it was before commenting. "But he takes up an awful lot of space. And you know, on our budget, we need that space to describe the contents. The way Mr., er, Twining does. Only with a little more sparkle, perhaps."

Asking Sonnabend for sparkle was a fool's errand: the tension ran down Brian's back and buried itself in his backside. Bending over Philo's desk was making his spine ache.

Philo wouldn't give up. "To tell you the truth, Brian, I seriously question that policy. I think there are lots of people we're not reaching, lots of people who would really enjoy the magazine if we could just get them to buy it. I mean, that's just my opinion. My brother-in-law, for instance, genuinely enjoyed that number he's holding in the picture. He said he expected it to be stuffy, but it wasn't half bad."

"Did he take out a subscription?"

"Are you kidding? My brother-in-law? But he liked it and that's a tremendous thing, if you knew my brother-in-law."

"I don't see a market in him."

"No, O.K., but what do we lose? Twenty-one thousand

subscribers is what we've got. Don't you think it's worth trying for more?"

Brian felt a sudden scorching rage. Where the hell did Twining find people like this? Was Sonnabend really the best he could come up with? He straightened up; being bent in two seemed to cut the gland of patience in half.

"I'm sorry, Philo, but we'll have to play it my way. I'm afraid the kind of readers we want are not going to be gulled by big pictures of handsome readers: or look at this big, big, buy thing . . ."

Philo was not easily to be shamed. "Twenty-one thousand readers isn't much," he said.

"Well, we just have to improve the magazine. We can't make it on stunts."

"So the policy is, no change?"

"We can try to brighten the advertising copy."

"You want me to do that?"

Oh God, what was the answer to that? "I guess you could give it a try," said Brian, riven with self-disgust. "But don't be disappointed."

His cubicle was available now. He padded through the dirty newspaper, leaving a determined Philo already rolling up his mental sleeves. Brian felt that the conversation had been terribly messy; it had settled nothing, only getting them both further into the swamp. Eventually he would have to tell Philo to forget the whole thing. Otherwise, the guy would be in every second afternoon with a fresh sheaf of monstrosities, and Brian would go slowly out of his mind.

He could only take it out on Twining. What was his idea in hiring an advertising manager who couldn't write ads? Philo's salary was pegged at about $8,500, which wasn't the price of genius. But there must be some college boy somewhere who could do the job—and you could escalate him if he did it well. Why, Brian's nephew, Forrest Thirsby, could probably do it, smart little kid, Brian had dropped in on the Thirsbys last Sunday. (This branch of the family had moved East seven years ago, encouraged by Brian's success, and were becalmed in Yonkers, so he owed them a favor.) Or how about Forrest's big brother, Sam? Sam was right in the middle of relocating anyway . . .

It took a minute for Brian to realize what he was doing. He was actually thinking of firing people. Worse, he was thinking of firing one of his own supporters. Something about the prospect of Philo's pale, misshapen face craning in here every afternoon, with a new, horribly fertile batch of designs, had been briefly too much for him. "Philo old boy, these are perfectly rotten. Philo, my *dear* chap . . ."

Of course, there was really no question of firing Philo or anyone else; he might be a handicap, but he was a loyal one. If that was what Twining had bequeathed him, so be it.

All the same, he could barely look at Philo on the way out that evening. It reminded him too much of Bernice Fitzwilliam in accounting, the girl he had made the mistake of (accidentally) encouraging sexually so many years ago. The memory of Bernice, now that he had resurrected it, was almost as persistent as the real thing. Bernice had hung on through thick and thin; no coldness or rudeness could shake her off. She slivered after him like mercury, from the elevator to the water cooler, infesting the whole office with middle-aged desire, offering unspeakable love. It was in its particular way his darkest hour at *The Outsider*. Brian had been on the point of resigning when Bernice had announced her engagement to somebody else.

So maybe Philo too could be outwaited; his ardor would burn itself out like Bernice's, and he would shrivel back to simple space bartering. It was a tragedy to have no talent, but an unavoidable one. Brian's own illusions had been punctured once upon a time, and he couldn't afford to believe that the operation was fatal. It was part of growing up, wasn't it? Still, for the life of him, he couldn't look at Philo on the way out.

Fritz, with his silly half smile, shared the elevator with him and said, "How's it going?" You and your impeccable taste, *you* do the advertising, thought Brian. Fritz was the office wit, insofar as the office had a wit, but you knew that if he did ads they would be conservative and quiet. Something, possibly Twining, inhibited him; still inhibited all of us, damnit. "It's going all right," Brian said.

Courage. If you had too much of it, you surrendered something else—your watchfulness, your woodland instincts. George Wren, for instance, probably had lots of courage. Twining . . . stop thinking about Twining, he has no conceivable relevance to this discussion. The name was becoming a teasing obsession, like a tune. As a boy, Brian used to have this trouble with the names of ballplayers, e.g., "George Selkirk," "Mike Kreevich," "Boots Poffenger," saying them to himself right through the summer.

It was the same now with "Gilbert Twining." "Good night then, Fritz." Gilbert Twining Selkirk.

A country boy with city interests, that was the story of Brian Fine—baseball, gangster stories, politics. The Fines had never really belonged in Iowa. They had followed the Thirsbys west, and then the Thirsbys had followed them back east, and that was that. So much for family history.

When he got home, his little apartment seemed more than usually inadequate. It was built for the small morning worry, the loginess after supper, the sense of burrowing at night: it could barely house the mega-worries of an editor in chief. He wondered if he should move somewhere else, and discard these diminutive associations. A house in the suburbs like Twining's with a special worrying room, a gymnasium for worrying, he had been out to Twining's a couple of times at night and it looked enormous in the dark.

The scale of his life was just too damn small. The night burrowing had lost its warm flavor. Just sitting in an apartment reading the evening paper wasn't good enough any more. He should be making decisions, forcing the issue in some way. He drank his beer and stripped down his pork chop. He could handle the days if the nights were just a little better. If he could, so to speak, take off his girdle when he got home. But all he could think of was going to a movie or a bar, and these happened to be two places where office thoughts pressed on him especially hard. In the movies they filled the screen, in a bar they swirled into the bloodstream. As the chop hit the fizzing pan he felt the brief incongruous throb of defiance that had become another of his new habits. "I can lick them." Twining didn't let things get him down, and Twining was a decadent English fop. Confidence was above all a technique.

Flashes of defiance didn't get you all that far in this kind of situation. This one gave way to a mild spasm of nausea, so that he couldn't face the pork chop. He wrapped it in silver paper and put it in the icebox. This was worse than anything he had expected. For a moment he felt as if he was jumping out of his skin. Already he knew that he wouldn't sleep tonight: and what he was going to do between now and bedtime God only knew . . . But it wouldn't last: a few good issues would change all this. The first week or two was bound to be bad, terrible: but he had every expectation of coming through. If there was one thing his life had trained him in, it was survival. He could outwait anything, even his own nervousness. You'll see, Gilbert Twining and all of you.

2

He couldn't very well fire Brian *and* Sonnabend *and* Marplate. Bad for morale. Brian would probably linger on indefinitely, one of those gray defeated men. Relieved to be taken off the hook, poor little bastard. There was no saving Sonnabend. Philo was a gorgeous mediocrity: worse, he was sly and vindictive . . . Fritz remembered the night—hairy old office-party night—when Philo had unveiled his rare collection of resentments: they had gone down to Sweeney's virtually arm in arm and Philo had unburdened himself without warning. "Brian Fine, so high and mighty, Olga Marplate is another"—old Uncle Tom Sonnabend, Old Yas-suh Boss Philo, had been storing it all up, every slight, every indignity, for centuries. Well, we can't have that sort of thing in the magazine of the future. Philo must find a new ambience for his grievances. Olga, now, we might give a chance to. She seems to be an efficient little broad. Never had much to do with her, thinks I'm a libertine, I expect. May have a point there.

The feel of silk on the skin could change a man's character over the years. Fritz felt like a master of hounds as he sprawled among Harriet's chichi bedclothes. *The Outsider* was such a cut-rate organization. With a little real money to play with (thought: Twining had never dipped his fist in the honey jar all the way—why not?), they could carry a real advertising expert on the staff. Olga could be reduced to simple accounting, where her bad taste would do no further harm to the office walls. (Green paint, that's where you make your mistake with me, kid.) Fritz scratched himself. How much of this wisdom was it worth passing on to old Harriet? He would have to reidentify all the characters, before he could even begin to talk about them. Harriet lay on her side, her speckled back arched in his direction. Give her a few simple thoughts.

"Poor Brian seems very tense," he said.

"Oh yes?"

"You know—Brian?"

"Yes, I know."

"Oh. You do. Well, he seems tense. You know, he's running the magazine more or less, and he takes it all so seriously, fuss fuss fuss like an old hen."

"That's always a mistake."

"He's an old maid, that's the trouble with Brian. He has no real life outside the magazine as far as I know. He never does anything like this, for instance."

"Poor man."

"Yes."

Poor man. Old, fat colleague. His face in the elevator this evening was so frightened. How much could he take? —would he go home one evening and hang himself in his garret or wherever he lived? Or would he just take an overdose of syrup of figs? Fritz slithered toward Harriet. Brian wouldn't have to suffer much longer if all went well.

"The theater season will be opening soon," said Harriet. Oh God, he was hoping she'd forgotten about that.

"Yes, we must see a few things."

"I suppose that Wally Whatshisname will be reviewing as usual." She didn't know that Wally was supposed to be a leading critic; she would have said George Bernard Whatshisname too.

"I guess he will. It's up to Brian right now. I have nothing to do with it." He whispered this into her ear, as if it was a very sensuous message. She answered in a crisp voice that almost made him jump: "Why is it up to Brian? Aren't you equals, on the masthead and everything?"

"Brian wants so much to try running the whole book, dear. Divided command really isn't a good idea." He hoped that his sultry whisper would expedite matters a little while they were trudging through this foolish interrogation.

"How long do you suppose he'll last? I mean, he *isn't* the man for the job, is he?"

"No. But he deserves a chance."

He hoped for a surrendering sigh, poor little Harriet doesn't understand these things, but instead she rolled away and touched her forehead with a typically stupid gesture and he realized that she was closing up shop: this rich, lame-brained, overtrained, undereducated bitch was still blackmailing him, damnit.

He underwent the briefest twinge of liverish rage, that such a child, such a cretinous sub-schoolgirl should have money and a body and power . . . Nothing better illustrated the sickness of our society than finding yourself obliged to play children's games with the very rich. A human thing like love could be balanced against an artificiality like reviewing plays, in her pink chiffon brain, and reviewing plays could come down heavier.

He took a cigarette out of the pack marked H.E.W. and scraped a match across a box marked H.E.W., and watched her tottering off to the bathroom. She held her forearm dramatically against her forehead, as though she really did have a headache. Was that her idea of good theater? He was nothing like so impressed this second time. (But let's not get too righteous, Tyler—if she wasn't a chump, you wouldn't be here at all. Right?)

He wondered, no, he was only kidding—he could see Twining half smiling like mad, even half laughing, over this one, but he wondered if Harriet would settle for one review?

Harriet's tickle of a headache outlasted his interest. In

normal circumstances he would have consoled himself by saying something a little sarcastic; but in that particular bed his range of expression was somewhat limited. He couldn't afford to get mean or angry for a moment. She might have admired a display of masterful wrath, but he couldn't afford to take the chance.

And this had suddenly turned it into a very cheap, bad evening. It was degrading, not to be allowed to get mad even when the logic of the situation called for it. The silk sheets began to feel like a cheap bribe. The chintzy bedroom looked suddenly huge and bleak. He put on his trousers, not at all the master of hounds. To be trouserless in such a room was to be completely at its mercy. "I'm truly sorry, dear," she said. "You seem to be getting a lot of these headaches lately," he said.

"Yes, it's mysterious." Nothing less dignified than a man stuffing his shirt into his trousers in this kind of bedroom. She kissed him with a terrible untroubled coolness. It's lucky I'm the one who's using *her,* thought Fritz, as he headed sourly for the elevator.

The new issue had just come back, and he sat in his cubicle staring at it. It was uncanny. You would never guess from it that Twining had been away. In fact, you could almost swear that Twining had written the last editorial, the urbane one. (No, that was me, Fritz.) The only thing seriously below standard was a book review by one A. P. Single, an old friend of Brian's whose stuff they had been turning away for years. Every editor should be entitled to at least one old friend. Hard to see what Brian was so tense about.

Brian or someone had placed on his desk a dingy-looking article about the gold standard. Talking about gold standards—his mind sneaked back a moment to the frustrations of the night before. That was the gold standard, baby, and the sooner we get off it, the better.

He shuffled the pages around. You could read them in any order, the article was equally sexless from any angle. He went to the door of his cubicle, because you could get a little more air there. The fan in the main section of the office swayed toward him and bestowed a small gust. Brian was heading toward the water cooler, pale and slept-in; his thin hair had been plowed up by desperate fingers. Philo stood up to intercept him. Brian seemed to duck. He got past Sonnabend to the cooler the way a frightened man gets past a demanding bum—watch out, Brian, you're going to offend the silly bastard. Philo stood there waiting for Fine to drink his fill. Brian turned at last with a look of nervous defiance. This was pretty funny. Fritz stood in the doorway watching and trying to listen. But he couldn't catch it under the noise of the fan. Philo in left profile was smiling, as usual, with his teeth all over the place. Brian was moving his hands, and his stomach was going in and out irregularly. Brian probably didn't know how easily Philo was upset, and how deep and undying were his wounds. If he was talking as he looked to be talking, Brian would find himself with an ineffectual enemy for life.

Fritz went back to his desk. The small things that interest you when you're bored. He picked up the Gold Standard and began to cut, and tie things together. He liked editing, even bad pieces, and did it with care. Brian had reached his own cubicle door—and there was Philo right next to him, touching his arm for pete's sake, just above the roll of sleeve. You don't *touch* Brian, not unless you're desperate, not unless you touch everybody. Fritz strained his ears, but Brian suddenly darted into the sanctuary of his office, leaving his shirt behind in Philo's hands (not really, just an optical illusion). Philo turned away with the hopeless, incurable smile . . . I should hate to see into that dim, sewer of a brain, thought Fritz.

Well, back to the Gold Standard. When we fire Philo and demote Brian, what happens to George? Good boy, George. Looking a bit world-weary the last couple of days. Growing pains. Promote George. Bar Olga Marplate from all the office parties. Cripes, this article was impossible. It couldn't just be his mood.

He went in to see Brian, who still looked a bit agitated.

"Brian, where did you find this—this thing?"

"What thing?"

"This gold thing."

"You mean Culpeper's article on the gold standard? You know who Culpeper is, don't you?"

"He's no writer, that I know."

"Look, we're lucky to have him, he's one of Canada's leading economists."

"A commentary, a sad commentary."

"I've been trying to get something out of him for years."

"You've been wasting your time, is all I can say."

"We're running the damn piece."

"O.K., but you can do the edit on it."

"Fritz, I often wonder what the hell use you are? I mean, seriously."

Brian leaned back and shaded his eyes. Some private panic had squeezed the words from him. Now he didn't know whether to cut his losses or to plunge further in. Pathetic to watch a man who couldn't keep his quandaries to himself.

"You want to have that liver looked at, Brian."

"What I mean is, you haven't done a damn thing since Twining pulled out. You haven't come up with any ideas, you haven't brought in any new articles. That cooperation we talked about, the night we heard about Twining—what became of that, I wonder? Now, on top of everything, you come in here and sneer at Harris F. Culpeper's perfectly good article on the gold standard."

"Sorry, Mr. Fine, sir. I guess I'm just a useless lay-about."

"Cut it out, Fritz. I just want to know if anything's bothering you. Do you resent what I'm doing? Are we in this together? Level with me, Fritz. Don't," he lowered his voice, "fart around the bush, like our young friend next door."

"I don't know what to say, Brian. There's no substance to this conversation. I don't like the article you gave me to edit. I'm sorry I didn't give you a written report. Have things changed so much that I have to do that?"

"No, that's all right. It's just your general attitude that had me puzzled. Forget it. Bring me the article."

"Did you have a bad time with Philo? Is that what's got you upset?"

"What the hell gave you that idea? Just bring me the article, will you?"

"And you want me to be a member of the team from now on, right?"

"I don't give a damn what you do. Just bring me the article."

3

Polly Twining paused with the duster. There was a pile of old *Outsiders* on the coffee table which could either be dusted or thrown away. Dusting old magazines was silly, so she picked them up and cradled them out to the kitchen and dumped them all in the garbage can.

Gilbert's liberalism. Gilbert's *responsible* liberalism. Floating through the county sewers. She sat down in the kitchen and lit a cigarette, her hand shaking slightly. Had the magazine changed so much since the old days, when she had loved it almost indecently? Or was the change entirely in her? She supposed the latter. *The Outsider* was the Dorian Gray of which her relationship with Gilbert was the picture: if that was the right way round. She reached absently in the can and took out a copy and began to read it. It was really quite a good magazine, objectively considered: yet she saw Gilbert in every line, especially the ones with semicolons, and this made it all seem curiously pointless. She hadn't been to see Gilbert in his California hospital, where he still, apparently, struggled suavely for life. She knew that what she had to say to him would not be of much help to a man with heart trouble. She would just have to wait a bit longer, dusting and paying the bills and trying to restore herself. So that she would be ready for a decent life, when the time came.

Her subscription would probably lapse. The divorce—the beautifully inevitable divorce—included the magazine. She didn't know what would become of her shares—she supposed she would hand them in somewhere. (On principle she knew as little as possible about money.) She could picture Gilbert sitting up in bed, in his monogrammed pajamas, surrounded by admiring nurses. Smiling as she came in: "You see, Gilbert, it's impossible after this, isn't it?" "Oh quite. You mean the girl and all that." "Yes, that's it."

"There's not much to say, is there?"

"No." It would be a perfect scene, too perfect to be true.

"Goodbye, Polly." It's been—grand. Oh dear, that her life could come to such scenes.

One funny thing was that she didn't mind too much about the girl in Gilbert's room. She was in a curious way embarrassed, almost touched by the fact that the girl was apparently someone he had picked up in a bar. The girl wouldn't have expected very much from him, she didn't know who he was. Yet even so, he had had a heart attack. Trying to impress a nobody.

That was almost Gilbert's most lovable side. Trying so hard to back up his marvelous first impression—she wasn't angry about that now, although it might give her a handy, legally significant grievance later on. There were other, much better reasons to divorce Gilbert. Take for instance what he had done to Fritz Tyler. She hadn't seen much of Fritz in the last few years, and she wasn't all that observant, she supposed, so it wasn't until they had lunch together a few days ago that she had a chance to appreciate how much he had changed.

It wasn't just the rather affected way he ordered lunch— that was just silly, the kind of mannerism that came and went; it was a kind of interior brittleness, a spiritual smirk that he had picked up while working for Twining. Years ago, she used to stand on rainy corners with Fritz, handing out peace pamphlets; and later she had dried out with him in cafeterias, and laughed nonmaliciously about the people at the other tables. They had also been arrested together, for refusing to take inadequate shelter during nonexistent air raids, and they had picketed, good-humoredly, and marched and heckled together. Those were among her sunniest, and most solid, memories. Fritz seemed indestructible, in those days, one of those men you could leave for fifteen years with perfect confidence. He personified not only the right ideas but the right point of view—irreverent, kindly, stubborn—everything that made the Left right and the Right wrong.

But now, as she listened to his new jokes, and his fleeting sincerities, she realized that he had been as malleable as anybody: that the old Fritz was just a phase, and that you can't count on anyone not to change. What precisely *was* wrong with him now? He was very sympathetic about

Gilbert, and excruciatingly tactful—and yet she felt that he wasn't really talking about that at all, but about something else.

"So what's going to happen to the magazine now?" she asked him.

"We'll just totter along until Gilbert gets back, I guess. Brian is our current leader. If it's too much for him—" he gestured.

"Would you like to try running it yourself?"

"I might give it a whirl. If Brian drops the ball, that is," and so on, in a noncommunicative way. She knew that Gilbert didn't think much of him. It might be the saving of him, to run the magazine on his own. However, there didn't seem much chance of that while Gilbert was alive. What really distressed Polly was that for a moment Fritz sounded a little bit like her husband. He half sneered at Brian and the others, almost like an Englishman.

"Don't you think the magazine's become rather conservative?" she asked him. "I mean, the world had moved and the magazine hasn't."

She hoped that this would tap some of his old reflexes. But she suddenly got a feeling that the question didn't interest him terribly much. He said, "We're always worrying about that, of course. So many of the radical fights have been won—"

"And so many of them haven't."

"Well, that's true too. We should probably reconsider some of our stances."

It was profoundly depressing. He suddenly began to talk very enthusiastically about the magazine and its potential, and about how much it meant to him personally. And she thought, you don't have to tell me all this, Fritz. She also thought there was something tinny about his voice. And she certainly didn't like the way he dabbed his mouth with his napkin, or the way he called the waiter over. But these were silly things to go by, she knew that.

"Polly, listen, it's been great."

"I've enjoyed it too."

"We must do this again."

"Yes."

It wasn't the bow tie, he had always worn bow ties, or the summer straw hat. He had changed less, physically, than most people. Yet there was a real cheapening somewhere. He stood by the taxi door smiling in at her, and she wanted to, I don't know, snap his tie against his Adam's apple. He had been around her husband too long.

Dorian Gray was about right. The magazine went on blandly year after year, and all its sins accumulated in the staff. Brian Fine had changed too (she had a chat with him in the office that same afternoon), and even George Wren, who had only been there a few months, and Wally Funk with his pansy tantrums when he came to dinner these days, and Polly Twining, what had happened to her? She wasn't on the staff, of course, but she could hardly have escaped. She had been closer to the source of corruption than anyone. She threw the magazine back in the garbage can, and went on with her dusting.

Well, those were better excuses, better than his silly old adultery. If a person was to be judged by the quality of her excuses, these ones did her slightly more credit.

But, of course, the point was that she couldn't start again with Gilbert, excuse or no excuse. She could have *continued* with him, but she couldn't go back to him. He would understand the distinction—"even Eleanor Roosevelt, even Albert Schweitzer would have understood, my dear." Gilbert at his most whimsical. She could not allow that voice back into the house.

She was shaken by the force of this conviction. It was a

serious, unprecedented thing, for her to give up on any human being. She would not, of course, treat Gilbert cruelly, that much remained of principle: but that was all. She could not accept excuses for *him*, as she would for any other person in the world. She could not feel sorry for his emotional deprivations, his icy childhood, his present loneliness. She knew the excuses were there as usual, that he was no more to blame than a thug or a drug addict for being what he was. (He had told her so himself. *Whimsically*.) And yet, although she knew she was being unfair and illogical, she could not accept any explanations that might let that voice back in the house.

She tried to get her mind onto something else—but Gilbert left this awful vacuum that only Gilbert himself could fill. So, helplessly, resentfully, she went at him again. He had promised so much, and he had defaulted on every penny of it. She had turned down or postponed so many people like Fritz (and she might have *helped* someone like Fritz) to be ready for Twining. She had almost fainted when she first met him: he was too perfect for this world. Why hadn't he admitted right then and there that there was really nothing to him, that he was only a dreadful little English boy, with a bagful of tricks? And then, he had courted her with such confidence (and of course such *amusement*)—it was an astounding performance for a man who was fundamentally weak and broken. But why had he bothered to do it at all?

And even that was not the worst of it. The worst of it was also the most surprising: his terrible pseudo-candor, the way he told you everything and nothing about himself. His own exquisitely tailored case history. . . . Anyhow there was nothing she could do for him, that was the point now. It wasn't a personal thing. After all, the poor man had had a heart attack; and he *really* couldn't help what he was. If the word liberal meant anything at all by now, it meant that you didn't hate people.

Dusting always induced a certain vehemence in her, and she found herself repeating grimly, "I will not hate him, I will not hate him." She could see Gilbert smiling at this. "Of course you hate me, my dear. Why shouldn't you? Even nuns have temptations, you know." He often talked about the pent-up violence of liberals, comparing it to a spinster's fascination with sex. For purposes of education, or punishment, he often used her as his stock liberal; and so she hesitated now to express any thought, even to herself, without first checking it against Gilbert's derision charts. Being married to Gilbert would eat into anyone's naturalness and spontaneity; it had, she knew, made her a little more clipt and careful. This was another of Gilbert's little legacies; he had left something for everybody. But she was darned if she was going to give into it or let it become a habit. Quite apart from anything else, she wouldn't give him that satisfaction.

4

"Lunch?"

"No, thanks."

"You feeling O.K., George?"

"Uh-hum. Feel fine."

Brian moved off, looking huffed and suspicious. People were so touchy. George shrugged. He wasn't the only one who was childish—*everyone* was childish these days, there *were* no adults any more.

Brian had put the new issue on his desk. George opened it, read his own editorial, counted the columns of ads, shuffled around here and there. It looked like a fairly good number. Brian was doing quite a sound job, although he didn't seem to be getting much fun out of it.

George bent back to work. "Our links with Canada," eh. Friendly giant north of the border. George was working hard these days. He was actually learning the business, and could probably, if everyone was wiped out in some cataclysm, even put the magazine together by himself. He felt that his face was heavier. Perhaps working hard, being efficient, changed your appearance. He avoided having lunch with people, because conversation had recently become an immense effort, and a totally unrewarding one. When Matty had people over in the evening, he just stared at the curtains until the people went away. It was personalities that he didn't like, that and the sound of voices. And, of course, faces.

Working quickly gave one extra time in the afternoon, and he spent it on long walks. His footsteps were heavier and he was thinking of buying a hat. He didn't make so many jokes to himself. He thought about work, and how foolish it was to sweat your guts out for particular people, how hysterical and feminine to make it a personal thing. You work for the sake of the work. Henceforth, he would do his stuff for anyone who happened to be there. Office politics ended at his door.

One afternoon he walked all the way down to Battery Park and another all the way up to St. John the Divine's. He got home late each time, feeling calm and numb. It was like some medieval disease, walking madness. Matilda said, "You're very strange lately." On Saturdays and Sundays he pushed Peter for miles along the desiccated Queens sidewalks, talking to the kid and enjoying him very much. At home, he was considerate about washing the dishes and putting out the garbage, but on the unspoken condition that he do it by himself and in silence. He encouraged Matty to go out to movies, or to friends, while he baby-sat. Since she had trouble about speaking first, she conveyed her concern about this mainly by looking at him queerly. But in fact he felt happy, in this new, sober way.

When he finished with Canada, he took it in to Brian's cubicle and slid it across the desk. Brian's upside-down watch said quarter to four. It felt like a pleasant autumn afternoon. He could take the bus up to Riverside Drive and walk by the river.

"You finished already?" said Brian.

"Yup. It was in pretty good shape to start with."

"You want to leave early, I suppose."

"If I may, sir."

"You know it isn't too good for morale, George. The girls in back would like to leave early too. What do you suppose they think when they see the editors pulling out at four o'clock?"

"I've never given it a thought."

"Well, it's time you did. Look, George, we're a partnership now, you and me and Fritz. We have to take responsibility for the magazine. It's not just something we work for, it's *us* now. It's—am I boring you?"

"No, not at all." George cut off the yawn. He still felt pleasantly tired from *yesterday's* walk.

"Couldn't you sit and read something until five?" George didn't answer. The question was almost unendurably uninteresting.

"O.K., it's no business of mine, I guess. I'm not going to start giving you orders at this point. If you don't have any feeling for the whole organization, for the team—"

George mooched on out. It was all so incredibly childish. A man of Brian's age, talking about the team. George grabbed his hat and headed for the elevator. He couldn't imagine that those nice girls really cared when he left. (Do you, girls?) He did his job and they did theirs. Fine arrangement.

He took the number 5 bus and pushed the self-service door soon after the bus had swung north along the river. He delved down into Riverside Park and began to stroll along the winding lanes, between shrubs, past furtive couples on beach blankets, past a drinking fountain that offered him a tiny spurt of warm water like the office fountain, and on down towards the river and up again, like a roller coaster.

The problem, as he saw it, was this one of identity. As long as you worried about who you were, you took the most terrible beatings. As long as you wanted to be George Wren the promising writer, the mentally healthy editor, the good husband, you were in a box. Conversely, as soon as you saw that it didn't matter a damn who you were, you were out of it again. If people lived out here on the grass, instead of in two and a half room apartments, they would see this more clearly. Out here, you were really nothing at all.

In fact, George didn't even want to philosophize about it, it was such a very lucid conviction. As long as he could keep it in mind, he was beyond humiliation, beyond horrible discovery. And it was best thought about without verbalizing. (Words were for magazines.)

Suppose, though, that someone of Brian Fine's age learned that it didn't matter who he was—he simply wouldn't believe it, would he? People like Brian remained at the mercy of every revelation, of every candid stranger. All you had to say to Brian was, "Let's face it, you're not really a good editor," or "Have you ever asked yourself, Brian, why you never married?" and Brian would fall apart. Because he still thought that those things mattered; he thought that the world cared, that the planet stopped in its gassy tracks, out of grief and surprise, every time it heard something disappointing about Brian.

The world doesn't give a crap about you, Fine, or you,

Wren. Or you, Twining. Humility and self-abnegation, all the Sunday school cant—nobody had ever bothered to tell him that they were really strategies of survival, that they might even keep you from blowing your brains out some day. The pain of self-discovery could not be borne, if you really cared; but if you had become nobody, you could take it. Or, at least, he hoped you could.

He got up as far as Grant's Tomb, and his feet ached voluptuously. It almost seemed that this new point of view depended on his keeping moving. But he couldn't keep moving forever. He climbed up to the street level and began looking for the subway.

"How long do you expect to go on being like this?" asked Matilda, with such a pretty frown, over dinner.

"God knows," he said.

It isn't much fun for me, he could imagine her saying. I'm sorry, there's nothing I can do about it, he could imagine himself saying. Buy yourself a new dress, or take in a show until it blows over. Oh George, what use is a new dress, it's *you*—

"Are you still upset about Mr. Twining?"

"Hell, no."

"Do you think he'll come back to the magazine?"

"No idea. I couldn't care less, one way or the other."

"Do you like this particular avocado?"

"Very nice."

She didn't say any more, and he finished his dinner in dreamy silence. It was impossible to convey that he was very, very happy. He just couldn't see a way of bringing his wife into the picture. That was probably why monks never married. He put his hand on hers and smiled; she gave him a worried smile back and said, "I wish you'd tell me what's troubling you."

171

He knew it was hopeless, but he owed her an effort.

"It's not the kind of thing you, women that is, ever have to worry about. It's a value question. Let's take an example: the office. A, let's say, wants to get rid of B. C agrees, but not on A's terms. They both approach D—"

"Couldn't you give their real names?"

"No, that's the whole point, the names don't matter. This equation goes on all over town. All right, let's say that I'm D. A comes to me, suppurating with grievances. He's fat and uncomfortable, you see."

"I think I know who that is."

"I told you, the names don't matter. C is an adventurer—"

"And I know who that is, too. Look, George, I'm sure it isn't exactly the same in other offices. Doesn't it matter that C is *better-looking* than A? Wouldn't it be better if you gave them names?"

"Oh, it isn't *exactly* the same. But, O.K., look, just go down to any playground, and what do you find? A, B and C again. One leader, one whiner, one mischief-maker."

"I'm sure it isn't that simple. I mean, there are real issues, aren't there, between Mr. Fine and Mr. Tyler?"

"Sure. Sometimes there's a tricycle to fight about on the playground, and sometimes there's a nickel on the ground. But the jockeying of ego is the real story."

"And you're above this whole thing, yourself? D is the adult that everyone appeals to finally?"

"I don't know how to say it without sounding ridiculous, but yes, in a way. The only thing is, anyone can be the adult who wants to be. Anyone who sees that the tricycle isn't that important can be the adult."

"Are you sure it's always only a tricycle?"

"What else can it be? Look, the earth is millions of miles away from the sun, and the sun . . ."

"Yes, I know. If the sun is a basketball, *The Outsider* is a ping-pong ball." He realized he had talked like this before, and that it must be boring for Matty.

"I told you, these things don't matter to women. Women don't worry about proportions."

"But isn't *anything* important to you?"

"Not very much, I guess. A, B and C think it's important who edits a magazine that 21,000 people thumb through, leave coffee stains on, read while they're on the john. D doesn't. D thinks it's just another tricycle. So if they come to D suggesting some brilliant maneuver, some glorious new caper—"

"You don't think *anything* is important?"

"Well, you and the baby, of course."

"Why 'of course'?"

"That's different. That's what life is all about."

He didn't want to talk any more. The more you talked, the further you drifted from what you really knew. You got into wrangles, you tried to score points, and before you knew it, you were miles out to sea and someone had stolen your pants. Keep quiet, keep your eye on the target, don't get distracted. Matty, poor Matty, let's face it, not cut out for this kind of thinking, said:

"Are you sure it wouldn't matter if Mr. Twining came back? Are you sure you'd still be Mr. D the adult if Mr. Twining was around?"

"You're damn right, I'm sure."

"You don't have to get angry."

"I'm not the least angry."

"I don't think life is like that at all. I think you've got it all mixed up, with your nonsense about tricycles."

Arguing about it was a tremendous and futile effort. If they must talk, let it be about something trivial.

"I think you're still under his spell," she said, "trying to see things the way he does, pretending to be bored with everything . . ."

Well, he was that, he was bored enough for two, but he let it pass. And waited for a chance to ask some question about, say, Peter's teeth.

It wasn't the best time in the world for Brian's second editorial conference. George contributed nothing at all, while Fritz kibitzed shamelessly. Brian seemed uncertain about the tone he wanted to set. At first he joshed with Fritz, and tried to draw George out; but when he found that Fritz couldn't be stanched and that George couldn't be persuaded to start, he became cross and the illusion of a happy ship vanished.

"Seriously, Fritz—what do we want to do with the back of the book?" he said at last. "What do we think it's for?"

"Sorry, Brian," Fritz looked up from his scratch pad, which was covered with clown's faces. "What was the question?"

Brian gripped the desk. "What do you think, George?"

"I'm with Fritz. I mean, I didn't get the question either."

"The back of the book—what's it *for?*" said Brian.

"I don't see much point in questions like that," said Fritz. "It's all too abstract. We've got so and so many good reviewers and we send them the books they like, and what comes in is in the back of the book."

"What about Wally then?"

"Yeah—well, there's always Wally."

"Do you think he's more trouble than he's worth? Is a stage column an anachronism these days? What are you staring at, George?"

"Nothing. I'm sorry."

"Look, we don't have to have these meetings if nobody wants them. I thought you'd prefer to make this thing a little more democratic. But if you find that it's all too boring, we'll forget the whole idea."

"The meetings are fine," said Fritz. "Dreamy."

George nodded.

"Well, I guess that's about all, then. I'd been hoping to talk about some layout changes as well but I can see it would be a waste of time."

"Don't feel too bad, Brian. Democracy takes some time to get used to. Maybe we're not ready for it."

"If you and George were a little less flippant, we might get used to it a lot sooner."

Me—flippant? thought George. What is the man saying? He doesn't think that Fritz and I are alike, does he? He doesn't think we're in cahoots, does he? It was a comical misconception, but it didn't seem worth bringing up. George picked up his scratch pad, which was covered with sketches of trees and vintage cars, and wandered back to his desk.

It was a creepier place in the dark than you would have suspected. Gilbert Twining had once said that there were no haunted houses in America ("Your *insects* are too uniform—no earwigs or unclassifiable spiders"), but he had done his damnedest to make an exception of the *The Outsider* office. Every paint job he had postponed, every new piece of equipment he had considered unnecessary had helped the spooks to accumulate. George bet they even had earwigs by now. ("The earwig is the Volkswagen of insects," Twining's recitation continued. "Your American cockroach is a piece of mass-production.") Marplate's green paint had not been enough—in fact, it had been assimilated into the general fug. After going home early three afternoons in a row, George had irrationally decided to work late. Then, tiring of that, he had turned off the light and sat now at

Twining's desk staring at the neon sign across the street (Bert Stark's C-o-hes) and soaking up the emanations from Twining's swivel chair.

The old boy was taking a lot of exorcising. For a man with a light manner, he made a heavy imprint. It had nothing to do with running the magazine (in the seventh mansion of Nirvana or wherever the hell he was by now, George could see that running a magazine was simply a metaphor for something else anyway); it was a question of aesthetics. By keeping the place blowzy and old-fashioned, a Victorian music hall of an office, Twining was making sure that the setting suited him better than anyone. Who else could wear those high-button shoes? Who else could work at a typewriter mended by string and not lose face? Olga Marplate, forever muttering about new this and new that, was wiser than any of them. She knew how ghosts hate fresh paint and modern furniture. Olga should be made chief exorcist.

George sensed that the others were beginning to worry about Twining's silence. Twining's health was characteristically vague, but surely he was now well enough to speak. Brian and Fritz were hardly the psychically receptive type, but they must begin to feel the poltergeistic force of this silence. At the twitchy conference this afternoon, for instance. Or on the way out. Silence could be a solid factor in office life, a large object that you had to walk around like Fred's packing boxes. George was getting mesmerized in the dark: he sensed the stirrings of another unpublishable poem. Time to go home, no doubt.

He went instead and sat for a while in Fritz's office to feel Fritz's emanations. He thought of rifling the private correspondence on the desk and found to his interest that he wasn't tempted. People's letters were metaphors, people themselves were metaphors—the human race was a joke in

176

remarkably poor taste. He did notice a letter from California dated three days ago—so Fritz *had* heard something from Twining: the master was communicado. George was faintly puzzled that Fritz hadn't mentioned it. But perhaps he had and George hadn't heard him.

Anyway, this one was worth a glance. He opened the blue paper and started to read. It was sort of like holding a sea shell to your ear—a pleasant distant sound. The first paragraph thanked Fritz for some letter of sympathy he had apparently written (George had thought of writing one of those himself, but had decided against). The second described in some detail his removal from the hospital to a nursing home. Nothing very controversial about that. He folded the letter, mildly annoyed that Fritz had received it and not he. He had a picture of Twining wrapped up like a mummy—his bandages in perfect taste—writing these little notes with a lumpy white fist: he didn't want to think about it.

The terrifying thing about Twining, absent or present, was that nobody knew what, or how hard, he was thinking; whether, or how much, he cared. You couldn't read his thermostat. His amusement and his sincerity were just two ways of saying the same thing—nothing. What was he planning now, for instance? He must have a lot of time for planning. And he surely wasn't going to let the whole thing go by default. George remembered his catlike defense of the magazine at their last meeting. They were all waiting for some such quick lunge now. And they got letters like this.

George shook his head, as if to the office sprites. He supposed they all, Brian and Fritz and everyone, had different pictures of Twining. The long silence would allow each of these pictures to expand to its own nightmare limits. Waiting like this in the dark could turn timidity into fear, slight awkwardness into total paralysis. Twining often used this tactic on a small scale, pauses, postponements, slow answers to questions or no answers at all. So that was probably the story now. Silence *was* his plan.

George stood up again and rebuttoned his jacket. None of it mattered very much. Twining at this range was a nine-parts mythic figure. He affected the office as an established old religion might—seldom mentioned but always there, keeping new forms from emerging, conveying the message somehow: if I die, you die.

George had found that things went better if you didn't think about him. But in this building, Twining's temple, that was easier said than done. Nobody mentioned him here these days if they could help it, yet he was here all the time, and he really came out after dark. George hadn't thought about him so much in weeks. It was probably better not to come here at night.

On the way out, George almost bumped into him—no, it was that damn packing box. The old Druid was disguising himself as a crate of magazines. The elevator sounded like Scrooge's old partner Marley, dragging his chains wheeze-thump up from the basement. George was intentionally heightening the situation, he supposed—but there was an element that wasn't quite intention and which he couldn't immerse in gags, and he was glad to get out on the street.

5

Brian was also concerned about the prolonged silence of Twining. It was the subject of his prickliest night thoughts. Gilbert must surely be well enough to write letters by now. Brian had sent him a semi-humorous get-well card a few weeks ago (and afterwards had wondered about the wisdom of this) but had so far received no response of any kind.

In his better moments, Brian hoped for a simple note of abdication ("doctor's orders, the old ticker," etc.). At his more frequent worse ones, he braced himself for a long list of instructions, a veritable master plan, which he would at least have a chance to defy. The one thing he had no answer for was silence. On his third twist of the night, the exasperated one that loosened his pajama buttons, he thought of forcing Twining's hand with a direct question of his own. But this was a counsel of nervousness—why *should* he force Twining's hand? His own *de facto* position was strong and presumably getting stronger. If Twining didn't strike soon, the magazine would have drifted beyond his reach; the new regime would be secure. *Viz.,* Red China.

He told himself this at one, and again at two. But patience was the hardest part of this job to learn: the understanding that political situations take time to ripen, and that there wasn't much you could do about them at 2:00 in the morning. He pictured Twining as gaunt and feeble from his illness, and then he pictured him as robust and reborn; and he knew it didn't really matter what he pictured. Time alone would tell.

The morning after the abortive conference he phoned Polly Twining, and was dismayed to find that she didn't know much more than he did. "It really isn't so long since his attack," she said. "The doctor tells me he is still quite weak." "When did you hear from the doctor?" "Well—two or three weeks ago, I guess."

It bothered him. Twining's silence, stirred into his other worries, made a gaseous brew. It was going to be tough enough dealing with Fritz and George and the others without having this thing hanging over him. Twining's presence seemed to get bigger every time the mail arrived without a letter.

Fritz had omitted to mention his own letter. But a couple of days later there was one for Brian Fine, Esq. Brian seized it from the pile and went squirreling off with it to his cubicle. The handwriting on the blue paper was neat and charming. For no very clear reason he closed the door before slitting open the letter. Now then.

He read it slowly. Medical report, satisfactory. Surroundings, cheerful. Not far from a delightful Spanish chapel. A rather unusual sort of hospital, actually a gift of a certain Mrs. Soames, herself a cardiac victim. He got to the bottom and read it again, with unbelief and something like shock. "Hope all goes well." Other than that, not a single word about the magazine.

That evening he had what was turning into a weekly dinner with Olga Marplate. She lived in a brownstone on West Eleventh Street. The living-room ceilings were the highest Brian had ever seen, and covered in dim white scrollwork. The walls were paneled and the bindings were of red leather. It was Brian's idea of an Edith Wharton type scene, and it was constantly resurprising him, because it proved that Marplate wasn't totally modernized yet, and it proved also that she had money. Everyone said that Olga was married to the magazine, yet, so far as Brian knew, she had never invested a penny of money in it. Rum, as Twining would say.

She came swinging out of the kitchen with a plate of sticky hors d'oeuvres. She was wearing a gold dress with a low neckline. Since he had just come out of the bathroom, where the most enormous brassière in the Western Hemisphere hung dripping over the shower rail, this aspect of Marplate was rather on his mind at the moment. For all his own chubbiness, he was rather disconcerted by flesh masses. He looked away and said,

"I think things are beginning to shape up. At the office."

"Yes, I think they are."

"George Wren is still a little snot, of course, and Fritz, well—" He paused.

"I rather like Mr. Tyler," said Olga, "to tell the truth. I think he's very polite and clever."

She went out to the kitchen again, leaving Brian to mull over the unpredictability of human chemistry. Why in God's name should Olga Marplate like Fritz Tyler? It was simply pointless . . . made a hash of human engineering. Brian finished the toasted cheese and licked his fingers. Where did you begin, if someone like Olga could like someone like Fritz?

"How are things in your department?" he asked when she came back, with a plate of little frankfurters on sticks.

"Oh, much better. The electric typewriters are a great success."

"How about the intangibles—morale, etc?"

"Morale is good, I would say. But *can't* you get your Mr. Wren to keep some sort of normal hours?"

"I don't know," Brian shook his head and waved his hand, "I really don't know. Why—have there been complaints?"

"No, not actual complaints. But you can guess what they're thinking, can't you?"

"I certainly can. I really don't know about Wren. I don't know whether he's retarded or simply spiteful. I shouldn't talk like this, I suppose."

"You have to talk to someone," said Olga. Brian thought of the huge brassière. "You can't keep it all bottled up," she said. He wished he had an intelligent ally. But Twining never hired intelligent people unless there was something else wrong with them. Unless they had evil characters. So Olga it was.

"I think George will have to go eventually. He doesn't fit in with us."

"He's awfully immature, isn't he?"

"Yes, that's it. And of course, one rotten apple affects the whole barrel. I think he's still Twining's fair-haired boy, and simply won't cooperate with anyone else. He won't even have lunch with me any more. And if that isn't childish—"

"Mr. Tyler comes and goes at normal times," said Olga.

"Well, that's true."

They had dinner in the next room under another vaulted ceiling, with an honest-to-God cherub on it. Where *did* she get her money? It would be nice simply to ask. But in Edith Wharton's world, you didn't ask.

He fenced around instead, inquiring how long she'd lived here, admiring various expensive-looking objects, wondering about her past. But she answered his questions with non sequiturs, and he had once again to put up with a mealful of childhood anecdotes and shopping anecdotes (she loved auctions, it seemed) which really told him nothing at all. Since more or less taking over the magazine, he had thought a good deal about money. It would be very helpful to establish a financial base of his own, but he didn't know any rich people. Harriet Wadsworth was the number-one backer at the moment, but she was simply impossible. She must have been introduced to him five or six times, without taking him in at all. (He wondered what was the first thing you said when you wanted somebody's money?)

Anyway, here was a source of cash under his very nose. A source that he could easily tap, brassière or no brassière; he shut his eyes and tried to clear his head. Possibly the reason she had never given money was that she had never been asked. Twining with his engraved class consciousness had never supposed that a subordinate could be loaded like this. He had never deigned to dine at her house, of course. Brian's humbler methods might strike pay dirt.

But he couldn't find out any more about her fiscal attributes, hard as he scratched for it. He switched once more to the question of the magazine's finances. This might smoke her out—although, come to think of it, it never had before. "I don't know what we'd do if Mrs. Wadsworth ever decided to pull out," he said. "Even with her support, it's touch and go every month."

"We always come up with something," Olga said brightly. "We're lucky people."

"You mean, Mr. Twining always comes up with something. We can't all have his success with rich widows, you know."

"Oh, Brian."

"I'm serious. Mr. Twining is a quality import. Like Harris Tweed. Rich Americans go for him."

"Perhaps we should broaden our base," said Olga.

She went out and brought back a rich-looking creamy dessert and they talked for a while about getting fat, and Brian had two helpings. His diet these days consisted mostly of worrying. Trying to get his hooks onto Marplate's money, for instance, should take off a few pounds.

"I know this," he said desperately. "If I had any money, it would go straight into the magazine."

"I bet it would, too," said Olga.

"I really believe in that damn magazine. Don't you?"

"Definitely."

"It's my life. With a little money, we could change the whole format, Olga. And you can't change a magazine without changing the format. Maybe you could even help me to find a new design. As I say, if I just had a little money of my own . . ."

Oh God. What did the experts do? Gimme the damn money, you stupid broad. In one-dollar bills.

"You're dedicated too," he said.

"Not as dedicated as you."

He had eaten the dessert too quickly, and his untranquil stomach had flung some of it back halfway up his chest. He supposed it would burn itself away eventually. Olga was already pushing a wheel of camembert toward him. He wasn't the eater he used to be. The pleats on his pants would hang in listless folds when he stood up. And yet his shape was not getting any prettier. It was a frustrating life.

"I think rich people are all basically selfish," he said. "I suppose that's why I believe in the magazine so much and all it stands for."

"I agree," said Olga. "Rich people are funny."

Of course *she* doesn't think she's rich, they never do. Brian had to fight a tide of irritation. He thought, she isn't really interested in the magazine, she's just interested in new typewriters and green paint. Her office-beautiful whims, which he had been slyly catering to, had already taken quite a belt out of the treasury. Her loyalty was costing him plenty.

There seemed to be a strange, subterranean connection between eating too much and thinking about money. The bill for Fritz's lunches had come in this morning—a harrowing document indeed. The till would be empty by the end of the year. He thought of Fritz eating his way through it like a rabbit in a lettuce patch. And Marplate papering the walls with money. And George Wren flushing it down the toilet, as a gag. Q: Fritz, how *can* you? A: All the best editors are fat, Brian. Brian had signed the restaurant check morosely, briefly envious of the good food it spoke for, and given it to Fritz to countersign, and neither of them had said a word.

Right now, with capon-lined belly, he could think of nothing but melting down Olga's candlesticks and selling them, melting down Olga herself—his dinner would never go down if he went on thinking like this. Melting himself and his dinner down, selling his baggy trousers . . .

I've never worried about money before, he wanted to say, but now I could almost cry. Up to now I have always earned so much every year, and spent a little bit less, and that's money. That's all there is to it. The bank statements have been replicas of each other. Cancelled checks—dentist, landlord, telephone company. And now this crazy situation. Palm-sweating calculation. And now I'm trying to wheedle money out of *you*, my dear. But I can't tell you about that, can I?

He moved over to the sofa and she sat a decorous distance away on the other end. It was no use making a speech about it. If he wanted the money, he must be nice to her, nicer than ever before. The apartment responded by seeming suddenly quite musky and intimate. Olga must have drenched her bosoms in 90-proof perfume. The ceilings were high but the lights were heavily shaded and suddenly the room was small and getting smaller. What would Twining do here? How would he get the money?

God, what a revolting thought. There must be an easier way than *that*. He excused himself and sashayed past the pendulous brassière and stood for a moment, leaning against the washbasin, settling himself. There was some Alka-Seltzer in the medicine chest, and he took some as quietly as he could, although the two discs went off like depth bombs in Olga's tooth mug.

It was a dirty, dirty thing, worrying about money. If only there was some way of getting it without worrying. He would have to say something to Fritz about those lunches, and brace himself for the return sarcasm. His flesh already dripped harpoons, like Moby Dick's. One more wouldn't hurt too much. (He wondered, as he flushed the toilet, what kind of thing Fritz had meant when he talked about cooperation the evening they had heard about Twining's heart attack.)

Olga waited for him, her knees crossed squelchingly. "I'm afraid the bathroom's a mess," she said. Now. No use getting testy with her, no use letting his nervous stomach be spokesman. She was a touching, limited woman. Probably her money was tied up in a trust fund anyway. That's what you would do if you had to leave money to Olga.

She took off her shoes and retracted her legs. Really if it was absolutely necessary, he supposed he could—but this was probably taking a rather distorted view of fund raising; it couldn't often come to that.

The Alka-Seltzer plunged through his system, spreading beneficence. Cool, sea-green bubbles. He wrenched his mind off the silver coffee spoons which he had melted halfway down, and tried to treat Olga as a person.

"Capitalism corrupts people terribly quickly, don't you think? I find just having to deal with money for a short time coarsens you, makes you terribly cold."

"I suppose so. It wouldn't do that to you, I'm sure. But I hate to give opinions about things like that."

"No, go ahead, Olga. I'd like to hear your opinions."

"Well, I think, wouldn't it be the same under any system? I mean, it isn't the money so much—"

He shut his eyes mentally, fanned his steaming ulcer. Alka-Seltzer couldn't compete. What with her opinions and Philo Sonnabend's ads (was there any other terror he had failed to unleash?), it looked like being one hell of a long winter.

Trust fund, shmust fund—what kind of person was it who wouldn't give her money to the magazine? What unfathomable, willful stupidity kept her from connecting the two ideas: her money and her, well, life? His eyes searched her stodgy flesh for an answer. For a moment he thought, my God, she's eaten the money. Like a spy swallowing the secret plans. God, I hate fat people, he thought.

Then again, his other ally was thin. He thought with even more desperate gloom of Philo Sonnabend. Twining hadn't told me (why should he have?) that Sonnabend would keep asking for raises. Two weeks running now, a list of Philo's rising costs: sending some imaginary son to Andover, etc.—no sign that they were allies at those times, hell no. Look, Philo, we're going through a difficult patch. C'mon, Philo, nice Philo—and all the while the thin fingers digging like a mechanical crane into the till, into the magazine's vitals. "Mr. Fine, I don't know if I can go on at this rate."

"Why don't you cut out the brandy for a while"—but you couldn't say that. You could only stew and say, as soon as we can, you'll be the first, Philo baby. O.K., kid, understand perfectly . . . And five minutes later, those bloody, bloody ads, blackmailing him like a whipsaw, ads–raise, raise–ads, "Mr. Fine, Mr. Fine, Mr. Fine."

He was sweating. He had no allies. Olga was keeping the apartment hot to inflame his passions, but it wasn't inflaming the right ones. "Are you all right?" she said. "You're perspiring, Mr.–Brian. Would you like to take off your coat?"

Hell, *no*. But talking about allies, he did have that brief idea, one he had dismissed several times before, but which kept coming back, and which looked a little better every time around. Really must get out of this stupid place and think about it, one more time. It had seemed out of the question, but was it really?

He stood up rather abruptly, rather rudely. Olga was surprised and said, "You aren't going?"

"I really must, I have a lot to do, to think about."

She took him to the door, with heavy bad grace. He was

carrying off about $20 worth of her food rather curtly. "You work too hard, Mr. Fine," she said. But mentally he was already gone, and the hand she shook was a plump shell.

6

"Mrs. Wadsworth is not at home," the doorman told him. And he wondered why such an old man should be asked to transmit such a silly message.

"Tell her I called," said Fritz.

The doorman was a friendly old fellow, but this didn't mean you were in good with the building. Fritz turned away. He was never sorry not to get into that apartment. It was an uncomfortable place, until your lungs got used to the altitude. He picked a random side street and strolled east towards Lexington. He liked the rich parts of town, no doubt about it. Too bad about the Revolution. No more rich part of town. Bang bang.

He laughed. He could still make fun of himself anyway. As a matter of fact, there was no necessary connection between socialism and austerity. Good times for all was the cry. And furthermore, he didn't *need* luxury, he certainly didn't need Harriet Wadsworth. He only needed to get hold of the magazine, get it away from corrupt old Twining and bumbling old Brian and give it some air. That was all he needed.

But Harriet Wadsworth wasn't helping any. Since her bed had been declared off bounds, through a series of headaches, cancellations and awfully-sleepy's, he had found it increasingly difficult to deal with her in any capacity at all. Handling her body at regular intervals had given him confidence, the whiphand. But without that support, he found himself fidgety again in the rich apartment, and uncertain of his moves. She in turn was vaguer and less responsive. They sat silently in those dreadful restaurants, and he found himself cancelling sentences in his head, because she wouldn't hear them anyway. He knew she was just a greedy child who wouldn't talk until she got her own way, but he couldn't dismiss her as lightly as he wished. Her will power at least was formidable. A grown-up child could be frightening, like a giant beetle in a science-fiction story.

He sometimes wondered how he had gotten into this mess. In the old petition and protest days, he had never imagined that radical politics could lead to this. The sexual profit system. Had it changed him? Since his lunch with Polly Twining, this question had been flirting with him. Polly had obviously disapproved. And for several reasons, he didn't want Polly to disapprove.

He wondered if he could explain it to her. He didn't think he had changed, basically. The same *willingness* that had sent him protesting missiles had sent him rocketing into Wadsworth's boudoir. Other times, other methods. Polly had asked after old friends, Pete Samuel and Sally Morehead for instance, as if that was some sort of touchstone: and he had been forced to say he hadn't seen much of them, and she had looked very knowing: "You see, you *have* changed." But a man knew his own identity, he knew whether the links held up. "Do they bore you now?" said Polly. "Do the old faces seem rather dull after Gilbert?" She sounded so righteous about it—one must never be bored with the old gang, even though they carry the same placards and the same dirty fingernails year after year and never grow an inch in any direction.

Yes, they bored him. That's how he knew he was alive. They were still stuck in the same groove of protest, a little older, a little scruffier. God help him if they *didn't* bore him. Pete Samuel's Utopia would be as dull as Pete Samuel's life. Folk songs around a campfire, indigenous culture, everything dead and authentic. "So that's how it goes,

Polly." Fritz yawned and thought about phoning Harriet, bypass the doorman and turn her flanks, so to speak. But he wasn't quite sure what he wanted to say tonight, and walked on toward the East River instead. Chintzy new apartment houses along here, new, stupid money. Decent architecture was something people should be made to care about. Utopia should be a bower of beauty. The poor should be introduced to loveliness. The old gang must be taught to scrub their nails and have their teeth fixed, for the Shining City.

He thought next about phoning George Wren. George was onto his wave length. No dingy old pamphlets, no half-assed soup kitchens for George. Open up the Waldorf, you bums—Fritz's mind capered. It was a nice autumn evening, with a breeze flicking off the river and swarming between the granite walls. Unfortunately George Wren was phasing, he was still young enough to change from one day to the next. At the moment he was acting remote. If he was an older man, you'd say that his feet hurt. Possibly having domestic trouble, with his flat little bourgeois B-average wife. Or possibly still blinded by Twining's stardust. Fritz remembered how forlorn he himself had been when Twining first dropped him. He could still remember the smell of Sweeney's that evening, the taste of the half-finished martini. It was as if Twining had taken him up to a great height, flattered him, confided in him, shown him the world below—and then said, but on second thought, you wouldn't really do; you're not quite good enough, are you? Not officer material.

The blinding humiliation of that dismissal: it had seemed to come in midsentence. Where had he gone wrong? Was it a flashy opinion or a split infinitive? Fritz had been too fuddled to know for sure. He remembered Twining looking at his watch and saying something preposterous about running for a train (or was it haring after a bus?) and leaving, with his third drink hardly tasted. Fritz sat alone for half an hour after that, too weak to move. *You're not what I took you for. It's so hard to tell with Americans, isn't it?* Fritz had phased then and there. Like Fine, and like Wren, his spine had been cracked. No one who had not experienced it could imagine the finality of Twining's disapproval. It was not brutal, it wasn't even personal, it was simply the last word on the subject. You were henceforth, in your own eyes, a rather inferior sort of person.

But unlike Brian, Fritz had recovered. The old resilience and openness had saved him. He would not let another man be his judge. He had taken a fresh tack. He would beat the master at his own game. In the dressing room and in the bedroom, if necessary. He might not have Twining's languor, but he had courage and resourcefulness. He couldn't talk such a good game as Twining, but by the end of the night, Harriet Wadsworth might agree to his other merits. By God, he would see to it that she did.

No, he hadn't changed. He still had courage and, if he said so himself, humor. He had survived Twining's evil eye. And he would eventually do more for the right causes than all his dingy old friends put together.

Having nothing better to do, he retraced his steps to the Lexington Avenue subway, and took a train down to Union Square. He hadn't been down there for a while, it was just outside the groove he had worn for himself. The Square was an extinct volcano by now, a symbol of the gutted thirties spirit, but it did remind him of beginnings. You could easily fool yourself, as Twining had done, into becoming a Park Avenue radical, if you forgot your beginnings.

It was light when he got on the train and dark when he

got off. The breeze had chilled, and the bums on the benches were crouched against it, the first serious coldness since last winter. To be able to come from Park Avenue to this without feeling displaced was probably an important secret.

A large Negro in a shiny brown suit was talking about Red China, and Fritz parked on the jagged rim of the crowd and listened for a minute. It was weak stuff, cranky, irrelevant. The Chinese had superior bone structure, and would prevail, said the Negro. Fritz looked around for something better.

A tattered, greedy-looking man came over to chat. His breath was terrible, not only stale booze but advanced moral decay. "If God is so daddamn good," he said, "why does he allow something like *me* to happen? Hey," his hand festered on Fritz's sleeve. "You ever read Genesis, Mac?"

Public protest had certainly gone to hell down here. Union Square was just a freak show now. The grim men in the threadbare suits had beaten a path to Westchester long ago. There wasn't a proletarian face to be found any more, just a clown's face and a clown's talk.

It bore out his point about how you have to change your style . . . Fritz detached himself, aware suddenly that he was the only man present who was wearing a post-1955 suit. The Genesis buff shadowed him over to the railing. Fritz fished in his pocket for change. A ring of bright-eyed Puerto Ricans watched him hand over a shiny new quarter. The Ricos were a new factor, oddly playful-looking, not bums or cranks, not looking for politics but for some kind of private fun. Fritz turned and walked abruptly out of the Square. It would have been poseurish to stay.

This sideshow had no bearing on anything, he had reaffirmed that: the ground had shifted. Union Square was in the dustbin of history, right on top of Columbus Circle and all those dusty little squares and parks where actual human beings used once to assemble to discuss tangible, honest-to-John grievances. Genesis for Godsake, and Chinese bone structure. It wasn't necessary any more to feel comfortable among these people, these dead souls. They were beyond politics, beyond poverty or suffering; drifting along in a slobbering purgatory of their own devising, through a maze of half-understood ideas, bad dreams, clammy stinking clothes. He took the subway uptown, a little puzzled by this curiously negative episode—perhaps he *had* lost something, some strain of sympathy, life was an endless shedding of dead skin—but glad to have been honest about it.

And to help produce a magazine that was carefully read by Madame Pandit and Adlai Stevenson was not nothing, as he had often remarked. He must have laughed, because an old man next to him grunted in eerie unison and then looked round with an encouraging smile. As long as he could still laugh at himself, he had kept his link with the old Fritz Tyler: he hadn't lost his soul.

"So many kinds of cultural shock, Polly—I feel ill at ease with the people who smell bad, and twice as ill at ease with the people who smell good, I mean Harriet Wadsworth smells fine. I must be getting old, Polly." He was going to have to explain himself to Polly Twining and he thought that this was a better way to talk than the way he had talked last time. If memory could be trusted, it sounded more like his old self.

7

Brian was determined to call one more editorial conference. And if it went like the other two, he would quietly offer to resign. "Gentlemen . . . what do you make of that?"

That would leave it up to Fritz. (George Wren didn't count one way or the other.) Fritz could then either accept the job himself—and we would see how well *he* stood up to pressure; or he could say, "No, no," in which case Brian could reasonably insist on more cooperation.

Done and done. Brian sat at his desk in the early-morning coolness. The clock said 7:30. His best hours were the ones before the others arrived. While the dew was still on the filing cabinets. He wrote up an agenda for the conference, and then threw it away—informality was best at these affairs.

From 7:30 to 8:10 was good. As good as it ever was, in the old, simple days. From 8:10 to 8:35 was so-so. After that the panic started. The elevator began to clank, taking people up to Murray's imported fabrics on the ninth and Osgood's wholesale rugs on the eighth. The fragile early morning peace was fractured. Brian lost the sense of weightlessness and poise. He didn't really feel like a meeting with those jokers. Not today.

It wasn't the work any more, he was on top of that as much as one ever was in this crazy business, it was the people. Every time the elevator started up, he was afraid it would stop at his floor and somebody he didn't ever want to see again would get out. Olga Marplate was usually the first, or else Philo—the stupider they were, the earlier they seemed to rise in the morning. Until recently, he had enjoyed going out and perching on the desk of whichever came in first and having a fraternal cigarette. But those days were gone, with both of them.

With Olga the problem was her insatiable craving for new office equipment. He had thought that having the place painted would satisfy her gorge; but in fact it had given her fresh appetite, and every day now her handbag teemed with news, pictures and text, of new dictaphones, atomic hand-dryers for the washroom, insulation devices, executive carpeting, air fresheners. She seemed to feel that Brian was put on earth to cater to her trivial whims. Quite apart from the fact that new equipment was out of the question, just looking at the ads was getting on his nerves. "Look, Olga, we can't afford so much as a new roll of, you know, towels." "I understand that, Mr. Fine—it's just in case we ever can."

Why can't one just put out a magazine without people? Olga's money was something he just wouldn't let himself think about any more. She must have been hired originally as one of those rich girls who are happy to work for next to nothing if the cause is a good one. But annual increments had gradually whetted her appetite there too and now she drew one of the largest paychecks in the place, and didn't refuse a penny of it.

He didn't want to think about anybody's money this morning. If he was going to conduct an editorial conference, it was advisable to keep his mind uncluttered. That was surely the secret of leadership—to be able to turn your whole attention to whatever came up: not to worry about this when you ought to be worrying about that. Not to listen to the elevators or the ominous shuffle of feet. He started to draw up another agenda, and in shuffled Philo.

"Hey, Philo, how's about knocking, huh?"

"The door was open," said Philo, not too deferentially. "Can I talk with you a minute?"

"Must you, Philo? Can't it wait?"

"I came here early especially to see you. Mind if I sit down?"

Brian felt the rage starting from down in his legs. What a relief to let it go all the way up someday. Instead he trapped it in his stomach and waved at his spare chair.

Philo pulled out a letter and handed it across portentously. It was typed on Andover Academy stationery. Brian gazed at it briefly. Something to do with money no doubt. Philo had so few interests.

"I've told you a hundred times, Philo . . ."

"I know, but this is serious."

Brian shut his eyes. His anger was billowing wildly. If he looked at that face a moment longer, he would say to it: "Why do you send your stupid son to Andover anyway? If he's anything like you . . ."

"Look, Philo," he said slowly. "This is serious too. This magazine is serious . . ." If he could just get one of them to see that . . .

"Oh, I know that," said Philo. "I wouldn't work anywhere else for this money, I can tell you that for openers."

Brian shut his eyes again. His rage howled wantonly. How had he allowed this to happen? And how dare this lame-brained incompetent talk as if he was doing the magazine a favor working here? It wouldn't cost anything to let him think that, of course, but Brian could not bring himself to make the right noises.

He said, "I'm sorry, Philo. That's my last word. If you really think you can do better somewhere else . . . perhaps. You. Should, *you* know, look into it."

Philo stood up stiffly and walked out. Wounded, profoundly shocked. Nothing settled. Now he would sit out there, staring like an idiot, sealing Brian into his cubicle. Marplate would join him. They would whisper. Brian would try to concentrate on something else, but all the time seeing their faces, caring about their whispers.

If, only just once, the elevator would yield up a friendly face. Someone to help him to worry, someone to watch the money while he watched the staff, or watch the staff while he watched the editors. In this special imported English fog, one friendly face was all he asked . . . The next off the elevator was not a friendly face at all but just Fritz. Looking even smugger than usual. Christ, I can't have a conference with him. Not with all these other things on my mind.

"How's it going, Brian baby?"

For a moment Brian literally couldn't speak. "Going all right," he said. Fritz looked like a winner, looked as if he wanted to strut a little. But he sheered off and went into his own cubicle.

A typical morning so far. He was still waiting for the tension to go away. One of these years. Meanwhile he could comfort himself that not one reader had guessed (out loud at least) that anything had changed at *The Outsider*. Well—maybe they're all dead out there. Maybe that's it. It was rather a soothing idea. It made him laugh. Maybe they've all been dead for years.

VIII

1

No one seemed to know quite what to do with the new man. A space had to be cleared for him, crunching Olga and Philo even closer together, in a steamy huddle. He didn't seem quite clear about himself, but was extremely amiable meanwhile, talking to everyone who went by. "How's it going, that's good, that's good." George Wren, who was no good at mechanics, supposed that the new man was meant to be some kind of coordinator between what happened in the rear of the office and what happened in the middle. He made, at any rate, many sorties back and forth, sitting down again afterwards in a peculiarly businesslike way. "Hey, Brian, who's the fat guy?" he heard Fritz ask. "Where did he come from?"

"His name is Sam Thirsby and" the partition door shut

and Brian's voice dropped to confidential. George wasn't curious. Sam was a good name for the new man, though. You could reconstruct the history of the name from looking at him.

Then later in the morning, George's Zen-trance was broken into again. He was thinking that death wouldn't be so bad if you died in installments, shedding a little of your self every day, until at the last gray moment there was nothing left, when they loomed into his doorway like Tweedledum and Tweedledee.

"George—I'd like you to meet Sam, Sam Thirsby."

"Hiya, George. Howya doing?"

"Fine, I guess."

Sam reached across for a handshake. "Glad to know you, George." Brian seemed to try to restrain him, as if to say, we don't do that here. But his hand never quite reached Sam, now or any other time.

"I see you got a window, you lucky so and so. How does this guy rate a window, Brian?"

George stared at him.

"I'm only kidding, George. Say, that's a nice view you got."

Brian led Sam away before he could say any more. George had never seen anyone like that at *The Outsider* before, but he supposed they might keep some of them in the back. Fritz was out in the corridor, laughing and shaking his head, but George didn't want to laugh it up with Fritz at the moment: he wanted to get back to his thought. Death, fifteen terrible minutes he imagined: your soul suddenly draining out, while the management tries wildly to plug the leaks. And there it goes, gurgling under the city streets like dishwater and dispersing out to sea. Terrible, if you really thought you were somebody; if you thought that the shape you assumed in the washbowl was a real shape. But of course if you knew that you were just meant to be part of the sea, and not washbowl-shaped at all, you might rush out with a *happy* gurgle—

"Hey, George, can I bother you for a minute?"

Sam was back. George blinked at him. Sam was supposed to coordinate the back with the middle, not with the *front*.

There was rigid stratification at *The Outsider* as between front people, middle people, and back people. Visitation rights were sharply limited by custom. No class system was ever more total. Surely Brian hadn't hired this fat-faced clown to democratize the whole damn place?

"I'd like to get some idea what you do, George. What's your end of the operation exactly?"

"He collects the used string," Fritz howled from the doorway. "He does the first aid. You know, splints, tourniquets, and so forth."

Brian came tumbling in behind Fritz. "Is everything all right? Are you getting acclimatized, Sam?"

"Brian Fine fixes our teeth—that's his end of the operation. Me, I—"

You could tell that Sam knew he was being kidded. But he offered only the same indecisive response to it that you might have expected from Brian. His face was zoned like a weather map, with angry depressions around the eyes, c'mon fellows, at the mouth, indecision streaking the middle. Brian did everything but lead him out by the hand this time. Fritz stood aside, grinning at them, the coordinator and his patron. King Twining used to coordinate better without even trying.

"What's all that about?" said George. He supposed that Brian had hired this nudnik to do what Twining used to do—to weave the place into a unit and give it some honest-to-God morale: "Like a cruise captain, or something," he said. But Fritz said no, he didn't think it was that; he thought that Sam was on hand mainly to weave Brian into a unit, etc. Brian needed someone to relax him, to make the place seem human, and not an endless nightmare.

"Sam makes the place seem *human?*" asked George.

"Sure, why not? You know who he is, don't you?"

"No. Who the hell is he?"

"He's Brian's lousy nephew, that's who he is." And Fritz doubled over with dry, soundless laughter.

Sam Thirsby seemed awfully big for a nephew. George found himself putting his metaphysical murmurings to one side and taking a reluctant interest in these two bottle-shaped men. Brian seemed alternately to be protecting Sam and to be seeking his protection: Sam's broad style constituting at once an embarrassment and a comfort.

"What's *your* end of the operation, Sam?" he felt like asking. It seemed to consist mostly of shuffling papers and frowning. (But then, that was what most office work looked like to George.) Every ten minutes or so, Brian would waddle across for a short conference: much grave nodding on both sides as if they were really getting to the heart of things at last. Brian must have had a much older sister who had looked after him as a child; and now this task had devolved on her son. That was the only way you could account for Sam.

George thought that he had received his last personal visit from Sam, but Sam had still not caught on to this particular nuance of office life, and in the early afternoon he was around again. This time he said no more than "How's it going," and then waited to see what *kind* of thing George talked about. George had stopped thinking about death and was quite glad to see him.

"Where were you before this, Sam?" he asked.

"All over. You name it, I've done it."

"Journalism, for instance?"

"No, I guess that must be about the one thing I haven't done. Maybe that's what makes this job such a challenge."

"Yeah, I can see how that might be. How did you decide finally to make journalism your vocation, then?"

"Well—er, vocation, yes, well the thing was, I was kind of between jobs anyway. The savings and loan business isn't exactly stimulating; tell you the truth, I was fed to here with it, so I asked for my release one month ago. You know, I'm over thirty now, and what the hell, if I don't gamble now, I might as well give up. Right?"

"Right. I guess."

"So anyway, at about that time I got a call from Brian saying, 'Sam, do you want a challenge?' and my ears picked up right away, and I said, 'You name it.' "

For all his bounciness, the tissue around his eyes was old and tired. He had obviously made this spiel about challenges in a dozen offices, but never more inappropriately than in this one. Whatever *The Outsider* was, it was not a challenge. Sam had overplayed his hand.

"What exactly does Brian want you to do here?"

"Well, it's not too precise, and *that's* part of the challenge too, learn the whole operation to begin with, I guess, and then see what needs doing—"

Christ, Brian must be desperate. George felt sympathy for him—what kind of pressure melted you down into hiring a permanent loose part like Sam? Yeah, George suddenly knew this guy all right. He could just see Sam's hands beginning to shake as the afternoon wore on, and the tic in his cheek coming to life. "Sir, I think I can do a job for you. Savings-and-loan is a real challenge, selling securities is a real challenge, never tried it before, which is challenge challenge challenge—"

"Mr. Thirsby, Sam, I'm sorry, but we're cutting down

staff, and your department seems to be the one." Sam's whole style was geared to the anterooms of business; he was totally lost inside. George knew, because his own father was a bit like that, a lot of people got like that in the Depression: only, for some people the Depression never ended.

"Oh, there you are." Brian had come to call for his nephew again.

"Yeah, I'm talking to George here."

"Could you come out a minute, there's something I want to discuss with you."

That bottle shape was no accident: it was a surplus of resignation flowing constantly into the hips. Sam wasn't a stupid man. His methods were a bit garish for this gray old place, but he would doubtless change them if he stayed here long enough—might even become a bit like Brian in the process. What wouldn't change was the basic sense of defeat, the inability to grasp a situation and do anything with it . . . what was it about the Fine family, anyway? Was it the sister who had fixed Brian and then Sam? Or was she bottle-shaped too?

When he tried to think about death again, he found these soap-opera particularities in the way. Death seemed rather pale, rather uninteresting next to Brian's sister. Mabel, he bet her name was. Be great to see all three of them together—well, maybe he would have the pleasure soon; maybe Brian would hire Mabel next, to coordinate Sam. Old Brian couldn't face the office by himself any more. Eventually everyone there would be replaced by bottle-shaped Fines.

"Hey, George, what are you looking so pleased about?" asked Fritz.

"Nothing."

"How about lunch tomorrow?"

"Fine, I mean great."

"You been in a fog lately, George. You know that?"

"Yes, well, that's how it takes me sometimes."

"Still in mourning for our beloved leader?"

"Christ, no."

George had eventually received not one but two cards from Twining and hadn't answered either of them. He hadn't kept the commander hep to the ups and downs of office politics. He hadn't even thought about him since that evening alone in the office. Whatever had been happening in his mind for the last few weeks, whatever clunking about in wet caves, he was sure he was purged of Twining now.

"I don't think he's coming back at all," said Fritz.

"No?"

"It's something about his letters. The strength doesn't come through anymore."

"I guess I'd noticed that." George thought vaguely of the cards.

"It's all, give my best to the chaps, send me any news about the chaps—no force at all. Even his handwriting. It's as if he suddenly got very old out there and doesn't care any more."

"How old *is* he, anyway?"

"I really couldn't tell you. Englishmen are like Negroes as far as I'm concerned, the old ones look young, and the young ones look even younger."

"Yeah." George paused. "So—you think he's not coming back?" he said, for something to say.

"That's right. I don't feel his thumb on my shoulder blade any more. He hopes that we chaps are carrying on spiffingly in his absence—"

"Does he really keep saying 'chaps' like that?"

"He doesn't have to any more. It's, how you say, implicit. —But otherwise, he doesn't talk shop at all. He just keeps collapsing into senile happy talk, as if I was one of his old school chums—I think we've all blurred on him, he writes to Brian exactly the same way he writes to me. We're all back at St. Dominic's together, having a giggle."

George had to admit to a certain exhilaration about this. Commander Twining was like the New York Yankees or the Taj Mahal—to watch him simply falling apart would be a beautiful thing.

"Of course," said Fritz, "he isn't that far gone. Lots of Englishmen sound senile when they're just trying to be funny. 'What, what, eh.'" Fritz puckered his nose and spluttered.

"They don't really talk like that and you know it."

"Well, maybe not, but that's what it sounds like to me. Anyway, I think the old boy is pulling away from us. It's part of his technique, to do it with jokes. The English and their jokes . . . I grant you, he's not like the other Englishmen I've met. He has to do it from memory, y'know. Pre-1914, punting on the lawn and croquet on the Thames. Then again, in the middle of all those frightfully extraordinarys, and the jokes about having his temperature taken, he'll suddenly insert three or four pages of *nature* writing. Forsythias, hollyhocks, the-gladiolus-is-a-perfect-poem-at-this-time-of-year kind of stuff. Who the hell does he think he's writing to? His Aunt Maud?"

Fritz was being a little cruel to a sick man. They both felt it at once. Scoring off Twining now was a little too easy. It had suddenly turned dark and Olga Marplate was coming through, turning on lights. Fritz said, "Englishmen and nature, that's a weird one. But I do think he's pulling away from us."

"It looks like snow," said Olga to no one in particular. The snow would play perfect hell with the forsythias. George could see the commander covered in frost, sitting outside in his dressing gown, jotting down notes about it.

Quite barmy, you know. Poor devil. When the malaria gets
to the brain—

"I guess that leaves it up to Brian, then," he said.

"Brian and *Sam*," said Fritz.

And he slapped George's shoulder and the two of them
laughed and laughed, until Brian came in like a schoolteacher to see what the joke was.

2

Matilda Wren had been dramatic, even tearful, about
their unspoken reconciliation last night, as if it had been
something serious. It hadn't been, but George was content
to let her think so. He woke feeling very unphilosophical:
death was back where it belonged, a thousand years away.
His son was just learning to edge around the room without
touching everything. George sat up in bed to watch as
Peter came weaving in through the glass door. To worry
about Peter's mortality while life jerked and waddled in his
rubber pants was a kind of sickness. In fact George felt this
morning as if he was convalescing from something. Sense
impressions were very sweet. The smoke from his cigarette
formed a sinuously beautiful line. Objects were clearer.
The fat roll of plastic and cloth around Peter's hips, for
instance; the floppy line of his mouth. It was the kind of
mood in which one might conceive a new child.

He breakfasted quickly and quietly, kissed Matilda in
her sleep, and Peter, and started for the office. Peter would
wake his mother when he needed her: when he got bored
with waddling. It was a sharp November day—probably
weather had something to do with these cycles. He wondered when his next bout of mysticism would occur. Eleven,
sixteen, skipped twenty-one, and now this one. Every five or
six years perhaps. The real mystics got one of these moods
and just kept going; people like George Wren were seduced

out of it each time by ordinariness, a story about somebody's sister in the hospital, a visit from your uncle. That's
a journalist for you. Today he didn't give a crap about
time, eternity, the great continuum. It was all gone, like a
thief in the night.

He felt as he hit the office as if he had missed several
chapters in a story, and was anxious now to catch up. What
were Brian and Fritz up to? What about Olga and Philo?
After fasting so long on abstractions, he felt a craving for
solid dirt, the lower the better. He greeted Sam boister-
ously, which left the big fellow more uncertain than ever.
What kind of place was this anyway?

Since he was, by his standards, splendidly on time, he
expected at least a civil greeting from Olga Marplate. But
he didn't get one. She looked red around the eyes and nose,
as if she had been, implausibly, crying. But she said it was
an autumn cold, and glared at her watch anyway—why
hadn't he been here at 8 a.m.? Why had he bothered to go
home at all? Philo looked excited, as if he had witnessed an
event, or entertained a thought. People had faces again,
with real expressions on them.

Another good sign was that he was bored with his work
again. For weeks now, the stuff on his desk had been
neither more nor less interesting than everything else. An
article on the bank rate or a pasquinade on neo-plasticism
shared the same undifferentiated "thingness" as the trees on
Riverside Drive. All were part of the great flow. But now
these stuffy, airless articles were definitely themselves again.

Brian Fine came in with a piece on population.

"Gee-sus, Brian, spare us population."

"What's the matter with population?" snapped Brian.

"You know, it's like the Catholics say, if everyone stands
sideways, there'll be plenty of room for all. Father Frog-

binder, S.J., the sainted demographer, made a good point about that just the other day—"

Brian's hands were trembling. He shoved the article at George's chest. "Here, take it." The pages got bent in the meaningless scuffle. Brian seemed suddenly at his wit's end. George braced himself for a scream or low moan, but Brian turned and left quietly. George was heightening events through his own filter.

Good grief, charts, graphs, $13\frac{1}{2}$ men to an acre: the printers would have a great time with this one. Somebody was shouting outside. Brian had combusted, he knew it instinctively. George sprang to the doorway and there was Brian, standing next to Marplate's desk. He was breathing hard as if he'd run all the way from George's cubicle. "We'll talk about it later," he said, as he saw George. Olga's eyes and nose were purple, as though she had been slapped across the bridge with a wet paintbrush. She dabbed around with a squashed-up Kleenex, and then picked up her purse and flounced to the ladies' room. Philo Sonna-bend had an unnatural glitter: he appeared in an ecstasy of excitement. Brian stood by Marplate's desk flexing his fingers, as if he was wondering how to get back to his cubicle without being seen.

Big Sam Thirsby came rolling up and put an improbable arm around Brian. He glared round at the onlookers— George, Fritz, Philo and two suddenly materialized secre-taries—like a policeman presiding over an accident. "Have you no homes?" Sam seemed to say. George went back to his desk. He heard the two men shuffling into the next com-partment, whispering. Fritz across the way winked engag-ingly. You couldn't dislike Fritz: and on the other hand you couldn't like him either. That was the kind of fellow Fritz was.

George went back to his graphs. He added up the nourished and the undernourished in China. They came to 103.5 percent of the population. Fair enough. Things were supposed to be pretty rough out there. Brian and Sam were still whispering when he went in. They looked up with the guilty irritation of lovers. If Brian was taking Sam's advice on how to run the office, he had every right to look guilty.

"Excuse me. Percentage trouble."

"Did you ever hear of a little thing called knocking?"

"No—it sounds like fun, though."

George had thought that he might have changed, even matured, during the last few weeks. It was obviously a false alarm. The American male doesn't mature until he has exhausted all other possibilities. Half an hour till lunch, and the driest martini ever devised.

Fritz had anticipated George's whim and was laying on another enormous lunch. Mr. Tyler, why you so good to me? George bit into a big, black olive and said, "Is it just me, or is our group a little tenser than usual today?"

Fritz crashed into a stick of celery. "Something between Brian and Olga—you know how they open the office every morning? Well, I could hear them screaming from two floors away when I arrived. I looked through the cage at them, they looked through the cage at me. Very funny. The oysters here are a treat, by the way."

"What were they fighting about? Could you make it out?"

"Mumble, you're hateful, mumble, take that—was the subject. I guess Brian made a pass at her, and she said, 'Let's not spoil it honey,' and he said—"

"Yeah, yeah. So, he's been trying to keep a lid on it, and it keeps popping up."

"Right, every time he passes her desk, their lower lips quiver like harp strings. I wonder what Fine does do for

sex, anyway. Covers himself in printer's ink, but then
what?"

"I guess his nerves must be in pretty bad shape. How can
you get mad at Marplate? Look, the oysters are two bucks
extra, I'll have the soup du jour."

"Have oysters, go ahead."

"O.K., if you say so. But listen, frankly—can the magazine really afford it? I remember the commander took me to
Schrafft's for my interview; we had the housewife's special,
as I recall. Have we gotten that much richer since I
arrived?"

"False economy, kid. Eat at Schrafft's and you begin to
write like Schrafft's. No, to tell you the truth, I hope to
bring some money into the magazine shortly—money such
as you've never seen, in fact."

"O.K., I'll have the oysters. Where is this money coming
from, and what's holding it up?"

Fritz looked at him with sly friendliness. You could feel
quite chummy with this guy without really liking him.
They had a congruence of tastes and amusements; they
enjoyed each other's company; and there was no danger of
any real friendship. You wouldn't ask Fritz out to Queens
for dinner, for instance. You wouldn't talk seriously with
him. Maybe they were too much alike. George was occasionally disgusted by glimpses of himself in Fritz, a feeling that
since coming here he'd actually begun to phrase things like
Fritz. He knew he was still young enough to copy people,
and Fritz was a natural for him.

"Second question first. I don't get the money until I get
the magazine. That means waiting around for Brian to
throw in the towel."

"Sounds pretty brutal."

"I know, but it can't be helped. This party won't give the
money to Brian. And I don't have to tell you what's wrong
with Brian, do I?"

"I thought he was doing a pretty good job."

"You've gotten habituated to mediocrity, George. Wait till we really start to swing. And I've got plans for you, too."

"Yeah? How they go?"

"We'll talk about it soon. Brian won't last much longer. Sam Thirsby is like a death-watch beetle. Brian has just about had it."

"And then the money comes rolling in, and it's oysters all the rest of the way."

"Right. Oh, there's one rather amusing stipulation that I won't bore you with now. I'm still hoping to get round it. How's your wife, and kid, by the way?"

None of your business. "Pretty good."

"Kid walking yet?"

"Yeah, he gets around. Empties wastebaskets and all that. So where is the money coming from, I forget if you told me?"

Fritz had the Chateaubriand again, which ought to make Brian snap that much sooner. George shared it with him. What the hell? Fritz didn't answer this last question right away. But George got the impression he wanted to talk about it, that he'd been nursing his secret too long. They eased through the lush mountain of food. "I've cooperated with Brian, and so have you," said Fritz. "I haven't tried to grease the slide for him."

"You were going to tell me about the money."

"Oh, yes. Well I guess there's no special point in being coy about it, you'll find out soon enough. It's our old friend Harriet Wadsworth—a dull answer, I grant you."

George thought about it for a minute. "That's not so dull. I mean, it grows on you. But how come *you're* the one who's getting it?"

Fritz looked a little embarrassed and a little pleased with himself—answer enough.

"Was that how Twining got his money too? And is that how all progressive causes are supported, I wonder."

"Probably yes and probably no," said Fritz. "It wouldn't be my choice, by the way, but it's hard to get hold of money without getting a little you-know on your hands. It flies around a lot at those altitudes. And as fund-raising methods go, I think mine is relatively sincere."

"That's one way of looking at it."

"You disapprove?"

"No. No." Magazines had to live. Editors had to eat. Oysters, if necessary. Fritz even had the correct amount of qualms about it. The dreary thing, if you had to pinpoint it, was that Fritz so obviously enjoyed sharing it with somebody. That made old Harriet look a bit silly. It made it a slightly less classy operation all round. But George really didn't give a damn. It was the kind of story that amused him today.

"I hope she doesn't bore you too frightfully," he said. "I remember you saying once that she was a rich bore."

"No, I've changed my mind about that—she's really quite a fine woman, many fine qualities. Otherwise, I just couldn't, not even a certified rat like me."

Hey, this is bad, thought George suddenly. This is very bad. You don't think this helps, do you, Fritz? feeding me this line of crap? feeding yourself? Hump your way to riches, and good luck to you, but don't give me Harriet Wadsworth's fine qualities.

Fritz left it like that. "I'm sorry, I shouldn't have talked about her. She's not what you might think. Some day, we might even—who knows, there have been stranger alliances."

George said, "I don't want any dessert. Let's get back to the sweatshop." He was honestly embarrassed for Fritz— that he should say such things to me, his friend, his well-wisher. Wedding bells, with that stupid broad.

Say, that couldn't be the other stipulation, could it?
Could Fritz be paving the way for a wedding announcement? The things people would go through for that crumby
magazine. He wondered whether Fritz's alimony would
really be enough to support *The Outsider,* and keep the
staff in oysters.

"What are you grinning about?"

"Nothing. Mrs. Wadsworth's fine qualities."

"Yeah, well." Fritz spread his hands and smiled almost
apologetically and said no more about it.

3

Brian had apparently boiled over again during the lunch
hour. Sam seemed to be holding him back, though the
action was obviously symbolic. Brian was not a physical
man. Olga Marplate was staring at him in bleary shock. Oh
hell, we've missed it again, thought George.

Sam was apparently trying to ensure just that: whispering God-knows-what incantations into his uncle's flaming
ear. Brian brushed at him impatiently. He must have made
up his mind, to do whatever he was doing, over the midday
pasta, and Brian's mind was not easily reversible.

"I'm talking to Miss Marplate," he said tensely.

Sam shrugged. O.K.—but did you notice, we've got
company now?

Brian looked around and saw Fritz and George standing
by the elevator. Philo looked at them too, peeved at the
interruption. Brian paused for only a moment, and then
went on in a comparatively ringing voice. "And that, my
dear Miss Marplate, is *one* reason why we cannot afford
new furniture," and turned and marched into his cubicle.

George and Fritz laughed. Office furniture yet. "Hey,
Olga, has the afternoon mail come in yet?" asked Fritz.

Olga nodded dumbly and pointed. Now that the scene

was unfrozen, her eyes were beginning to leak at the sides. She punched at them with the same chewed-up Kleenex.

"You're doing letters to the editor, right?" said Fritz.

"Right." George went over and gently detached the editor's letters from the business letters. "You all right, Olga?" She gave a nod, which cost her a shivering snort. Brian must have made a heavy pass indeed, to reduce her to this.

George fanned the letters across his desk. The childish handwriting on the left. The California addresses and the indefinably queer-looking typing on the right. He opened the ones in the middle.

"Dear Sir, I remember when you used to be a liberal magazine. I suppose you still think you are." George skimmed: "Soft, safe, established," here we go again. "Editors, a bunch of old women," that's you, Brian. "Never go north of 125th Street any more," that's you, Fritz. "Stuck in last year's liberal attitudes," ah, you talk too much. You're just pleasuring yourself, Major.

George cut the second and third paragraphs by formula. What about this, "When did you last have a decent labor report? Do you think the labor problem is solved, or what?" Well, isn't it? only kidding. George left it in. It made him think of Fritz—coming in every day with a French poodle and this dumb babe on his arm. Mrs. Harriet Tyler, our new labor reporter. Mrs. Van Tyler has been living in the South for the last six months, with her face dyed pitch black. Who says we ain't a liberal magazine, boss?

Olga Marplate kept on sobbing, intermittently, right through the afternoon. Fritz came in and muttered, "Can't anyone shut that dame up?" It was the devil's own work to concentrate in this rat-trap. Just as you dipped your face under the surface, she would burst out again. "Oh dear," grim sounds of pulling self together; then tap, tap, tap, twenty sharp steps to the ladies' room. Brian, you *scoundrel.*

By four o'clock, he could stand it no more. He went out and asked her what was the matter and could he do anything. (Dammit, why were there no decent informers to tell a fellow what had happened? Even in a small office, no one's Intelligence Service was complete.) Poor old Olga's face was a shambles when she looked reluctantly round. He had never seen anything so disorganized. "It's nothing," she said.

"Well, thank God for that," he said, and wandered frustratedly back to his desk. To have to read about politics in Uganda, while some unforgettable drama was going on right here—

She left at five sharp, and George hared over to see Brian. "What did you say to her, you horny bastard?"

Brian looked gruffly embarrassed. Marplate probably hadn't cried for twenty-five years. It was like the bursting of some great dam. And every sob had made Brian seem a little more ridiculous.

He had obviously had a terrible afternoon: he gave a curious effect now of not having slept well. He hadn't been able to comfort her, to stop her, could only sit here and take it, while her groans derided him. George was about to rub in some salt, tell him to keep his hands off that poor woman, but it looked as though Brian would shoot straight up the wall if he did. Marplate berserk was enough excitement for one day.

Fritz's voice came mournfully over the partition.

"Christ, Brian, it wasn't just office furniture, was it?"

Brian nodded, as if Fritz could see him.

"What was that, Brian?" said the voice.

"I said yes, that's all it was, office furniture."

"Has everyone gone crazy around here? Where's your sense of proportion, man?"

George looked on with horrible fascination as Brian tried to fend off the disembodied voice coming over the partition. No one had spoken to him all afternoon, except Sam, and heaven knows what had passed through his head during that time. He had presumably never made a woman cry before. He thought it was difficult; he thought it took some unspeakable provocation and required some desperate defense.

"Furniture, Brian," Fritz's voice prodded at him. "This is worse than Captain Queeg and the strawberries. Get a grip, Brian baby."

"It isn't me who needs to get a grip," Brian snarled. "It isn't me who cried like a baby—I just told her she couldn't have the furniture, that's all."

He looked up hopefully. Perhaps the voice would be satisfied with that. "Oh, come on, Brian," said Fritz from over the wall, "Olga's been going on about furniture for years. There's no need to make her *cry* about it."

Brian—don't take it so seriously. We're not the cops. If you could see Fritz's face, you'd see him trying to keep from laughing—George wanted to say something like that, but he would have had to hurry. Brian was already saying, in all seriousness, "Don't make *me* the heavy, Fritz. Olga could buy enough furniture for twenty offices if she wanted to. That kid is loaded, she's dripping with money. If she gave a shit about the magazine, we'd never have to worry again."

There was a short pause. "You didn't tell her that, did you, Brian?" Fritz had bounced out of his chair and was standing in the doorway.

Brian looked defiantly guilty. "What if I did?"

"You told her what to do with her own money? You

insulted her about it? Brian—you're getting this thing out of scale. It's only a magazine—"

Somewhere in the distance they heard a great rushing of waters. Sam Thirsby made a complicated toilet before leaving in the afternoon. The belt slid back and a moment later he stood radiant in Brian's cubicle. Brian looked at him desperately, as if Sam might have an answer for the whole question. Sam could only look puzzled: "Is everything all right?" he said.

Brian looked at Fritz. "To you it's only a magazine—" No one answered. It wasn't just that Brian was trying to defend an impossible position. He was completely lost. He obviously didn't know whether he was right or wrong. There was nothing to do but wait for him to dither in the direction of silence.

"If you think you can do better, Fritz, you're quite welcome to try. I've sweated my guts out for this magazine, but nobody else seems to care."

I care, George wanted to say. But it would have sounded absurd. By Brian's standards—he didn't care.

Fritz took a deep breath. "You need a rest, Brian. You haven't had a vacation this year. Your nerves are a mess."

Brian looked at Sam. Still no answer. Sam barely knew what they were talking about. Brian set his mouth for a moment, in a small firm line, and then suddenly relaxed and waved his hand as if he was handing something to Sam: "I can't do it by myself," he said.

It seemed more like the middle of a scene than the end: but the other two seemed to feel that something was settled. Fritz and George trooped out. Sam appeared to have caught up with the bidding. George could hear him talking to his uncle in a pleasant everyday voice. Sam was quite a subtle fellow in certain peculiar contexts. George felt like the girl at the movies who asks at the climax, what happened, what are they saying now? He wanted to ask Fritz in particular whether Brian had actually handed over his sword or whether he had just agreed to go on vacation. Fritz seemed to understand perfectly, whichever it was.

George stood in Fritz's doorway, watching him put papers away. Very neat fellow. There was a solemnity in the air, and the only sound was Sam's gentle voice, and Brian's very low responses. It was like listening to a church service.

After everything was cleared away, Fritz sat at his desk and waited. Finally Brian looked in and said good night. George imagined all kinds of exchanges. "You win this round, Holmes." "Yes. Match and rubber, I think, Dr. Moriarty." Or, "I tried to work with you, Fritz, I wanted to make it a team effort." "Sounds like a cute idea, Brian baby. You must try it on your scout group sometime." "Grow up." "You grow up." ("No, *you* grow up.") Or how about, "It would never have worked, Brian. We're two different breeds of cat." "Still good friends." "The best." But they just said good night, Fritz soberly, Brian rather malignantly, and Brian and Sam walked to the elevator.

"The elevator's off for the evening," said Fritz.

"Thanks," said Sam. They went out under the red light and George could hear them clattering slowly down the stairs.

Fritz got up to follow. He linked his cuffs and reached for his jacket.

"Tell me something, Fritz"—George felt limited to one question, and this was the one that interested him most—"were you really so outraged over what he said to Marplate?"

Fritz paused a moment. "Yes, I was. It was a terrible thing to say to the old broad. You coming down now?"

"I guess you really were, huh? Yeah, I'm coming down. In a minute."

"You want to have a drink at Sweeney's?" Fritz laughed. George laughed. "Not tonight, sir, if you don't mind."

Fritz dwindled off. "Very well, old boy, as you wish. See you at the shop tomorrow, then. Cheerio."

"Cheerio, old boy." And Fritz went out under the red light too.

4

Matty had a huge dinner for him, but this time he was ready for it. His lunch had long since floated down like a feather and he was ready for more. Steak again, not Chateaubriand exactly, but a nice little try. He thought of his old salary, and his present one, of how much he had sacrificed for his ideals, and how little his ideals actually entered into the situation now. The only trace of them was the cheaper cut of meat, the blown-out television tube, the slightly moth-eaten upholstery that his salary left them with.

"It was a funny kind of day," he said. "Maybe you can make sense of it." He described Fritz's financial methods, Marplate's tears, and Brian's ambiguous collapse. Matty didn't smile at all, didn't see it as human comedy.

"It sounds as if Mr. Twining's being away hasn't helped at all," she said. "The others are just as, I don't know . . . strange."

"It's all in the selection of details—I could give you another account of *The Outsider* that would make it sound delightful."

"You're not going to tell me that Fritz Tyler isn't a monster?"

"A monster? *Fritz?* Yeah, I can see I've told it wrong. You'll never get the picture straight if you think of Fritz as a monster."

"Well, he's been a monster to Brian by the sound of it."

This groping for precision was always frustrating. "That's the trouble with these third-person descriptions," he rambled. "If you knew the two of them, saw them in action every day, you wouldn't use words like 'monster' at all. I don't know what the hell Brian was up to this afternoon, but I'd say that if he quit, it was because he wanted to. He was looking for an excuse."

"It sounded much healthier at C.B.S."

George laughed. "That's an original point of view anyway." He had a feeling that Matty had mythologized C.B.S. into the Great Good Place; perhaps he had selected different details to bring home in those days.

You could turn off a conversation with Matty simply by passing up your turn. Sometimes he wished she talked more, as women were supposed to do in the jokes, but tonight this arrangement semed a good one. He felt drowsy and oddly receptive to fantasy. He went to his armchair, pretending it was in his private study, and lit a genuine 75-cent cigar that he had hijacked from the restaurant where he had lunched. Fritz's turn at the helm now, and with it, his turn. All the ideas that Twining and then Brian had kept him even from having—the satirical, irreverent ones, and also the ones that were too *heavy* for the company style—could bloom like a hundred flowers. He puffed a lush ring into the lampshade: it exploded gently and curled its way up in blue tendrils. He was still seeing things with the morning's sensuous clarity. Wonder how Fritz likes poetry, he thought.

Too bad Brian had to *look* so pathetic. That kind of bottle–shaped body confused the issues, by looking so insufferable when things were going well with it, and so touching when things were going badly. George pictured him now, shuffling to the staircase (even the elevators don't work for losers), his shoulders sloping down into his belt, his useless nephew towering over him, and he thought, maybe Fritz is a monster after all.

Of course, it hadn't looked so touching at the time, memory had done a trick. It was really just a fat man descending a staircase. In real life there were no monsters, Matty should get out more. See the funny way the world really works. George could remember how a short time ago he had chosen Brian as his own private underdog. Then when Brian had become a sort of top dog, he had forgotten all about it. And now Brian was underneath again. Someone had given the little puzzle a shake and *Fritz* was on top.

Backing underdogs was futile, if they were going to keep changing positions like this. Brian looked appealing when you looked down at him but awful when you looked up at him. Therefore it was almost a duty to keep him down. Fritz had been charming in the middle of the puzzle but on top—George blew the metaphor away in a purple cloud. It had occurred to him that in this particular formation you might almost call Gilbert Twining an underdog—and that was ridiculous.

Insofar as George had expected things to be clear-cut now at *The Outsider,* he was disappointed. Fritz seemed to be in charge of the dummy now, but Brian didn't withdraw into the shadows. On the contrary, he was noticeably pushier than before. George could hear him heckling Fritz about details, the way he used to heckle Twining. The question now was: was he doing this to save face, or had he just taken a step backward, the better to harass Fritz?

Fritz took it all in very good part. He winked at George over Brian's shoulder—as if to say, this is how Brian should have handled minor irritations when he was in charge. Fritz was also much politer about George's poetry; he said it looked like pretty good poetry so far as he could tell. But when you got down to it, he said, poetry in *The Outsider* was just another of Twining's rosebushes: poetry, puzzles,

chess problems—it's a wonder he hasn't tried knitting di-
lemmas and gardening quandaries. The magazine would
have to go on with all that cozy crap for a while, but when
old poets and puzzlemakers gave out, they would not be
replaced.

"You want to make me happy, Fritz? Publish the damn
poetry." But Fritz said no, if we publish you we have to
publish Philo—he writes poetry too, you know, and the
only excuse we have to offer him is that we don't take that
kind of stuff from the staff.

Give a man a little authority around here, thought
George, and he just becomes impossible. The poetry excuses
George was used to: they wouldn't let him read his things
over the air at KXB, the voice of Tewksbury College,
because, because . . . never mind because; and they had
even cut the last three lines of his sonnet in the Tewksbury
Yearbook to make space for an undertaker's ad. The poet in
the twentieth century had to acclimatize himself to incredible pain. But Fritz was also evasive about his satirical
ideas, and this was decidedly discouraging.

"It's not the kind of thing we do," said Fritz, and then
catching George's eye, added, "I'm sorry to insult you with
a standard excuse, George. What I really mean is that it
isn't good enough. Jokes about the Bomb, yeah yeah yeah—
they have to be great, fantastic, at this point. And you
wouldn't call this great, exactly. Would you?"

Nothing was more impossible than trying to defend a
joke—that was why you gave up even suggesting them
under Twining and Fine. But with Fritz, his old buddy in
charge, he had hoped no defense would be necessary. Fritz
used to *laugh* at his jokes. That must have been before he
became editor in chief.

To George's yellow eye, as he sat there with a sheaf of
hopeless outlines in his lap, Fritz appeared to be in favor of

changing everything; but, for the time being, nothing was actually going to be changed. His only positive idea so far was to drop things. As for Fritz proper, he was still the same old kidder, but George imagined spitefully that there was something a little impersonal about it now. He seemed to be looking just behind you, in case there was someone out in the hall who might benefit from hearing the joke too. It was institutional kidding.

George was getting sick of doing the Falstaff–Henry V bit with everyone around here. There didn't seem to be one man in a hundred who could assume leadership gracefully. They all went stiff as marionettes and began goose-stepping all over you.

"I'm sorry, George," said Fritz. "But just because I happen to be in this position doesn't suddenly make bad ideas into good ones. I have to react as if I didn't know you. You can see that, can't you?"

"Oh, sure." There was nothing as boring as good sound common sense. George felt as if he had wandered into some government office, and had just made a joke about, oh, the flag, or Communism, and the official in charge was patiently putting him right. It was as if they had never met before. All Fritz really needed to say was, "You come in here with a pile of crap and you don't even bring me a shovel," or words to that effect. By God, when *I'm* editor—about two months from now, by the look of things—I'll know how to talk to people. If there is anyone left to talk to.

"By the way, Fritz. What the hell is your position around here?"

Fritz looked cautiously at Brian's wall. They could hear Brian's voice somewhere out in the lobby, indulging his new style—the small gust of rage. Having intimidated Marplate so successfully the day before yesterday, he had apparently decided to make this a regular feature of his day and his little flare-ups were already part of the office noise.

So there was no question of Brian ever hearing anything, and Fritz said, "I'm not sure I know, to tell you the truth. I wanted to be delicate—you know, not make it anything too official. I thought Brian would just fade out—that's how it looked the other night, didn't it? But he seems to have changed his mind, and now he won't let go. It's a hell of a silly position. He wants me to take the responsibility and to make the decisions, but he also wants me to clear everything with him. In a way, I guess he's got the two of us working together after all."

Brian's voice went up a notch. It sounded as if he was roasting the inoffensive Sonnabend this time. Today Sonnabend, tomorrow the world. Soon no librarian or small delivery boy would be safe. It was a funny reaction to defeat—if it was defeat. Fritz continued: "I can only say, to hell with delicacy. I should have dictated terms when I had him on his knees. You should come to the office on time sometime, George, you miss a lot. This morning he threw one of his little tantrums in here. And I can tell you, a Brian tantrum is a strange little thing. You don't know whether to laugh or cry. I guess he's still at the practicing stage."

"Did you throw one back?"

"What's the use, he wouldn't have heard me. Anyway, you feel kind of sorry for the guy. It's an escape for him, to flail around a little. He said I had to clear articles with him, and I said O.K. with me, and showed him some stuff, and he went through it very solemnly and said hem, hem, 'That seems to be all right.' No reference to the other night. In fact, when I tried to bring that up, tactfully, he acted (a) as if he didn't hear me, and (b) as if he would get terribly angry if he did. It's going to be quite a proposition getting through to him from here on in."

"So he's a rubber stamp now, our gracious queen. You can give him that much, can't you?"

"Yeah, but he's so pick-pick-picky over details. This morning for instance we had a thing about putting the semicolon inside or outside the quotes on stuff that comes from England, I can't even remember which side he was on, and something else about changing the typeface on editorials. I can't tell you how that stuff wears you out."

"I can imagine."

"And you say, do it your way Brian, and he says no, I think it's up to you, and so you say, O.K. change the typeface, and he says, but that might confuse the printer, and, oh God, I don't know—so then you try making fun of the whole thing, and he does his new bit, looking angry and not quite hearing you at the same time—"

"I must try to catch that. It sounds a riot."

"It's an impossible situation. I'm going to have to do something about it."

"What? Lean on him some more?"

"No, that's hopeless—besides, I'm no sadist. He loves this kind of situation, it's his perfect damn niche, two feet from the top and burrowed deep. You can't ask him to move down, and he hasn't the guts to move up. He'd like to go on like this forever, I bet, the way he did under Twining."

Fritz was George's old buddy again. Their friendship was really political—it had no other serious frame of reference.

"So what are you going to do, Fritz?"

"I'm going to have to get him out of here altogether. For that, I need a lever and, as the man said, a place to stand. You watch."

So George took his poems and his new ideas back to his

desk, and decided to await developments in a spirit of malevolent neutrality.

5

It arrived on his desk a few days later, without fanfare or warning. It was neatly typed, which was a switch for Wally. George started to read it with no more than half his attention: across the way a small wrangle was in the works, and he didn't want to miss any of the high points.

"Honestly, Brian—*what* does it matter?" (Twining had left that sentence in the air, and Fritz had simply set it in motion again.)

"You know what I resent about you, Fritz old boy?" said Brian—it was funny how people used their Twining-imitations *against each other*. "You're making me out an old woman—but you're a fussy guy yourself, Fritz. Your stuff is always impeccable."

"Is it, old boy?"

"Oh, for crapsake—"

Good point, thought George: I wonder I hadn't thought of it myself. Fritz gave a great effect of casualness, but he was a neat, scrupulous soul at bottom. He was exaggerating the difference between himself and Brian to make a point.

George went back to his reading. Wally had done something strange to his style. It was simple and fresh. Almost *too* simple and fresh, a bit dewy, in fact. Sporadic attempts to eavesdrop had slowed his reactions to a crawl, and he was halfway down the page before it struck him that this probably wasn't Wally at all. He flipped the pages. Harriet Eustace. Who she? Brian's niece? Brian's old granny, more likely.

Now that he was alerted, he was in a position to read the thing with a little intelligence. It was girlish all right, but old and fragile at the same time. Miss Eustace sounded like a little old woman who had never quite grown up—who still wore ankle socks and practiced tennis shots in front of the mirror. Her phrasing had frozen back in the nineties, and her response to the arts went back even further than that. (You couldn't have Tennessee Williams "weaving a spell of enchantment," could you?)

He was about to go in and tax Brian with it. But he paused by the side of his desk. Brian was still whining at Fritz, a note of real hysteria in his voice. His nerves must be in terrible shape. Miss Eustace wasn't some little mistake you could tease somebody about; she might be a symptom of real trouble. The poor little bottle-shaped bastard was calling in all his friends and relatives to save the day. What could you say to a guy like that?

George stared at the green blotting paper, deciphering an upside-down phone number. Fritz's voice came in now—like Twining's, only chillier, crueler: keeping Brian's nerves stripped. It was bad enough for Twining to talk like that, but probably everyone in his family talked like that, it was an heirloom. For Fritz to use another man's voice, though, seemed terribly perverse.

Had Fritz seen this Eustace thing, he wondered. Was he letting it go through as a final humiliation for Brian? George could just see the letters coming in the week after it appeared. 21,000 trancelike readers stirring in their sleep, where's Wally, who dealt this mess—Fritz would take the letters round to Brian: "Shall we forward these to Miss Eustace and let her answer them?" Might as well hand Brian a revolver and leave the rest to him.

Staring at the green blotting paper and listening to these two talk made him feel curiously seasick. Fritz imitated Twining so often these days that it wasn't an imitation any more but a legitimate aspect of his own voice. And Brian was now answering in kind, because the only way to foil a

Twining sneer was with another Twining sneer. The effect was of two Twinings where there used to be one—and no doubt the thing would spread, Philo and Marplate would turn into two more Twinings as Fritz's scorn licked at them . . .

This was a hell of a place, you know? You would have to clean and scour the building to make it livable again. Or was Miss Eustace really just a practical joke? Was Fritz having him on? He read the piece again—of course, that was it, it was a spoof. Nobody wrote like that in real life. It had to be a joke.

So he went in and interrupted their argument about subheads and waved the column at them.

"Very funny, you guys," he said.

"What's funny, old boy?"

"This thing, old bean. Harriet Eustace, God bless her violet woolies. I suppose her name is an acrostic for 'Up yours, George Wren.' "

Fritz looked only the lightest shade embarrassed. "Oh, that's Harriet Wadsworth's theater column. I thought I'd give Wally a fortnight off."

George looked quickly at Brian: you're always bitching at things these days, bitch at this. Here is something worthy of a man's powers. But Brian had nothing to say. Fritz fingered his bow tie.

"I'm sorry you don't like it, George. I thought it had a certain freshness. After years of Wally's browbeating, it seemed to me that our readers might welcome the feminine touch. Anyway, we're running it."

Now, come on, Brian. This may be your last chance. It isn't only about commas that you bite and scratch, is it? It isn't only, who's stealing the pencils, who forgot to flush the johns?

Brian's tantrum never materialized. Rather absurdly he

avoided George's eye. "Well, I've got to get back to work," he said. "I'll leave you two to settle it."

George looked at Fritz. It clarified matters slightly if you thought of him as a grade-A shit. Fritz was looking as friendly as hell, as if to make positive that George didn't see him that way. And George suddenly felt himself beginning to smile back out of habit, enjoying the old political complicity. He skipped back to his own cubicle before this went any further.

Harriet Wadsworth. It was too bloody much. He didn't think *The Outsider* was the end of the world, but it had some value. That was the fiction you agreed to when you worked here, these were the terms of the engagement. You didn't run stuff by Harriet Wadsworth. You took a certain minimal pride in those pages as you might in your own bedsheets: you drew some sort of line on what was allowed in.

. . . This was, he supposed, probably the way some drunken old bum of a doctor must feel about the Hippocratic oath. He picked up Wadsworth's column and took it to Fritz and said, "Here, you edit it." Fritz didn't say anything. He had obviously given it to George to get George's tacit compliance. Well, he hadn't got it.

George looked in at Brian. You're another disgrace to the medical profession, Fine. But the two of us can take a stand about this at least. Brian didn't look up; George knew he wouldn't look up until George had gone, even if his neck burst with waiting. What's the matter, are you afraid of Fritz? Is that hot little temper a small cover for a big fat chicken heart? Or is it just a case of more politics—that you want to see *Fritz* make a fool of himself for a change?

Whatever it was, it just about made him sick. Twining had told him that these two were "small," but he hadn't said *how* small.

George realized from the uncomfortable silence in the corridor that they were waiting for him to do something. He had pushed himself center-stage. Was he going to go along with them, or was he going to stage a miniature walkout? Tune in, my tiny friends, and see.

He sat there for what seemed a long time thinking about it until the silence broke: somebody coughed and everyone started moving about again.

For some wayward reason, he began thinking about his wife instead. Did she look better in short or long hair? That was beside the point. This job was costing her upwards of $5,000 a year walking-around money. Easy to talk about making sacrifices, but it was much more her sacrifice than his; and it wasn't just a given number of sacrifices: the whole texture of her life was slightly crumby. Walking the baby from one small room to the next, and back. Pulling up the blind to look at the other pink buildings—500 sets of Venetian blinds, 100 air-conditioners. Buying a new dress and feeling nervous about the money. None of it was very terrible in itself—but that's all there was.

Face it, men, Matty was an idealist only by marriage. Under their agreed-upon rhetoric lurked a normal American girl. She never complained, but he knew that she went in for regular housewife reading and viewing, and this must prime her with constant reminders of what she was missing. A dishwasher would be nice, a vacation in Cape Cod would be nice—again, no one of these things was irresistible; but having to say no to *everything*, again and again and then once more at bedtime, must get you just slightly down.

She never complained—what a horrible phrase. Those open copies of *House Beautiful* and *Stately Mansions* were complaint enough. She often said that she didn't care about those things, and he was sure that she tried not to—but why surround yourself with pictures, if you didn't care? She cared all right. Even the strain of not admitting it must add to the burden. And if he was going to make her go without everything more or less indefinitely he should have at least a fairly good reason. And this meant some attempt to define what he was doing here.

He passed Fritz's door on the way out to lunch and Fritz looked up and watched him go by. Still waiting for something. Look, George, this is just a temporary expedient. Once we've got Harriet on our side— Brian was standing by Sam's desk: Sam had a look of borrowed time about him now. Fritz would probably purge him in a week or two. When George looked back at them from the elevator cage, they seemed to be a long distance away. They looked like small china figures, artfully bent towards each other. Fritz might come over at any moment and turn them around so that Sam would be sitting with his back to the desk and Brian would be bowing to the opposite wall. This effect was the result of breathless immobility. Brian refused to stir until George had passed and Sam, with his unfailing sympathy, refused to stir either. He must have supposed it was part of a plan.

George stood by the grille, waiting for the elevator to wheeze into place. The whole office had shrunk. When Fritz popped out for a second, presumably to see if he had gone, it was clear that he was much too small to turn the two figurines around. Marplate was smaller still, no bigger than a man's thumb. And Sonnabend was maybe half of that. You're all nothing but a pack of cards, thought George, as he slipped into the elevator.

One thing you'd have to say for Twining—he would never have let Harriet Eustace Wadsworth into his magazine. He might give himself a heart attack trying to raise money, but he wouldn't stain his pages with Harriet. So—that was one thing.

I wonder who I should hand my resignation to? Supposing I wanted to? Old Arrogant out on the West Coast would bust a gut laughing at the chaos we've made of things. Fritz, really—no, you *didn't*. And Brian—*poor* Brian. And George, what did little George do, I wonder. All right, condescend for all you're worth, Commander, we've ruined your magazine for you at least. He rather pictured the commander turning serious at this. Yes, you have, haven't you? I must say, I rather mind about that.

He hated these imaginary dialogues with Twining. As a schoolboy, he used to try out new ideas on a mental picture of his father. In real life, his father was an abrupt, inattentive man: but in this mental picture he was wonderfully receptive. And it was precisely the same way with Twining, sitting next to him now, on the next stool, in his floppy hat and the gardening shears on his lap. However impossible he was in real life, he was a wonderful fellow to talk to in imagination.

George turned to the affable, eighteenth-century slattern behind the counter and ordered a ham sandwich. None of Fritz's ill-gotten banquets from now on. You were absolutely right about that guy, Mr. Twining—what did you call him? I forget, but you were absolutely right. Ham on rye, a humble dish. I wonder what makes some people good imaginary company and other people not? Something about the shape of the ears perhaps. One always felt with Mr. Wren, Sr., that one had had a really good conversation once upon a time, and some day might have it again. Had there ever been such a conversation? or was it constructed wholly of imaginary ones?

Same thing, anyway, with Twining. George had managed in the last few weeks to blot out the imaginary Twining, but now the old spook was back. This was the commander as one had first seen him, bright with possibilities, apparently the most understanding man, the one who imposed the fewest barriers, and who gave and received in the most perfect proportion—well, it was all a trick of course, Twining wasn't like that at all. But the version survived in the memory, next to the primal version of Mr. Wren and the Good Conversation. And George could suddenly see that version being crucified by little maggoty men called Fine and Tyler; and Twining suddenly seemed helpless in their hands, as he never had in real life; brimming, grotesquely, with good will and a crazy kind of innocence. He turned to George now with a face of the most wistful betrayal. Fantastically, he *was* the underdog, in this particular situation.

George walked out of the drugstore hurriedly, leaving half the sandwich. This was sentimentalism of the most paralyzing kind—seeing crucifixions under every bed, the great liberal vice. It was essential to see it as a simple question of practicality, of judicious choice. Tyler, for instance: Fritz's lack of class would hurt the magazine eventually: his lack of any center of gravity. In some unforeseen situation, and after years of unfaltering, too-perfect taste, Tyler would do something incredibly wrong and out of tune: had just done so, in fact. He had no real instinct for the thinkable and the unthinkable. Not exactly that Fritz lacked convictions: but the deeper you went, the filmier the convictions got, until they were like an underwater picture, shifting, dreamy, out of focus. Brian might be better at that level, but something had gone wrong with him up top, near the skin: during these solitary evenings, he had missed some routine connection—but George didn't want to analyze them even that personally, but only as magazine creatures. Brian would be O.K., except that the whole office would stiffen and die under him: you couldn't breathe the air that Brian doled out.

George detoured ten blocks, to work out a position to walk in with, but was now heading inevitably back. Reduce it to the simplest terms. Whether or not one could see any point of virtue in *The Outsider,* and he was so confused about that by now as to be almost beyond caring, one, that is, you, had certain professional obligations; you had to keep it up to its own standards, and to do this, you had to back Class, as his father (who played the horses) used to say—Class in terms of the particular situation. Make it a simple formula like that.

So he decided to write Twining a letter that afternoon, and tell him what had happened and how things were, exactly as he had promised four months ago, and see what that led to.

IX

1

Gilbert Twining had had his lunch, in the warmth of the window, and now the blinds were down and he was ready for his nap. The harsh sounds from the next bed died away. His roommate came from Oklahoma, and his voice combined the worst of South and West—to Twining's ear, anyhow. Funny about accents. You couldn't think my thoughts if you had his accent, and you couldn't think *his* thoughts if, etc., etc. The day nurse came from Ohio, for some reason. California was a jungle of transplants.

Why do Englishmen keep their accents wherever they go? Is it that they don't listen to other people? Or is it so welded into their thinking that, *you* know . . . he was already drowsy, and finishing sentences was a bore. Think English, talk English. Accentology, or whatever you called it, was really quite fascinating.

My wife Polly and my friend George have warm American accents. (Why do they call it warm, do you suppose? Coldest people in the world, Americans. National style founded on commerce of course. A banal thought, worthy of a Brian Fine editorial.) (Not without relevance though.) (And so forth.)

The blind flapped very gently against the window. Outside were two huge geranium beds and a grove of eucalyptus trees. Strange combination. California for you. Yes, warm accents. George Wren hadn't written once, not once. And Polly's letters had to be defrosted. She signed them "affectionately." These were his friends. His enemies didn't bear thinking of . . . although, come to think of it, they probably had warm accents too.

He didn't understand the first thing about this country. Polly and George, let's call them Pollygeorge, shall we? had such open, friendly expressions; and they had that solid, motherly American quality: naturally one confided in them. One hated to mislead people: especially one's friends.

One didn't want Pollygeorge to think one was perfect. He had wanted them to know his weaknesses, know that he was human, etc. (he yawned) people were supposed to prefer that kind of thing. Instead, instead—he shut his eyes, and let the train of thought drift easily away. Although it was all a fake, he liked this bloody country better than England. Missed England of course, various sounds and smells. Missed being a small boy in Wellington boots. Missed Lord's cricket ground. Missed the feeling of certain streets, town streets, suburban streets, railway carriages, frozen guest-rooms, green-line buses, bathrooms with washbowls— he found himself deep in one of his lists. Soon he would be naming Cup champions and Derby winners. Then sleep.

But he had been miserable in England. His clique had grown older and cliquier and clogged with mannerisms. For instance, one didn't have tastes any more, one had attitudes. One liked, oh, plain chant and the Beatles, Gorki and Thelonious Monk. It didn't have to be that particular cluster, of course. It might be William Byrd and Miles Davis, Gogol and Acker Bilk. It might be Buster Keaton and Alban Berg, Orlando Gibbons and Salvation Army bands. It might be—he was off on another list. Point was, one was forever pruning the taste buds to make an amusing point. "Middlebrow, middle class, romanticism, oh dear. I mean, *he's* the sort of chap who likes Rupert Brooke, late Beethoven, middle Louis Armstrong." And meanwhile they grew older, and their voices scratched at your nerves, and their jokes; and marriages got messy, and old friends announced that they were turning homosexual (practically took space in the *Times* to announce it) and everyone seemed to get shriller and more desperate . . .

Except for old Gilbert. Old Gilbert never grew shrill. He remained a boy for a very long time, and the things he did didn't count against a boy or show in his style. You'd never suppose, would you, that Old Gilbert is already a man in his late thirties, heading toward a singularly corrupt middle age. Yes, fact. Habit is no longer something he can flirt with; I mean, one no longer boasts about one's hangovers. Gilbert Twining, 1945–55. There were places one couldn't go, things one couldn't do, because one no longer had the pride and vitality to resist the feeblest kind of temptation: one acquiesced like an old man acquiescing in death . . . still, he was boyish: his face in the looking glass was the face of a sixth-form prefect.

Better to make lists. He was sweating slightly. The point he had been trying to make for the thousandth time was that America had freed him from all this: by changing the setting, by flattering him, by, in some curious way, clearing his head. He was a whole new thing here, come of age and respected—fantastically respected: he thought of the early parties, receptions, panel discussions, with a hopeless tenderness and gratitude.

It was, one told oneself, rather a lark. (As usual the English idiom sounded grotesque to his inner ear—cheerio, lark, half a mo: was it possible that he had made all these words up?) But it didn't do to pretend to one's wife. Positively not. Marriage was impossible if one of the parties was posturing. He wasn't going to act the public figure in his own house. So one evening he told Polly . . .

Oh dear, he would never get his nap at this rate. His friend from Oklahoma would wake up soon, full of talk, ugly horrible Western talk. Twining burrowed into the pillow. Insomnia, his old trademark, had dwindled to the point where he fussed if he didn't get a two-hour nap every afternoon. Polly had, all right, go on with it, already been slightly disturbed by the other factor. It was as disappointing to him as it was to her—America hadn't made him a completely new man, after all—but it might as well be faced. "Polly"—shameful confrontation by the fireplace. Polly had staged a candlelight dinner that evening and was obviously working into a romantic mood. He really must explain things before it went any further. "Dear Polly—"

He might, on the whole, have been better advised to cut his tongue out. Polly sat very quietly, nodding, asking the occasional question. And he told her the whole story, told about the curious wound in his psyche, asked for her help and forbearance. She seemed to stiffen slightly at certain points and he wondered whether he was going too far. But the confession gave him confidence, it was the kind of thing he did rather well, and when it was done, he would never have to refer to it again. He would have nothing to live up to any more . . . Besides, Americans were always telling each other dire psychological secrets. It must be all right. As he finished he moved to her side, a free and freakishly ardent man.

To his surprise, she drew away with a kind of revulsion. "You don't want to make love *now?*" she said. It was honestly as if a leper had touched her. (Was there anything he could swiftly unsay? No, that was hopeless—and not his way.) She went to the bedroom in a terrible cold silence, shutting the door behind her: leaving him shrunken and dismayed by the fireplace, confidence leaking like gas all over the room.

Since then he had inflated, and punctured, a good many aimless generalizations about liberals and women and Americans and liberal American women. Partly vengeance, he supposed—but she really should have understood a little better. It was indecent for a grown woman to be so innocent. What was Radcliffe coming to? Or Wellesley or Bryn Mawr, for that matter?

. . . And then, *mutatis mutandis,* he seemed to have gone and made the same mistake with George. Nothing so spectacular there, the disgust was fainter. He had actually supposed that George and he were still good friends when he came out here to the coast. But George was the only person at *The Outsider* who hadn't sent him a get-well note of some kind; and George hadn't answered his postcards, or sent that report either. So—George was disgusted too. God would doubtless explain these people to him on the Last Day.

He *had* parted with George on good terms, hadn't he? Twining's memory for recent events had become a touch woozy, and he didn't want to put pressure on it. One's head was easier to live with in this kind of soft shimmer. Pollygeorge didn't want him to have any weaknesses at all was what it came down to: his particular purpose in life was to be perfect. It had something to do with Wilsonian white American liberalism, etc., etc., but probably not very much.

The fact was (California yawns were surely the world's biggest and best) that this drugged refusal to concentrate was the closest thing to pleasure that he had experienced since he was a boy eating caramels in Wellington boots. There must have been politics then, even in the nursery. But they weren't everything. There was, let's see, chocolate and sleep and the smell of clean white aprons, this was undoubtedly the silliest list he had thought of yet. He felt like an old soldier dying of fever and talking disjointedly about Nanny, and tea on the lawn and the peculiar smell of Daddy's white gloves. He brought his knees up into a snug ball. For too long, his mind had been exclusively concerned with the political—and the sexuo-political—side of himself. He had worried about things like ascendancy and betrayal. A fig for all that. Ascendancy had no meaning in this context, and no one could betray him now.

Frankly he didn't give a damn about the magazine either. Worrying about it would only make him excited again. It was splendid to realize that he could be happy without *The Outsider*. And he was beginning to feel his age, which was, let's face it, excessive. He wasn't sorry now that he hadn't heard from George, or that Polly was probably preparing to leave him. It all served to free him from fret.

He had a feeling, from certain shaded hints, that he was expected to leave this place in the near future. He didn't want to a bit. Even though he couldn't afford a room to himself, he was very content here. Fine and Tyler and Marplate could plot away to their hearts' content: he would just lie here and talk to his friend from Oklahoma and read detective stories and keep an eye on the garden. He should have been doing this years ago.

The nurse came in with his tea and toast and asked how he felt. She was not at all bad-looking in the afternoon sun. Her uniform turned a very radiant white as she snapped up the shade, and her skin was made of sheerest gold.

In his present state of calculated torpor, Commander Twining hardly minded one way or the other.

2

At what point in this protracted twilight George's letter reached him he wasn't quite sure. California, having no weather to speak of, was the ideal place for a man in one's condition. Time lost its pressure. Place had no special characteristics. Instead of the geraniums and eucalyptus trees outside, one might easily have had, say, mimosa and chestnut trees, or palm trees and columbine. Or—and instead of patients from England and Oklahoma one might have had—all was arbitrary, nothing was necessary, under this pale, featureless sky.

But here was George's letter, and it looked like a long one. Five pages at least of George's rustic prose. He decided, in deference to an old custom, to have his breakfast first.

"I see you got a letter," said his roomate.

"Yes."

"It's like getting a letter in the army. God, that was exciting. Were you in the army, Gil?"

"No. The doctors found a heart murmur. I was with the Ministry of Information right through the war."

"You people were great in 1940."

"Thanks. I haven't heard that phrase in years."

The army would have made one of these nice, logical breaks. Before 1940 I was such and such a man, after 1940, *such* and such a man. As it was, everything had been frozen, suspended for the duration. Personal growth simply ground to a halt. However—not very interesting to think about now. That long gray business. His memory tended to skip it.

"You seem like a military man, Gil. I don't know what it is."

"My nanny used to make me stand up straight. That's all it is, I expect. And sit up straight and lie down straight." His roommate, whose name was Charlie, went on for a while about the war. He had been in England a while and had found it exhilarating. His reminiscences brought back the dank feel of those days, however hard one set one's mind against it. Waiting for buses in the dark. Watching the Yanks enjoy themselves. Charlie talked about the group spirit in England, but Twining remembered the war as a peculiarly solitary affair.

"Aren't you going to open your letter?" Charlie interrupted himself.

"After breakfast."

"I guess that's what I mean by military."

Charlie had felt enlarged, liberated by the war; Twining had felt ever so slightly diminished by it. It was a cramped, psychologically squalid time. On the one hand, boredom, boredom incredible; on the other hand, little fever zones of pleasure. Desiccated jests at the Ministry and the nighttime prowl—it was a bad time altogether. He wished that Charlie hadn't brought it up.

"One felt about six inches high out of uniform," he said, "an absolute moral and physical dwarf. I can't tell you how I loathed myself at times."

"But you were in an essential occupation. And it wasn't that safe in London."

"Yes, I know."

The subject had brought a faint unease to his mind. Those years of restless boredom had done him no good. He was already a rather overripe bachelor by then, oozing ideas and energy. He had, three months before war was declared, been appointed editor in chief of *The Watchman,* the youngest editor in chief of anything in recorded history. But now *The Watchman* lay in a deep coma, a dead mouthpiece for elderly patriots; and Twining was obliged to put his ideas and energy into storage, and simply mark time for six interminable years. He was conventionally anti-German, of course, and outraged at all the right things, but there was little room for growth in that. Any other kind of thinking seemed remote and unreal. His radicalism grew stiff from lack of use, and when the war ended, he had a curious feeling of being out of date. Some socialists were, some weren't, on what principle it was hard to say.

In 1945, *The Watchman* came back to life as if nothing had happened (rather reminding one of elements in the Christian church, which had become once more a great force for peace). He knew that he personally had spent those years badly. That he had lost something in the process. But nobody else seemed to notice, and life was sweeping up all the war's cripples and carrying them forward. Gilbert's marriage in 1946 seemed now like a gesture of compliance with this. He moved out of London and put his name down for a car: trying by main force to bring about the logical break in his life that the war should have occasioned.

Well, of course, either Hilda was the wrong girl or 1946 was a bad year—whatever it was, it hadn't worked at all at all. That frightful winter in the frightful country; trying to keep excited about the Labour government over an electric fire with one bar working; the first tentative London evenings—this was a thoroughly unpromising line of thought, and put him in no frame of mind for George's letter.

"I don't much like to talk about the war," he said.

"It must have been pretty bad," said Charlie.

"Yes. It was pretty bad."

"Buzz bombs, doodlebugs . . ."

"A bad dream in every respect. But somehow, you know, waking up was even worse."

"How do you mean?"

"Well, you know, everything was going to be all right after the war, that had always been the feeling. Peacetime life looked so magically simple from that vantage point. And then you woke up and found that the monster you'd been dreaming about was still there at the foot of the bed."

"You mean rationing and all that. Shortages."

Twining was always amused by cross-purposes.

"The whole wartime malaise," he said. "The feeling of second-rateness. Yes. All that." He hadn't been able to look at his wife Hilda, after a while, without thinking of the Woman's Territorial Army. Her role was to serve tea in a canteen forever and ever. In shapeless khaki uniforms and utility underwear.

Going to bed with Hilda was like going to bed with the war. She had as a matter of fact spent five years in the army, and a kind of institutional dinginess had rubbed off on her. She liked to sit in the kitchen and listen to dreadful variety shows until the house echoed with the second-rate heartiness of those days. "We've set the microphone up in this shed . . . and now a request from Corporal Robinson of one nineteen Bumby Road Harrogate and all the lads in the mess. 'Keep the home fires burning' . . . And here to sing it for you is your own Sweetheart of the Forces (and let's give her a great brainless roar of love while we're about it)." The kitchen was the only warm room in the house, and he hated to ask Hilda to turn this awful stuff off: it was her world, it was many people's world—and not all of them were stupid either. It just happened that these jokes and songs and this cheap fellowship, the self-satisfied *amateurishness* of it all, were somehow bound up in his mind with the war horrors, the lonely, jealous years.

This sudden priggishness was rather alarming for a man in his position. He suddenly didn't like the feel of England any more. The faces had changed, the shop girls were cheekier and wore their hair differently. He began to hate the sight of massed bicycles and the sound of football scores. He was a prewar object, you could tell that by the way people talked to him. (Americans didn't know that, of course; he seemed like the last word over here.) He had never caught up, and even now the thought of postwar England, mods rockers fab grotty, made him wince slightly. He had missed some trivial step during the war, the band had changed tunes, and everyone had heard it but him. (More than anything else, it reminded him of spending the holidays at school and then watching the other boys returning: V-day was a shattering invasion of privacy.) And his marriage to Hilda, which might have brought him into the swing, only completed the alienation. For, of course, he was a failure with Hilda from the very first night, as he was with all women he knew "personally" so to say or respected even a little bit.

A most unpromising line of thought. It left one in no mood at all to face the boyish challenges of George's letter. Breakfast was unmistakably over and Charlie was full of life, and could adapt anyone's affairs to his purposes . . . Whatever George says in this letter, I shall do nothing about it. There is some chance of peace if I keep out of things now. . . . On that understanding Twining took the envelope and zipped it open with an unused butter knife.

3

One must resist this kind of thing at all costs, he repeated. He put the letter in the envelope and out of sight.

With a mind so deliciously full of failure, and resigned to it, one didn't want to flirt with the illusion of competence. Much better to watch the flowers and chat with one's friend Charlie. He got his bathrobe and went and sat by the window.

A heart attack in those particular circumstances was rather conclusive, wasn't it? Self-esteem was all too happy to retire permanently after such a ludicrous drubbing. Oh, it wasn't, he knew, really Hilda or the war or this or that. It was, as I have told you a thousand times, dear, something that happened in the fifty long years of boyhood; he had been humiliated once too often by his snotty godlike cousin, and then had tried to set the bone himself and had set it wrong. He tried to postpone the challenge of the letter by striking out on this familiar line of thought. But it didn't get him very far.

He did not share the American passion for Freudian self-analysis—which struck him as not so much inaccurate as desolately uninteresting: if the secret of life lay in the moist half-witted world of infancy, let it lie. He preferred to think of his troubles as a scrap of social history. He had been brought up in an intolerable fashion. He wondered if Charlie would be amused to hear about "nannies" and the English public-school system? Probably not.

Charlie was talking about the Anzio beachhead. He said that war was a funny thing: that shortly after the landing he, Charlie, had turned an Italian family out of their house on a bitterly cold evening at the point of his rifle, so that he and his men could sleep in comfort for a change; and that he had felt no remorse at all. He could picture them still, and he felt lots of remorse now, of course, but at the time he felt nothing but a kind of bleak pleasure. Twining could see it all, rather as Charlie must have seen it. Black shawls and toothless bewilderment and "mother of God."

"Yes. I suppose it was not being able to do things like that that made one feel so inferior."

"That's a funny point of view."

"One wants to be in the swim. What did you do after you got out of the army, Charlie?"

"I married a German girl. It seemed like the thing to do at the time. A washout, a very big mistake."

It was good to have Charlie back in the postwar period. Twining knew all about Charlie's present wife and three children, but the German girl was a surprise. This, however, turned out to be something that *Charlie* didn't want to talk about. Fair enough: one respected these sensitive areas enormously.

"Do you ever think of retiring, Charlie?"

"Not too much. My wife wants to go to Europe the minute I retire, and I'm not too keen about that. Of course I'd like to see your country again, but the rest—I don't know. How about you, Gil?"

"I think it isn't something you plan, you suddenly find it's happened. Like an old athlete, I suppose. You wake up one morning and you don't feel like running a hundred laps. You roll over and go back to sleep."

"How old are you, Gil?"

"Fifty-four, actually."

"Hell, that's no age to retire. That's young. Run fifty laps tomorrow instead of a hundred and you'll be fine."

"Fifty laps is no good for my particular sport. You make the full effort or none. After all, who wants to run the mile in 4.30?" He enjoyed talking to Charlie, a patient man, and not unintelligent. "I might retire and become a lecturer. Or a Personality."

"That's work, isn't it?"

"No, not really. Not really." He looked back over his

shoulder at George's letter. "Work is something quite different."

I expect you'll find this all very amusing, said the letter, *and quaint.* Oh dear me, no. Not amusing at all. George must have a queer notion of me indeed. But then, no matter how assiduously one tried to explain oneself, one couldn't help giving these false impressions. Again a question of education. (Are you sure you don't want to hear about the public-school system, Charlie?)

"What does your wife think of your retirement, Gil?"

"I don't think she cares one way or the other. You've seen the number of letters I've had from her. I daresay we'll be separating as soon as I get better."

"Gee, that's too bad."

"No, I think it's rather a good idea. It'll all be part of my retirement. Don't you find marriage an awful strain at times?"

"I never know when you're joking, Gil."

That was enough of Charlie for now. He shut his eyes in feigned sleep. Actually, it was his theory that for the last year or two, Polly had simply been looking for an excuse to divorce him. It was rather charming of her to need an excuse. Being made uncomfortable by a man wasn't enough, being criminally disappointed in him wasn't enough. But give her one technical "good reason," and she was off through the door.

Poor Polly.

They had an early, hospital-hours lunch, and the nurse reminded Twining of how well he was getting. His bills had so far been divided between hospital insurance and, rather surprisingly, the countess, who felt obscurely guilty, so she said: so there was no concern on that score. But this was not the kind of place that relished looking after healthy people, and the staff had begun to apply a steady pressure of hints. He supposed he should be making plans. "Perhaps I should hire myself out as an English butler," he said to Charlie. ("You're not the type," said Charlie.) "Or as an English character actor. Gentleman of the old school type of thing." ("Or as a gigolo," said Charlie, rather unexpectedly.)

He had real trouble sleeping that afternoon. The letter had left a small deposit of excitement, and while he refused to address the question directly, fragments of it kept insinuating themselves. It was nice of George to write, for instance. That ass, Harriet Wadsworth, was another thought. So Olga Marplate got her green paint was a third. It would take at least 150 laps around the track by now, and a man of fifty-four with a weak heart had no obligations in the matter. Perhaps he had exaggerated *The Outsider*'s importance—was it George who had accused him of that? Well, now their positions were nicely reversed. George's letter reeked of concern, he himself couldn't care less.

His mind drifted back to the beginning. The reception in the Hotel Thingummy. They didn't know then that they were importing damaged goods; that Gilbert Twining was a slightly spent force in England, that nobody quite took him seriously over there. *The Outsider* patrons crowded around him in a peculiarly pleasant way, taking him as seriously as he could possibly wish. They had already given him a controlling share of stock, and now they were treating him in line with his price.

They asked him to say a few words, and he went and stood by the bar with a glass of champagne jiggling in his hand and said something like this (he had reworded it, edited it slightly, since the event): "You people don't understand the first thing about English notables. You suppose that all our Grand Old Men really count for something. You think it matters that Bertrand Russell thinks this, that Winston Churchill thinks that. You imagine that the honors under which we bury these men represent real coin." He would soon be asleep at this rate. Nothing like listening to a dull speech. Point is: "You pay, as a nation, dearly for these illusions. You force yourselves to listen to distinguished English lecturers who couldn't pack ten people into the Albert Hall, and who have come over here solely to restore their confidence; you quiver to politicians who are mimicked or ignored in every English pub from Land's End to, etc., etc." He yawned. "And you hire English editors with overblown reputations to dilute your journalism." They had taken it all for irony, of course, and had practically carried him out shoulder high.

Reading George's letter was like returning to the scene of a party the next morning. He had as he had humorously prophesied, made rather a sorry mess of things. He hadn't known how to pick the people or how to work with them or how to leave them on their own. He was a hopeless judge of Americans—Charlie over there was probably a homicidal maniac and one would never know it; and after he had judged them, he didn't know what to do with them next. Out of the question to go back, George. See what *you* can do about the situation.

Hush. Old Mr. Snow, the patron of those days, is making a speech. "We want to welcome to these shores a young man who"—once a boy wonder, always a boy wonder. Might be more accurate to call me a sort of boyish old man. Never mind, sorry, go ahead, Mr. Snow. "We have great hopes for Mr. Twining. We believe that he is a fighter. We believe that he has integrity and vision"—must remember not to giggle. Mr. Snow faded back and Gilbert Twining found himself standing in the empty room again. There were streamers on the floor and broken glasses and a chair upturned. The guests had gone and the place was unbelievably frowsy. We'll have to clean this up, thought Twining, and actually went out to the lobby to look for a broom.

X

1

The Wrens had to leave their Queens fastness over Thanksgiving to visit Matilda's parents. They were out of touch with each other again—it was exasperating how good things never lasted: girls reopening dead issues. . . . At the best of times, George didn't like to see Matty in her old setting—it seemed to set them both back at least five years. Her father disapproved of *The Outsider* ("Communist, socialist, whatever you want to call it") and Matty seemed to find this mildly amusing. George would be helpless—what could you say to your father-in-law? "Sir, you are talking crap. As usual."

"Why do they always have to bring it up?" he said as they wriggled into the tunnel.

"Bring what up?"

"Right-wingers. Politics up. Why?"

"I don't know. They like politics, I suppose."

"He knows I disagree with him. What pleasure does he get out of proving it over and over again? It's like some duty he has to perform. Unmasking the enemy."

Matty sighed. They were crawling along behind an oppressive truck with about fifteen small license plates tacked to the back. George read them carefully. He began adding up the numbers. Visiting Matty's parents was really neither here nor there, a minor irritation. The thing that lay between them now was his letter to Twining. The combination of *that* and her woolly-pated father would make it a miserable weekend for everyone.

"I still think it was the right thing," he said.

"What was?"

"It's *his* magazine; let him clean up his own mess."

"Oh, that."

"This isn't a kindergarten, you know. I'm not telling tales behind someone's back. God, I didn't think it was possible for anyone to interpret it that way."

Matty didn't answer, but began to fuss with Peter, who was sitting up in his baby chair and twisting his plastic steering wheel ferociously from side to side.

"I wish you'd talk to me about it, Matty. I'd like to understand your position, I really would."

"Oh, let's change the subject," she said.

He did understand her position of course. She wasn't interested in details, so there was nothing to talk about: all she knew was that he had sent for Twining; he was resubmitting his will to the Master's.

"I know how you hate *The Outsider*," he said, "so this argument won't appeal to you. But the magazine is really lost without Twining. Brian can't make it. Fritz—oh God, Fritz. And then there's me."

"I'm sure you know what you're doing."

"*Christ.*" He gripped the real steering wheel. "Do you have to say it in that tone?"

She clammed up again after that, and he decided it was just as well. The licenses on the truck totalled 93,105. He began to check the number backwards, by subtraction. The Lincoln Tunnel on Thanksgiving evening was a terrible place to have an oblique argument with an illogical wife. "He probably won't come anyway," he said—that should be illogical enough for anyone. The right lane of traffic was sliding along splendidly, but the one he was in was frozen solid. "I think you really agree with your father," he said. "You think me and Twining are Communists." Silence. "What do you say, Peter? Beastly traffic, what?"

It was indeed a terrible Thanksgiving. Mr. Frobisher treated him throughout the labyrinthine family meal as if this was his first visit, and all his opinions had to be sounded.

"What do you think of Medicare?"

"I'm afraid I'm for it." "Oh." Pause: "Aid to education?" "Oh, I see."

No argument; just a most painful duty being done. It was like filling out a form for the State Department. And Matty, supra-political, watching satirically—you don't think you're really talking about politics, do you? Awful, woman's wisdom.

All the time, he was tensing and untensing over the letter he had written to Twining. If the commander hadn't answered by Monday, he, George, would surely have to resign. Two weeks of suffocating stillness had passed since the Wadsworth caper. He didn't know what the others were waiting for: but both Brian and Fritz were watching him like ferrets. He must be the winning piece that both of them needed.

One funny thing, which the gross and endless turkey reminded him of, was that neither of them had suggested taking him to lunch recently. Each had made his final bid, and had agreed to do no further canvassing—but he wasn't allowed to concentrate on this consecutively, for that gentle white-haired fool was sounding him out again. Mr. Frobisher's anxious voice seemed to follow him everywhere, out from the dining room and up the staircase, doing its distasteful job of inquiry.

"I can't stand it," he said to Matilda after dinner, "he's a nice old man and all that . . ."

Matilda stood by the bedroom window, wearing a totally unreasonable smirk. She had been a child in this place, and took on a character that George barely even recognized.

"What's the joke?"

"Nothing."

"You *stand* like that whenever I'm talking to him, by the window, by the fireplace, smirk smirk smirk, as if I'm making some kind of fool of myself."

Her smirk broadened.

"Do you know a better way to handle him? I wish you'd let me in on it."

"You're doing perfectly fine," she said.

She undressed complacently and climbed into the four-poster bed that was part of the house's charm. George had told the gang at *The Outsider* that he wanted the whole weekend off, for he had hoped to make up with Matilda, in the slow, groping way that was necessary with a nontalker; but now that he saw her, propped up like a doll in the big farmhouse bed, he began to lose heart in earnest. The wallpaper behind her was a mosaic of little girls wheeling baby carriages: there was a miniature baby-blue chest of drawers in the far left corner. He climbed into the big stupid bed and shut his eyes.

"I think I'd better go back to town tomorrow," he said.

"All right."

"I'll drive back on Sunday to pick up you and Peter."

"Fine."

He was too irritated to touch her, but he could imagine her smirking beside him in the dark like a phosphorescent statue. It was hard to sleep, hard to get his mind to fuddle properly. He thought she might be telling him in her silent way that if Twining came back, that was the end; but that didn't really sound like her. Anyhow, it was no use asking her. The droning of Mr. Frobisher had obviously killed her sense of words, years ago, and had forced her to find other means of making her point.

If he stayed here till Monday, he would probably wind up using sign language himself. Listening to that good gray man, you lost first the taste for words, and then any sense of their relative values, and finally their actual meanings; all lost in the gentle burble.

He got to sleep at last by pretending he was listening to Mr. Frobisher talking about the inflated dollar.

He left at first light, before anyone could get at him again. Mr. Frobisher heard a noise and came down in his dressing gown to talk, but George was halfway into his overcoat by then. Mr. Frobisher followed him to the storm door and waved a wan goodbye.

There was a blustery headwind all the way into town, and George found himself pointing ferociously into it. The muffled gray blast on the windshield and the sense that it was terribly cold outside the car invigorated him, poised him for happenings. It was only as he got within sight of New York that it occurred to him that he wasn't really going anywhere. He had no wish to spend the afternoon fencing with Brian and Fritz. The day after Thanksgiving was one of those nonexistent days; no crisis was ever resolved the day after Thanksgiving.

He thought of going to the Museum of Modern Art, to catch up on his general culture—amazing how journalism, even high-class journalism, thinned you out—but settled instead on an Italian movie. Sex *and* culture. The movie was full of big empty rooms and the sound of footsteps on tiles. He didn't even attempt to pick up the story but sat hunched among these bleak images and hollow reverberations, thinking his own thoughts.

Matty's inarticulateness gave her certain oracular powers. Silent people impressed him as having rich instinctual lives like animals. If Matty scented something wrong in a situation, it was probably there—though her verbal analysis would be disappointingly trite, of course.

People like Matty saw like Indian scouts and heard like blind people (was it true that blind people could "hear" a wall in front of them?) and smelt like retrievers—funny world they must live in. The screen showed an enormous white bedroom. A sexy scene was coming up, and he sprang to brief attention. Movies were certainly getting raunchier . . . but not raunchy enough. The scene dissolved into a long, empty vista.

Matty wasn't that good, he told himself severely. She was no Indian scout. Her instinctual life was corrupted and banal like everyone else's. Being bad at words didn't protect her from them—quite the reverse. She was, like most inarticulate people, completely at the mercy of clichés. Her interpretation of the current situation was an insult to everyone concerned. Matty must simply be ignored in this case.

After the movie, he killed some time at the Russian Tea Room, and after that he went and shot some pool. It was a pleasure he had missed lately: soft-shoeing around the green baize table, and listening to the old click-thud. He shot three games, and then began to get careless with his shots, and then bored. Every now and then, someone would come up and watch, and then try to hustle him, which was a king-size bore. At six o'clock he turned in his cue and, rather at a loss, strolled in the direction of *The Outsider*. Brian and Fritz would be off now, pacing their cages, planning more devilment for next Monday. The place would be deserted. He could sit at his desk and write letters, and go to the magazine rack and read back numbers of *The New Republic* and consider the day well spent.

He selected the right key and stabbed it into the outer door. An office at night, a city on Sunday, were real pleasures in a clotted life like his. He mustn't let the earwigs spook him this time. He switched on the light in the rattle-trap elevator and began the mangy ascent.

Goddammit, somebody was working late. There was a light in one of the editor's offices. He thought of reversing the elevator, but it made too much noise.

"Hello, is somebody there?"

Christ, and he knew *that* voice, all right. Standing by the door of his cubicle now, as if he had never left. Whatever became of the old-fashioned waistcoat?

"George—it's you. You gave me an awful fright."

All right then, but I'll not go to Sweeney's with you. Not for more than an hour anyway.

2

"You're looking well, Mr. Twining."

"Thank you, George. I feel very fit."

The Good Conversation—Twining still held out the prospect, dangled it on a golden string.

"It's good to see you here," George found himself saying. "You dress the place up."

Twining nodded, as at the sober truth. The ratty-looking office was one of his most amusing props. Without him, it was an abandoned stage set.

"I gather some rum things have been happening in my absence," he said.

"Yes. You could call them rum, I suppose."

"We'll have to see what we can do."

Twining picked up a copy of the magazine that he had left open on his desk, and began to read, making marks with a red pencil. His hip sidled languidly along the desk and finally dropped into the chair below, while he read obliviously on, and George stood by: waiting for he knew not what.

When Twining had finished every word of the issue, he reached for another. There was a pile underneath that, which would keep them here until morning.

"Is there anything I can do?" said George. "Do you want to have a drink downstairs?"

"Not at the moment, thanks very much. Perhaps you can tell me if Brian and Fritz have left town for the weekend? I'd like to have all this cleaned up by Monday if possible."

"By *Monday?* Are you kidding?"

Twining smiled. "Well, perhaps not. But we can make a start. How about Brian to begin with? I suppose he's spending the weekend with that frightful nephew of his, Sam Thingummy. The chap with the awful wife."

"Wife? I didn't know you knew them."

"Oh yes, I know them all right. I had to endure a whole Sunday with them once upon a time. Sheer torture. Taking Sam's measure, so to say: Brian thought he would be ideal for *The Outsider.*"

"I guess I didn't mention Sam in my letter, did I?"

"What—don't tell me he's been around again?" Twining smiled thinly. George felt sick with embarrassment, for all of them. He was now their representative, and was obliged to put a face on everything they'd done, even Sam.

"Sam isn't so bad. I'm sorry about his wife." George paused. "Being awful, I mean."

"And you mean to say that Fritz didn't raise any objections to Sam?"

"Not around me he didn't."

"Hm, I see."

Twining picked up another issue, and started to read. His damn hip began to sidle along the desk. He certainly knows how to hold a magazine, thought George. It was like watching a first-rate actor demonstrating magazine-holding.

"Look, if there's nothing . . ." said George pointedly, although he had nowhere else to go.

"What's that? Oh, I'm sorry. Do sit down."

The suggestion was unexpected and George complied automatically, flicking up the skirts of his overcoat. A few minutes later, Twining said, "That'll do, I think. I'll give Brian a ring now. He *might* be in."

He dialed Brian's number without having to check it. That was the kind of thing that kept one in his power.

"Hello, is that you, Brian? . . . Gilbert here."

And Fritz Tyler thought that *he* was good at looking amused. Twining leaned back in his swivel chair, removing his face from the glare of the desk light. George could just picture old Brian spluttering distraught greetings at the other end. Twining was smiling in the shadows.

"Much better, thank you. Yes, the heart is perfectly sound."

George felt he was being invited to join him in another delicate smile, but he felt too sorry for Brian; fancy putting him in the hands of this cruel bastard. Why did I have to write that crumby letter?

"I was thinking of dropping over for a few minutes. How

does that sound? . . . Well, I could make it tomorrow morning if you prefer; around breakfast time." Brian's voice came through as anxious static. "No good either? I see. Well, that *is* awkward." More static. "Are you quite sure, Brian? . . . Good, excellent . . . yes, George has given me an idea of what's been . . . very good. I'll be over in a few minutes, then."

Twining replaced the receiver gently and stood up.

"Would you care to come along? I'm going to see Brian."

"I don't think I should."

"Why not?"

"Well—I feel like a scab, for one thing."

"Nonsense."

Twining took his coat off the peg and shrugged it on. He didn't bother to explain why George's suggestion was nonsense. And George couldn't very well just stand there. Having called down Twining, he supposed he must take some part in the action.

"I'd be in the way," he said.

"Nonsense."

Twining helped him into his coat. "It may be quite useful to you. Some day you may find yourself in a similar situation . . ." He picked up his marked copy of the magazine and put it in his outer pocket. "I shan't be unkind," he said.

George felt like the Great Detective's stooge as he stumbled out after Twining, pulling the rusty chain that turned out the light in Twining's cubicle and steering across the foyer by strips of street light. "I think we'll pay a call on Detective Lestrade." "Very well, Holmes." And then the sense of panting to keep up.

Twining didn't talk in the taxi, except to say that he

found New York rather chillier than California. If you could call that talking.

George had never seen Brian in his native lair. It was a desolate new building with corridors like Reading Gaol; he felt like doom as he walked past the cell doors: 15F, 15G— Twining is the hangman and I am the chaplain. I should have a bell. He expected Brian to be quivering in a corner, but imagination had played him false. Brian came to the door of 15H in a velvet smoking jacket, and said, "Good evening, Gilbert," and threw in the barest of nods for George.

"It's good to have you back, Gilbert."

"Why, thank you, Brian."

"Let me get you a drink."

"No, thanks."

Brian looked slightly upset at this. He had a drink of his own, half finished on the naked mantelpiece. George decided that it would be a simple kindness to join him, would give so much pleasure, etc., so he said yes, and Brian fixed him one quickly—as if he was ready for his big scene with Twining, but wouldn't be ready for long.

"So—how are *you*, Brian?" said Twining. "Your back and so forth."

"I'm fine."

"Backs can be an awful nuisance. I ought to know." He gave his a rueful pat.

Brian's eyes bulged expectantly. But Gilbert took a long time getting to any sort of point. He talked amusingly about his own back—at least, *he* seemed to be amused—and of the effect of various types of weather on it. George's suspicion that the commander had lost his marbles was reactivated. Brian became totally bemused, and he nodded several times like a man in a dream.

George's mind wandered slightly. The austerity of Brian's apartment reminded him for some curious reason of an evening he had spent with his father a couple of years ago. Mr. Wren had come up from Florida for a few days, and had promptly contracted flu in a second-class hotel. George remembered sitting at the foot of the bed, talking very much as Twining was talking now about minor health problems. His father had a magazine on his lap which he was too tired to read; and he was looking altogether very old and moist, with a bad case of the gronking sniffles. The only other furnishings were a vaporizer on his bedtable, and a Kleenex box that he kept reaching for listlessly. And George had thought, I can't just leave him like this; a man of his age shouldn't be alone in a room of this particular type . . .

He noticed that Brian was staring at Twining with a look that might almost be mistaken for fear. It was as if he too had remembered that hotel room—but he was staring at Twining's hands; and George noticed for the first time that the commander was holding the marked copy of *The Outsider* and tapping it with his finger.

"Well now, the magazine." Twining sounded humorously businesslike, like a chairman on an amateur committee. "It looks to me as if you've all done quite a creditable job in my absence. Simply keeping the flag flying is no small triumph. I know how deadly those summer months can be."

Brian kept his eyes on Twining's fingers, as if they were a door opening on something horrible. Twining toyed with the pages, opening, closing, opening again.

"I imagine a lion's share of the credit goes to *you,* Brian. George tells me you were more or less in charge of things. Let me congratulate you on your presence of mind."

Brian nodded under the lash of the compliment.

"Everybody pitched in," he said.

"Indeed?" said Twining. "I'm delighted to hear it. Well, perhaps we should let it go at that. However," and the fingers wrenched the magazine open so sharply that even George jumped a little, "I did notice a few things in glancing through this issue—I mention this in no spirit of criticism, mind you." He turned the magazine round, and it was disfigured with red marks, as if Twining had been bleeding it back to health. "Considering what you were up against."

Brian opened his mouth, but Twining ignored him and said, "Could you come here a jiffy, or shall I come over there?" Brian said, "For godsake, Gilbert, it's eleven o'clock on a Friday night. The mistakes can't be that important, can they?"

The lines of authority were as usual so vague with Twining, the whole scene so ill-defined, that you never knew what was insolence and what was fair comment. It occurred to George that this might be why the British didn't have a constitution.

"We didn't do things that badly, did we?" he chimed in. "I thought it was the same old lovable magazine—"

"Still the court jester, eh, George?" Twining said sharply. George was needless to say taken off balance. A pox on all smoothness.

"I said it was creditable, Brian, and so it was. But in normal circumstances, this sort of thing wouldn't really do. We can postpone discussion till Monday if you like, but I'm afraid discussion there must be, at some point. It's fatally easy for a magazine to slide into bad habits, you know."

Twining had pulled this trick three times this evening, and so far it had worked twice. Offering to postpone the unpleasantness. Brian couldn't face waiting, couldn't live with something hanging over him, and Twining had spotted this.

"Let's leave it till Monday," said George quickly. "Then Fritz can join in too."

Brian dithered: "There's always that, of course. On the other hand, maybe we're making too much out of this. Hell, I've been in the business for how many years, and I know I'm not going to make that many mistakes. There may be a difference of opinion on what constitutes a mistake, eh, Gilbert?"

"Perhaps, perhaps not. Shall I come to you or shall you come to me?"

3

"You can't have been serious, Brian . . . honestly, Brian . . ."

After a few minutes, George knew perfectly well it was bluff. Twining's corrections were of a logician's triviality; the kind of thing a clever lawyer would use if he had to defend a hopeless case. The worst you could say was that Twining could have done precisely the same to one of his own issues.

George sat back benignly waiting for this farrago to cease: at which point he would make these very comments . . . It was a long wait, though, and he went to the kitchen and made himself a second drink. Twining was making up for the thinness of his case by stretching it to intolerable length. Brian's face creased in weariness; he seemed to be having trouble following the commander's tortuosities. "I'm sorry, I don't get that," he said at one point.

"You don't? My dear man—look, I'll explain it once more. And do try to attend."

Brian looked miserable. He must know that Twining was talking a lot of crap, but the sheer weight of it seemed to be getting him down. A little later he said, "Don't you think this is all rather picayune, Gilbert?"

"Frankly, no. I happen to think that these things matter. I happen to think—"

George was about to say, oh come off it, Gilbert old thing. But he was still smarting from that court-jester crack. Twining had made him feel silly, and robbed him of his magic powers, before starting on Fine.

The electric clock purred around twelve, swooped around twelve-thirty, flung itself around one. It was awfully stuffy in here, but George was awakened from time to time by the small schoolteacher asperities, patronizing and sarcastic, with which Twining spiced his analysis. Brian took them all on his bowed neck, not answering now, not looking up—my God, this was getting beyond a joke. George suddenly realized that Twining was cold-bloodedly wearing the man out. Since the specific criticisms were quite meaningless, it followed that the whole affair was an exercise in raw power. Twining could have made his marks at random on any issue; they were only a pretext for beating up Brian.

Brian looked up in puffy despair. He was smart enough to know what Twining was doing. His despair might come from realizing that he couldn't conjure up one of his special new rages. Twining's whole manner would have made it seem childish: but beyond that, he probably just couldn't do it, physically. It was as if Twining had his hands round his windpipe.

"For godsake, Gilbert, we're only at page 23," Brian said.

"Yes, I'll try to make my points a bit briefer. I know it's very tiresome for you." Twining looked at him almost fondly. "If your back bothers you, we can resume this discussion on Monday."

George was tempted again to intervene for humane reasons. But what the hell, he *had* called Twining back from the Coast; he *did* want to see Brian dislodged. Brian was underdog once more, but this rotation had to stop at some point: Brian would just have to stay on the bottom.

He dozed off on that thought, and when he opened his eyes the clock said ten to three. Brian and Twining were still talking but in the next room, Brian's small bedroom. They must have gone there not to disturb him. He could just see their knees and feet facing each other.

"Is it true," the mellower than mellow tones of the captain, "that you had a run-in with Miss Marplate?"

"Well yes," came the lighter, virginal answer—this voice had to lose to the first one, whatever the argument was about—"sort of. You know the tensions . . . summertime, small office . . ."

"I also heard—and this I do find it hard to credit—that you quarreled over money. Her money, this can't be true, can it?"

It sounded absolutely insane when put like that.

"Well, I guess it did come up," Brian fluted. "I didn't know she had so much of it. I was shocked for a moment."

"Honestly, Brian. I can see that it's high time I came back." He said this with good-humored indulgence; annoyed? my dear fellow.

"I guess you're right," said Brian. George wanted to cover his face in his hands.

"I could have told you about Olga years ago." Twining stretched his legs. "I thought of asking her for a contribution myself, once upon a time. But one could see at a second glance that she was, well, not the type. What's the American phrase for it—tight-assed?"

The knees uncrossed and Twining was standing in the doorway smiling to himself.

"I'm afraid you'll never make a fund-raiser, Brian old boy. I only hope you haven't impaired Olga's effectiveness permanently. I shall have to have a special talk with her."

That should have been enough; but if Twining seemed to have a little weakness, it was not knowing when to stop.

He said, "I also hear that you hired your nephew Sam . . . can this be true?"

God, how he hated that voice, those indecently modulated noises. A voice that held in it the promise of the Good Conversation should not be used for this cheap bullying; it was a monstrous perversion. There was absolutely no need to throw in Sam. George stood up and said in a loud voice, "I'm going."

Twining turned round and said, "Ah, you're awake, George. Yes, that's an excellent idea. I'm afraid I've kept you up, Brian. I hope your back doesn't protest too vehemently in the morning."

Brian led them mutely to the door, as if he was trying hard to remember what he'd said—knowing that it was bad, but not yet sure how bad. "I'll see you on Monday," said Twining. "And perhaps we can discuss a well-earned holiday for you then."

"This jacket was a gift," said Brian aimlessly as he showed them out.

They strolled back along the corridor, and Twining said, "These buildings never seem to get properly finished. Have you noticed that?"

"No," said George. He was weighing his own complicity in this scene, the curious sense of being victim and oppressor all in one.

"Bits of plaster on the carpet, ladders lying about—however, perhaps my experience has not been typical."

They rang for the self-service elevator ("I hope the last one hasn't left," said Twining), and when they were safely on board, Twining said, "There, that wasn't too bad, was it?"

He leaned against the plastic wall and added, in a meditative voice, "One tries so hard not to hurt feelings, but it's difficult to tell what's right with Americans. I know I've made some terrible mistakes. With all of you."

Thanks a lot, you're a big man, Commander.

"But I did praise his efforts," Twining brightened, "and I think he liked it when I mentioned a holiday. So perhaps it will be all right."

His back hadn't troubled him in years. It would be attributing too much power to Twining to say that it troubled him now: but he did in some obscure way feel *physically* defective now. He moved slowly, although the limp was in no specific place, into the next room, where he took a clean pair of pajamas from the drawer and put them on, infinitely laboriously; and felt an incongruous wave of sexual longing which passed. He thought limply of the many ways of killing oneself, and slid like drowning into a delicious sleep.

4

George slept by himself in the Queens apartment feeling disproportionately lonely. There was an effulgence of street light and neon, and the bars of Peter's empty playpen were starkly visible every time he opened his eyes, until he finally got up and moved the pen into the living room.

At eight o'clock the phone rang, with early morning briskness. "George, is that you?"

"Yes, that's me, all right." It was nice to talk to anyone, after such a desolate night. "What's on your mind, Gilbert?"

"I was thinking of paying a few calls, and wondered if you'd care to come along?"

"You going to call on Fritz, you mean?"

"Probably, yes."

"I wouldn't want to miss that."

"You will come along, then?"

It was unusual to have two days in a row as indefinite as this. He could go with Twining to another bloodletting, or he could see another Italian movie. He savored the experience of choice briefly.

"If you haven't had breakfast yet, perhaps you'd care to have a bite with me."

"All right."

"See you at Schrafft's in half an hour?"

"All right. Better make it forty minutes."

So much for *that*. Choice, indeed. He shaved morosely, listening to the rasping buzz on his chin with more than usual attention. His skin felt raw and a tuft of his hair wouldn't stay down when he tried to comb it. Those were the surface effects of solitude.

Twining looked as if he'd been up for hours. He had a slight tan, from drinking tea on some damn patio, and his hair shone from thousands of crisp brushings. Goldback military brushes. Thirty times on each side. It was all curiously depressing.

"I've called Fritz and the others. I don't know how much we'll have time for today . . ."

Twining had had his own breakfast long since and was toying with a cup of coffee.

"What do you plan to tell them?"

"That depends on what they tell me."

George had his mouth full of pancake, so Twining did such talking as there was. He said, "It's curious that you're all in town for the weekend. I think it says something about the magazine that you all cling to New York so obsessively. *The Outsider* has become more New Yorky than I had realized . . .

"Have you ever been West, George? You should. You should make it a point. A fascinating experience . . .

270

"Have you by any chance seen anything of my wife? I talked to her this morning and she told me she'd been to the office. She's divorcing me, you know . . ."

"That's too bad," George managed to say.

"I suppose. Yes, I suppose."

The commander ordered more coffee and said, "I'm not supposed to drink the stuff, you know, but I can't take Schrafft's coffee seriously. Yes, I used to cling to New York myself, so I know how easily it can happen. Many goblins lurk here . . ."

He said nothing at all about what he planned to do with Fritz; but George supposed that the basis of his strategy was to keep them all waiting in their various corners, not knowing when he would strike. There would be something specially awful about sitting around in a city apartment, feeling that you can't go out, that you can't make plans . . .

"I'm thinking seriously of taking up golf again," said Twining. "I used to play it at Cambridge, you know. Do you play anything, George? . . . you should, you know. It gives one a sense of proportion about things. I don't believe anyone at *The Outsider* plays games . . ."

George had some more pancakes, at the commander's insistence. "Build up your strength. I was going to propose that we use your car, if you don't mind." So that was what this was all about.

"O.K., sure."

"Should take up golf," said the captain.

They drove through pleasantly empty streets to an address in the Bronx. It surprised George to realize that he didn't know precisely where any of his colleagues lived. That was another mark to put against *The Outsider*, alongside the shortage of golf players and the refusal to leave New York.

But it turned out that they weren't visiting a member of the staff at all. The name blotched on tape and stuck into the dilapidated register was *W. Funk.*

"Wally saves most of his splendor for the public life," commented Twining as he exchanged buzzes with Wally's button. "The upkeep on his façade is quite ruinous, so his private life has to be somewhat penurious."

They climbed three flights of stairs, at the top of which stood Wally, tousled but regal in a monogrammed red dressing gown. "Oh, it's you, Twining," he said. George was beginning to feel slightly invisible. He said, "Hello, Wally," but didn't expect an answer and didn't get one.

"Christ, Gilbert," Wally said, and his fat lower lip began to shake right away. Gilbert touched his arm and steered him back into his own apartment. And all the way to an armchair by the window.

George looked around. An artist's studio in the style of, he bet, Louis Quinze. A gray window shaft beyond. Wally sat hunched and lost like a deposed monarch. Twining sat across from him on the daybed, tapping his finger patiently on the quilt.

"Christ, Gilbert, what's happening at your magazine?"

Gilbert shrugged.

"Well, if you don't know, who does? Does Wren here know?"

"Morning, Wally," said George.

"Christ, I may have slipped, but I haven't slipped *that* far, I haven't slipped beneath Harriet Eustace—whoever *she* is. And it isn't as if they had handled the thing *gracefully.*"

If you can't keep your lower lip in line, you'd better not talk at all, thought George. But Twining was quickly sympathetic.

"There's been a confusion," he said.

"I'll say there has. The plain discourtesy! That's what I can't get used to, Gilbert. I make no great claims for myself as a critic . . ."

Twining made a "not-at-all" gesture.

". . . but minimal courtesy . . . And I do fancy . . . and after all these years . . ." George tuned out. Losers were not one of his interests. He remembered how he had once quivered to Wally's weekly opinions; had watched his gradual descent into peevishness, the brocade thickening over his prose—but always with the thought that this was a great man going down, a whale capsizing—not a loser whining and fishing for compliments.

"Of course you're still a first-rate critic, Wally," said Twining.

"Some people don't seem to think so."

"Some people don't know what they're talking about."

"I never write where I'm not wanted, you know."

George said, "You got any coffee, Wally?"

"But of course you're wanted at *The Outsider*, Wally . . ."

George stood up and wandered into the next room. One of the advantages of being invisible was that it gave you the run of the house. Louis Quinze was putting it much too simply. The bathroom was a baroque bird's-nest. When he flushed the toilet he expected bird song, organ music, or both. The boudoir featured a serpentine green chandelier and a bowl full of tropical fish. He would never be able to take Wally's reviews seriously again.

It slightly bothered him, as a point of tactics, that Twining should take such pains smoothing Wally's fur. Wally was long overdue for a boot in the tail. This soft treatment had a sick-room flavor about it—it kept Wally sick, it kept him in his dressing gown all the time.

When George wandered back into the front room, the

atmosphere had sweetened even more. Technically, Wally was still pouting, but there was real pleasure in his small eyes. "You don't think I'm that good, judging by the way you cut my copy," he said archly.

"You're a Dionysian writer, Wally, as I've told you so often. We disciples of Apollo must trim the exuberances at times."

That's talking his language, thought George. I guess it is, anyway.

"But give me a Dionysian writer any day, with the blazing insights, the broad, flashing strokes. We drudges can do the pruning, the tidying up after the hurricane. But what can we do in the wake of a drizzle? How can you prune a tame writer?"

Wally wriggled shamelessly in his chair; he was so pleased he didn't know where to hide it.

"That's a very slick explanation, Gilbert," he said, and they both laughed.

"No, but it's true, and you know it, and I won't say anything more about it. The long and the short of it is that I'm an old pedant—but you're an artist. I couldn't do what you do. It's somewhat like a coach and his star athlete."

At any moment George expected Wally to lumber over and sit in coach's lap. The cadences were almost those of mother and son.

"Don't you ever open a window around here?" he asked.

No answer, of course. No wonder Wally was such a mess. George thought of the number of times that Wally had come billowing into the office, waving his mutilated copy. And then the simpering noises from Twining's cubicle. The "look here, Gilbert . . . but really, Gilbert"—Wally was allowed to play the little man, the bristling homunculus, so long as it was understood that Mother's word was final.

"You're very restless, George," said Twining.

"Yes." George turned with a snarl. "I think I'm illegally parked."

"We must go, Walter. We have some calls to make. Where did I put my coat?"

As Wally scuffled happily in the closet, the commander said, "So anyway, do send your next column to me, marked 'personal' or to George here . . ."

Wally turned and looked at George: rather insolently, now that he was back in Mummy's favor.

"I must apologize again for the unpleasantness—it's unforgivable, for a man of your stature. However, I shall see to it—" George started down the stairs. Wally had handed him his coat, but *helped* the commander into his. Catch me coming to see you again, Funk—a fellow has feelings, you know.

The commander joined him on the second landing. "Writers are a special breed," he explained. "You have to jolly them." George thought, supposing I throw up right here in the lobby, will he get the point?

"Wally is capable of fine criticism, on his day, and Americans seem to be impressed by him," said Twining. "It's worth making a little effort to keep him happy."

"Don't you think you laid it on just a teeny bit thick?"

"Not for a writer. You can't lay it on too thick for writers. Besides," added Twining, "there's a balance to redress here. I think that Wally has been treated barbarically."

George could picture Wally Funk sitting up there on his royal toilet seat, wallowing in praise for the rest of the day, spongy and spoiled like a child king; and he thought about Brian and how wretched he must be feeling today; and he thought, people take Twining too damn seriously around here.

"Where to, boss-man?" he asked, and Twining smiled,

not taking *himself* seriously in the least. The whole point of this rancid interlude might just have been to show himself off as a good fellow: to display the kindly side of power. He smiled at George. "Can you face Philo?"

They bundled back into the car. "Ominous-looking weather," said the captain. "Snow in the air."

"Where does Philo hang out, then?"

"Head for the Harlem River Drive and I'll show you." Twining lolled in the front seat. "Are you one of those who find the autumn depressing, George? Or does the prospect of winter exhilarate you?"

"Can't say I give much of a crap one way or the other."

"Ah, a philosopher."

Twining began to examine the dashboard. "Nice little cars, these. At least, when I say 'little' . . ."

"What are the tactics for Philo?"

"Tactics? No tactics. Find out what's on his mind, that's all. I hope this isn't beginning to bore you."

"No. Morbid curiosity should keep me going for a spell yet."

"You can wait outside if you like, or go to a bar."

"No, thanks."

George was hoping for some word of commentary to link the scenes. Why, for instance, was Twining going in this particular order? It sure as hell wasn't for geographical convenience; and Sonnabend came after Marplate in the alphabet.

"When I was a boy," said Twining, "I used to look forward tremendously to winter. Now I don't know."

And again—why bother to see Sonnabend at all? George hadn't said anything about Philo in his letter. So far as he knew, Philo was one of the few neutral zones at the office.

"We used to have a genuine Yule log, and my father invited the villagers in, they used to be tenants, but friends too, in a way. All that sort of thing has changed . . . for the better of course. But the fact is, I have never looked forward to Christmas since."

Ah, shut up.

5

Philo was wearing a tweed sports jacket with a mammoth flap in the back. "Where's your horse?" said George, and Philo smiled—a wonderful sport, Philo. You could say anything to him. Jane Sonnabend came up behind in a tweed suit. "Hello, Mr. Twining," she said. "I hope you're feeling better."

Gilbert shook hands very warmly with both of them, as if he had come to New York especially to see them. "It's good . . . to . . . see . . . you, Philo . . . Jane." He heaved across the foyer, like a man who had come in from the cold, rubbing his hands and puffing cheerfully. "I've missed you two, how *are* you both."

"Fine." "Fine." "We're both fine, I guess."

"Good, good." Twining hung up his coat, and stood back to let them lead him into the living room: which they did in rather confused tandem. George tried to catch Twining's eye, to exchange a quick smirk: but the old boy seemed totally sincere. He plunged enthusiastically after the Sonnabends, with his hand high up in his jacket pocket, asking questions about Jane's health, about Wilkins the cat, about Philo's trick knee. He must have been reading a book about the Sonnabends while he was in the hospital.

George sank into a big leather armchair. He had never met Jane before, and was inevitably amused by her teeth. Had they grown to look like Philo's over the years, or had they started like that and been attracted to Philo's by some orthodontic magnetism? One interesting difference was that they didn't smile as Philo's did while in repose, but looked rather schoolmarmish. George had an immediate impression of being personally disapproved of, for some trifling mistake in grammar.

"So, how has life been treating you in my absence, Philo—busy as usual, I suppose."

"Yes—yes. I've been keeping busy."

"Everything all right?"

"I guess so." He looked at George. And Jane looked at George. A smile from him and a frown from her—what are they trying to tell me?

"Don't mind George," said Twining. "If there's anything you want to say."

"No, there isn't anything."

George thought of offering to leave, and then thought to hell with that. Jane was really glaring at him now, and he was beginning to resent it slightly. He couldn't care less what was on Philo's mind, but he was damned if he was going to let this funny-looking woman stare him out of her living room.

"I gather Mr. Fine has been looking after things in my absence," he said. "I'm afraid I hadn't thought—one never thinks, does one—that anything quite so sudden would remove me from the scene. A lesson."

"We were shocked," said Jane.

"Anyway, you all seem to have done quite well without me. Not as much advertising as one would like to see, but that's an old problem, isn't it? And perhaps our own advertising has been a little pedestrian, another old problem. As a matter of fact, I've been thinking about that—"

Philo started to speak and then hesitated. Jane started too, and the result was a three-way jam. "Go ahead." "No, you go ahead." "I'm sorry."

"Say it, Philo," Jane stage-whispered fiercely. "You shouldn't try to cover up, after what he's done to *you*."

They looked at George again, but perfunctorily this time.

They were ready to talk now, whether he left or not. Philo took an unexpected meerschaum pipe out of his pocket and began fooling with it.

"Well, it's nothing really, nothing at all. But since Jane insists, no, I haven't got on all that well with *Mr.* Fine."

"What seemed to be the trouble?"

"I found him"—he began waving a sequence of matches over the pipe—"arrogant and . . . dictatorial and . . . difficult to work with."

"Do you think you can be more specific about that?"

"Well, yes. I began with every intention of cooperating with Brian. Until *you* got back, that is. And"—he pulled unsuccessfully on the pipe—"he did ask me for ideas at first. And"—he began waving matches again—"probably the ideas weren't very practical, I know you've rejected ideas of mine, I'm used to that"—Twining nodded approvingly, as if Philo had done just the right thing. "But you were always courteous about it, you always listened at least. Mr. Fine became very brusque. Then he began to avoid me altogether. And *then,* to top it all, he began to lose his temper with me."

Twining clicked his teeth sadly. "He must have been under a strain, I suppose."

"Well, that may be. But after all, all I asked of him was common courtesy. That doesn't seem like too much, does it? A man who won't look up as he passes your desk"—the pipe was drawing now, and sparking like a bonfire—"a man who won't acknowledge your greeting, or ask after your wife—and of course, he didn't ask my advice about the ads, *oh* no, not Brian, *he* knew all about advertising, just as he knew all about accounting—ask Olga about that sometime—and all about editing and I don't know what he didn't know all about . . ."

George felt faintly stunned. He had no idea that Philo

279

expected to be greeted every morning, or have his wife asked after. George hadn't even known he had a wife.

George remembered, a hundred years ago, sitting in Luigi's watching Brian and Philo and Olga, huddled together over lunch, and he remembered thinking, I'll make them my favorite underdogs. In real life, they were more like a pack of alley cats, weren't they? Almost undistinguishable from *rich* people.

"I didn't find Brian so hard to work with," George interrupted truculently. "Frankly, I think Brian is a pretty good man."

They looked round at him sharply. His words sobered Philo instantly like cold water. He said, "Of course, it isn't important, I wouldn't have brought it up if you hadn't asked, Mr. Twining."

Twining was silent a moment, and the Sonnabends watched him like musicians watching the conductor. It was up to him to approve or disapprove Philo's attitude: if he approved, it was a good attitude; otherwise, Philo had let himself go unforgivably.

"You were quite right to tell me," Twining said at last. "These things are unfortunate." He shook his head. "It's my fault for leaving things in such a confusion."

Philo relaxed and basked. Jane stopped frowning. It was really too much. Twining's methods were so goddamn threadbare. This must have been the way they dealt with Kaffirs in the old days, a little child psychology, a little bluff—but most of all, that godlike manner, that gift of absolution. Twining had probably treated Philo more contemptuously than Brian ever had, yet here was Philo licking his hand . . .

George reflected that Brian's ads were just the same as Twining's ads. It was only his bedside manner that had failed—maybe he didn't despise people like Sonnabend *enough;* maybe *that* was Twining's edge.

Well, it was late in the day to be sticking up for Brian. George had sent for the hangman himself—better let him get on with the job, in his own way.

Philo didn't say much more. He refused to be drawn out about Fritz—perhaps he was afraid that George would pounce on him again, and say, "Fritz is a *good man.*" Twining talked for a few minutes about advertising policy, pausing now and then to sound Philo's reactions; but Philo was mute now, even on his own subject. He said, "I guess you're right, Mr. Twining . . . why don't we try that, Mr. Twining?" He seemed to have forfeited his claim to an opinion about anything at all.

The Sonnabends invited them to stay for lunch but Twining refused for both. "We have some calls to make," he said.

They wolfed a quick sandwich at a nearby luncheonette, and George said, "I didn't know that Philo was such a crumb. Talking like that about Brian."

"Philo has a lot of resentments," said Twining. "It's like hay fever. It doesn't do to take them personally."

"Really? Philo has resentments?"

"Certainly. He resents me. He resents you. He resents everybody. You've got to learn to spot these things, George."

"So why did you encourage him?"

"I suppose you could call it a species of therapy. You have to release some of the excess resentment every few months. I gathered that no one's been doing it in my absence."

"You're a cold-blooded bastard, Twining. I'm sorry, but I mean it."

"Perhaps, perhaps." Twining rubbed his forehead wearily. For the first time, it occurred to George that these interviews might be tiring for him. "I won't argue the point. By the way, do you know a curious thing about Philo? He's actually a rather right-wing republican. I couldn't have been more surprised, when I discovered it. Why he goes on with us is one of life's more amusing mysteries." He paused and frowned. "Have you noticed, by any chance, how difficult it is to get a really decent ham sandwich these days?"

He seemed to be husbanding his strength for some invisible exertion. So George said no, he hadn't noticed, and they talked about ham sandwiches for the balance of the meal.

George decided to skip the Marplate interview, partly because the prospect was too grotesque even for his taste, and partly to save a little curiosity for the main event—the showdown with Fritz this evening. He drove Twining over to Marplate's house, and walked the few blocks to Washington Square and sat on a bench. He could see what Twining meant about the coming of winter. The children in the playground didn't seem to mind the cold at all. But suppose you were an old man who knew he was going to die before spring? The almost palpable shrinking of the days, the gray chill, everything closing down . . . George, neither old nor young, neither poetry nor prose, felt betwixt and between.

He decided to phone Matilda, for comfort, but it was a cheap impulse, and he wasn't surprised to find her dimly, long-distancely chilly. He knew he had ruined the dreadful weekend, she didn't have to tell him; he had also—what was that, Twining was back? She was silent. Oh, God. Oh double-God.

There were scratches in her soft voice like an old phonograph record. If you were an old man expecting to die before spring, that was just what people would probably sound like. "Do whatever you think best," she said. Outside the phone booth, the desolation of a large drugstore.

Matilda fell drearily silent at the other end. Just as she could never start a conversation, so she could never put down a telephone. "O.K., I'll see you tomorrow then," he said. "Tell your parents I'm sorry." A fishlike face appeared on the glass of the booth. Someone wanting desperately to get in. He hung up sadly.

He might as well get back to Twining, at this rate.

6

With any luck, the worst of the interview would be over by now. He imagined unspeakable flirtation. Olga, you've been a brick. Oh, Captain Twining. Oh, Captain—the pair of them draw closer, closer, as if magnetized, her bosom, his brass buttons—until suddenly they start to sing. "Ah, sweet mystery of life, at last I've found you."

He walked up the steps, and was surprised to find that Marplate apparently occupied the whole house. Business must be good. No, that's right, Olga has money. He could well imagine Brian losing his temper upon discovering this; he was vaguely annoyed himself.

"Oh, it's you," she said, and for a moment he thought she was going to say, "you're late." But for once she looked passably cordial; and her bark was quite friendly. (As well for you, kiddo! One more icy reception and he might just have bitten somebody's bosom.) She had a fire going in the living room, at which Twining was toasting himself. He had a ledger balanced on his knee and was sipping out of a porcelain cup. "Ah, there, George," he said.

George accepted a cup of tea, sank back, shut his eyes, squinted them half open to light a cigarette: in this particular underwater ballet, Olga Marplate seemed to be fluttering diaphanously around Twining, offering him bits of paper. She must have gone to the office this morning to get them. Twining was being very businesslike. He even had on a pair of glasses, as a sort of stage prop, halfway down his nose. George said, "I didn't know you wore glasses."

"I got them in California. Just for reading. I suppose vanity had kept one from doing so sooner."

It was typical of George's relationship with Twining that he still didn't know whether to call him Mr. Twining or Gilbert. When he asked about the glasses, Olga looked around, and she too was wearing spectacles: businesswoman spectacles. It seemed like a bond between her and the colonel. They put on their spectacles and made fiscal love.

He was beginning to spawn a sort of theory about these visits: perhaps Twining was restaging some bit of the past when things had gone well with each of these people, reestablishing each relationship at its Utopian best—with Olga, a curious financial camaraderie, a sense of real, shy warmth between them as they discussed figures; with Philo, the pleasure and relief of grievances discharged and received; with Wally, the simple insult of flattery—a writer need only be coaxed into loving himself, according to Twining: one's relationship was simply that of procurer, auto-erotic matchmaker; with Brian—and this was what made the theory impossible—the peak of their relationship had also been its cruelest point.

It was as if Twining had found that the best way to enjoy Brian was to humiliate the pants off him. For that's what he had done last night, in a way. He had gone and staged a rite of humiliation—as if he had remembered delicious scenes just like it, and had thought to himself, I've never been closer to Brian than when I had him on his knees; and had then thought, why, I'll do it again, I'll get down the whip and give him a smart crack on the bottom. Brian the underdog—Twining knew how to treat these wallahs, how to make them love one . . .

(And George Wren, what shall I do with him?)

His face was getting hot from the firelight and he pulled it back. Even Twining could not be as miserable as that. The captain was in fact being courteous and jolly with Olga, pointing out items, suggesting by his whole bearing that everything was all right . . .

Next question: Why had Olga and Philo rebelled if he treated them so well? (And why would Brian have rebelled, if he enjoyed being treated so badly?) Well, maybe they sensed that Twining was catering to their weaknesses, and was destroying them that way: or maybe Twining was fundamentally wrong about them. Whatever it was, they seemed happy now, after a whiff of independence, to go back to the old treatment. A Twining kind of love.

The room was muggy like all the other rooms—Olga had the heat up as well as the fire—and George was woozy from tea and cakes, absent-mindedly consumed. He found it difficult to shape his own policy, difficult to take his eyes off the snake charmer. Objectively Twining was pretty foul, and yet he was so pleasant about it—not just *seemed* pleasant, *was* pleasant about it—that George couldn't even make up his mind about that. Olga, Brian, Philo were not fit to run a magazine: then why not "handle" them? why not destroy the small independence bacteria that made them so discontented? (Put like that of course, one's liberal rhetoric cried out against it. Independence, rah rah rah. But perhaps it could be put another way.)

He took another cup of tea, in lieu of trying to decide. He couldn't hope to describe to an outsider—to Matilda, say—how different it all seemed when you actually knew the people. "The trouble with you chaps is that you don't visit one another's houses. You don't play enough golf or make the proper ham sandwiches. I've been thinking about those things a good deal lately: while I was out on the Coast . . ."

The really intriguing question was this: If he uses this routine for Olga, and that routine for Philo, and the other for Brian and Wally—what is he going to do with Fritz?

Bastard or not, that was definitely worth waiting for.

They left Olga on a tide of good will. Her pleasantness with George seemed a symbol of capitulation—as if her hatred of him was bound up with her independence from Twining. She seemed a lesser person in peace than she had in war.

It was an awkward time, late afternoon, dark, cold—a bad time of day to start something new. The trees on Olga's street were stripped clean. Let's go home and forget about Fritz.

Twining also seemed tired, depleted. He paused by the door of the car, as if in real doubt: perhaps he was measuring his strength, dribbled away in these confrontations, against Fritz's, dribbled away in waiting. Was Fritz a nervous man? The commander appeared to give a small nod, as if satisfied on that point, and lowered himself into the car.

"I think the best plan is to take a short nap at my hotel, and then tackle Fritz over dinner. I got into the habit of taking naps while I was in California . . ."

"You want me to ring him?"

"Would you mind awfully?"

"Not at all. You want me to come to dinner too?"

"But of course, naturally."

"I guess I'm your principal source of information, right? You need me to keep them honest?"

"George," said Twining sadly, "have I really conducted these little meetings in that spirit? As legal proceedings? I'm afraid you've got the wrong idea altogether."

"I admit I find the meetings hard to classify."

Twining laughed at this. "Now let me see," he rubbed his chin, "I was most amused by your descriptions of Fritz's Lucullan banquets—I had pictured him as the more austere type of reformer—so I suppose we'd better choose a restaurant up to his standards."

George pulled on his headlights. This suddenly changed the time of day, made it a *good* time to start something. So Twining was getting nasty at last—that was more like it. No crapping around, no more psychology. Real blood.

The commander went up to his room for his nap and George rang Fritz.

"Have you any idea what the old bastard wants?" Fritz sounded tense but excited.

"Beats me to hell," said George. "I've been with him all day, and I still don't know what he's up to."

"Whose side are you on, George? Never mind, I don't want to know. Just tell me this—does he want me to bring Harriet? I've got her right here."

So that's where his confidence came from. Screwing gold. This might turn into a pretty good match at that.

"He suggested Le Pavillon—is that all right with you, old boy?"

There was a pause at the other end. "It's a long way from Schrafft's, I'll say that much."

"Or you can make it the Four Seasons if you prefer. Or—"

"You decide, George. I'm awfully busy right now."

George went and sat in the lobby. He found himself wondering whether Twining wasn't trying to cram all his business into one day because, like Brian, he didn't want to leave it hanging over Sunday; perhaps he didn't trust his own nerves.

And what about his heart? How much strain could that take? If Fritz put up unexpected resistance, Twining might just clutch his chest and crumple. George's picture of him permitted this now; there was something older and frailer about it. If things went badly, if Fritz refused to bow, Twining might begin to sweat: like an old man trying to impress a girl—

You're not so hot, Twining, you're really not—he found himself almost talking out loud. He had seen Twining in action all day, and seen how cheap the tricks were. Twining had never met anyone his own weight, that was all. (He had made sure of that when he hired the staff, hadn't he?)

But Fritz, immersed in Gold, up to his elbows in Power, all afternoon—this could be another story. Real potency vs. sham. This could be a contest. It was, George thought for a moment, a little like Russia fighting China; he hoped they both lost, in a way. On the sporting level, they deserved each other.

. . . Yet now that he wasn't with the arrogant old bastard, that curious vision that had prompted him to write the letter returned to him in odd flashes. He saw this older version of Twining slumped on the edge of a bed in real defeat, his face gray, broken, emptied of force; he saw him on his knees, in his shorts, trying to pray; he saw him gasping at the dinner table, while Fritz laughed at him. On *that* level it would be quite terrible if he lost.

Twining himself cut across these thoughts; he stood in front of George's chair saying, "Wake up, George," and he didn't look old and weak, but spruce and jaunty and quite young. "What are the plans?" he asked cheerfully.

"Fritz is meeting us here at half past seven. Then we can decide."

"Capital, capital." It was almost half past seven now.

What the hell, it was only a dinner. Nothing very terrible was going to happen at a dinner—a dinner, furthermore, for three editors of a minor magazine of opinion. You had to know the people, Matty, to understand how trivial it really was.

7

"Evening, Gilbert."

"Good evening, Fritz."

"How's the heart?"

"It seems to have recovered."

Fritz was also turned out very smartly, as if for a fashion contest. He had discarded his daytime bow tie, and looked rather more solid than usual. Twining stood silently gazing at him for a moment, but Fritz didn't dither: he smiled easily back, a replica of Twining's smile, and waited for the real Twining to say something.

"I thought we might just eat here, at the hotel. The cooking is quite decent—although I gather from George that you're accustomed to something rather better."

Fritz let his smile out at the corners. "We've had a couple of blowouts, yes, George and I—so George has told you about that, has he?"

Good old George. Making out his little report. They both looked at him with amusement. It was the first time he had been brought into the action, and it wasn't a hell of an auspicious debut.

"I guess I can manage to rough it here," said Fritz.

"Capital."

They trooped into the dining room. When the jumbo menus arrived, Twining said, "Don't stint yourself," and Fritz said, "I won't," and he ordered snails, vichyssoise and tournedos. And he said, "I see they have wild strawberries for dessert."

Twining smiled benignly. "And how are *you*, Fritz? You're looking quite pleased with life. Something must be agreeing with you. All that rich food . . ."

"Yes, things have been going pretty well." He paused. "I saw Polly while you were away."

"Oh, yes?"

"It must have been a blow for her. Your getting sick, I mean."

"Yes. I fear so."

"I took her to lunch."

"That was thoughtful."

They drank their martinis and Fritz ordered another one.

"What are your plans now, Gilbert?"

"I'm not quite sure. It depends."

"Depends?"

"Yes."

"On what?"

"On a number of things."

The meal seemed to go awfully slowly, and Twining talked about everything except the magazine. George got nervous, but Fritz chimed in good-humoredly enough. Twining's small talk was so incredibly small that you had to concentrate to follow it. He talked about a curious tribe of Indians living in northern California, about stucco architecture, about the magnificence of the redwoods. Even Fritz seemed to weaken after a while, under this torrent of inconsequence.

And then to George's amazement, Twining called for the check, and said, "I must make an early bed. I'm not used to being on my feet all day."

Fritz had been trying to signal the waiter himself for a glass of brandy. He said, "Don't you want to talk about the magazine, Gilbert?"

"Not tonight. Monday will do perfectly well."

"You're coming in on Monday?"

"Yes, if you have no objections."

"No—come in whenever you like," said Fritz.

"That's very good of you."

"I shall be glad of your advice. At any time."

Twining looked up. He put the check down and said, "I see. This is going to be tiresome." He signaled the waiter and asked for more coffee. Then he turned to Fritz and said, "Harriet Wadsworth doesn't own the magazine, you know."

Fritz smiled, more Twining than Twining. "That's what you think."

"Harriet owns thirty-five percent, isn't that right?"

"Yes. And Polly owns twenty-five percent. Or did."

"Did?"

"Yes, she sold them to me. Do you mean to say she hasn't told you?"

This was the moment for Twining's agony. George could scarcely bear to look at him. He expected the face he had been imagining, twisted, bewildered. But of course, when he did look, Twining was quite his old self.

"I see. That's very interesting. Actually, I haven't seen Polly yet."

"She needed some money for something or other—and Harriet loaned it to me, so there you are."

"Funny thing for Polly to do."

"Yes, it was, wasn't it?"

Twining smiled, quite unaffectedly. "Yes, that's very amusing. Well now, before we discuss this further, perhaps you wouldn't mind if we talk about some of the things you've been doing lately. Not the dinners, of course—I don't begrudge you those; if only you'd asked, if only I'd known you cared for that kind of thing—" he said lightly.

"Shoot," said Fritz.

"Now, to begin with—I gather, what we all care about is

the magazine. Is that correct? The magazine, and the things it stands for."

"Right."

"And we agree that personal ambitions are of little account, in comparison with this larger purpose?"

"Right."

Twining stretched himself. "Good—we have a base. Now, my interest at the moment is more to satisfy my own mind than to satisfy yours. After that, we can decide on a course of action."

"Excuse me, Gilbert, that sounds like a fascinating procedure." And more than ever, Fritz's voice was Twining's; he was picking it up just from listening to the commander. "But you understand that the key decisions have already been made. The transaction was completed only yesterday. Harriet has the stocks, and she wants me to be editor. (I was going to tell you on Monday, George.)"

"Thanks."

"We shall see," said Twining. "We shall see. But putting that aside for the moment—"

"Put it aside as long as you like, as long as you don't forget that it's there."

Twining nodded. "Now I understand, Fritz, that the actual editing in my absence has been done by Brian, is that correct? and not you."

"Yes, that's right."

"A pity. I'd like to have had a chance to judge your own performance. It would have helped . . ."

Fritz couldn't help looking slightly annoyed. "Look, Gilbert, you don't seem to understand—you don't have to judge anything. The ball game is over."

"As I say, I'm simply trying to satisfy myself at this point. We'll discuss the other question later. I find I have returned to a rather distressing situation, you know. I find

Brian on the verge of a breakdown; I find Olga and Philo desperately unhappy; I find—"

"George is happy," said Fritz. "Aren't you, George?"

"I understand your wish to keep things on a bantering level. But I think we really should discuss this matter seriously. As I say, everything seems to have deteriorated, including the magazine itself."

"Well, it was Brian's baby, not mine."

"Yes, you see, that's what disturbs me. You seem to have allowed Brian to get things into the most frightful mess, without lifting a finger to help him. This strikes one as quite irresponsible on your part—unless you have an explanation?"

"He wanted the chance to run things, he got it."

"But, Fritz, my dear fellow, I thought we were agreed that the good of the magazine was paramount. And yet you have allowed the most dire things to happen to it. Positively *dire*."

"He would never have been happy if he hadn't had the chance," said Fritz. "That had to be taken care of first."

"You think he's happy now, is that it, Fritz? If you ask my personal opinion, I would say that what you have done to Brian *alone* is one of the more wanton pieces of cruelty I have ever come across—and what that bodes for the new editor of a liberal magazine, I wouldn't care to say. But simply sticking to this one point, on which we have agreed, the good of the magazine—"

"Wait a minute, Twining, you can't slide over a thing like that, an accusation like that. Brian dug his own grave. It wasn't me."

"That's funny. I don't remember leaving him in charge. Do you, George?"

"Eh?"

"You know, Fritz, I sometimes think that people like you

forget what being liberal, being on the left, is all about. I don't care what your plans are for the world. If you aren't capable of personal decency—"

"Hey, this is rich," said Fritz, "this is pretty rich. We must ask your wife about this some time. Personal decency."

Twining didn't crumple, didn't even get peeved.

"I think you may regret that remark when you've had time to think about it, Fritz. It doesn't really help your case materially. Anyhow, be that as it may—the point I wish to make is not a fundamentally personal one. There have been many good editors whose beliefs were rather misty, or seemed so from the outside anyway . . ."

"Could you give me some idea when the lecture will be over? I have an engagement."

"But at least they believed in their jobs. They believed in their own magazines. To put it in the most temperate terms, they did not ask Harriet Wadsworths to write their drama columns for them."

"So *that's* it. That's what this is all about."

"That's part of it, certainly, yes. A certain rock-bottom pride in one's own pages—I can't conceive of an editor without it. Granted that it was against your policy to say a kind word to Brian—or Olga or Philo (and I must say I shouldn't much care to edit in such a chilly atmosphere myself—however, I suppose all that comes under the heading of 'giving Brian a chance')—I remain profoundly puzzled by your attitude to your craft. Do you believe in anything at all, Fritz? Yes, of course, that's the dreadful part, you probably have lots and lots of beliefs. More than I would care to admit to myself. But still, you allow your own magazine to be desecrated. I don't know, I really don't."

Fritz didn't answer this time, but he was far from giving ground. He sat looking stubborn, with the air of a union negotiator who is tired of talking.

"What do *you* say, George?" Fritz asked after a moment. George shrugged.

"If everything was as terrible as Twining here says, why didn't *you* say something?"

They both looked at George; he was in the action again, as inauspiciously as ever. No use explaining that he had been thinking about Death and such during the time under discussion. A real mystic keeps his eye on the ball. "I don't know," he said.

"I guess, from the things Twining has been saying, that you did say something to *him*. But why didn't you say something to *me* or, if that didn't appeal to you, why didn't you help Brian? instead of just farting around the place, taking notes?"

"That's enough," said Twining. "Let's not have a silly wrangle. I left a confused situation behind me. I did hope that my senior editors could contrive something between them. I see I was wrong. George has only been with us a few months. I don't see what he could have done. I asked him to send me a report, and he did so. If I have a bone to pick with George, it is that he didn't send me the report sooner. But I can see that he was in a difficult position. Conflicting loyalties, etc."

"Loyalties," said Fritz, "is very good."

George realized that his future at the magazine had just ended. The Golden Age that Fritz had promised him would never dawn now. He wasn't altogether sorry—but what a miserable exit. Scab, clown. Rotter.

"You won't believe this," said Twining, "so I don't know why I bother to say it, but I had actually reached a point of not very much caring *who* edits the magazine. So long as it is someone with a fair degree of competence and a fair degree of honor. I'm sorry you didn't have a chance to prove your competence at least, Fritz."

"You're right about one thing anyway, Twining. I don't believe you."

"Yes, if you and Brian had done a creditable job, we could have discussed the succession like gentlemen. And it might very well have gone to you. Brian is *not* a leader, is he? Even with your fullest cooperation, he would probably have realized that by now . . ."

"You were always big on irony," said Fritz. " 'Do you realize you could have had the job *without trying*, old boy? Fact. You needn't have killed all those people at all. I was just about to give it to you anyway'—I happen not to believe it, *old boy*. I believe I got it the only way it could be had. And I think it was worth it. A few bad issues, an embarrassing theater column—what is that, against years of excellence? I'm not a monster, I don't like to hurt people. But Christ, Twining . . ."

Twining smiled. "I didn't realize I was holding the magazine back from 'years of excellence,' " he said. "How little one does know. No, you're not a monster, Fritz. You're just a very confused young man. You've seduced yourself with trickiness. The obvious thing to do in my absence was to produce some first-class issues. But that was too simple for you—or too difficult for you—alas, we shall never know which. Anyone can talk about 'years of excellence,' but bringing out a good issue next week is something rather more difficult."

Fritz applauded sarcastically. "Thank *you*, Mr. Dale Carnegie. Don't you think I realize all that stuff, Twining? Don't you think I know that talk is cheap? I can supply my own truisms, thank you very much. If I don't start on Monday to improve the magazine—"

"It might be amusing to find out," said Twining, "but I'm afraid I know the answer already. I know an inadequate man when I see one. This thing about craft is important, you know. I shall have to oppose you, Fritz."

"Good luck to you, then. But I hate to keep reminding you, I already own the magazine."

"I thought you said Harriet Wadsworth owned it?"

"It's the same thing."

"Not quite," said Twining.

Fritz snorted. He had lost his cool at some point, in spite of obvious efforts to keep it. But he still had his shares. Twining began to stand up. "Is Harriet at your apartment, or her own?"

"Back at hers, I guess. Why do you want to know?"

"I'm going to call her. I think we should discuss the matter with her right away."

While Twining was out telephoning, Fritz sat staring past George. There was less than nothing to say. George toyed with the idea of explaining himself, but gave it up as hopeless. He had managed to do something indefensible without even knowing he was doing something slightly wrong. However, it finally occurred to him that perhaps this wasn't the first thing on Fritz's mind at the moment.

Just as Twining reappeared in the dining room, Fritz suddenly said, "Forget it, George. You probably had your reasons."

Twining came over to the table smiling broadly. "It's all set. She said she would be delighted to see us."

8

Twining gave the address to George, and all three of them climbed into the front seat. George braced himself for some more small talk, but for once Twining didn't oblige. He gazed mildly out the window, until it was time to say, "Here we are." Fritz was sandwiched in the middle, also silent. It took George a while to find a parking space, and

Twining took an intelligent interest in that, saying, "There!—whoops, sorry. It seems to be a church entrance."

When they got to Harriet's building, Twining greeted the doorman by name—and so did Fritz. Fritz talked to the elevator man about the New York Giants, and Twining passed. It was a funny old building. The ferns hadn't been changed in a hundred years, he bet.

"Gilbert, how nice to see you." *The Outsider*'s new drama critic swept toward them in a blur of chiffon; her apartment reminded George of a nineteenth-century stage set.

"Harriet, my dear." Twining kissed her so naturally that George wondered if he should kiss her too. Fritz stood back looking proprietary, but no more so than Twining. "Delightful," said Twining.

"Fritz told me you hadn't been well," she said. "I was so sorry."

"Yes, a slight heart seizure. The doctor says I'm perfectly all right now."

"Oh." She hesitated. "I'm so glad."

Twining and Fritz both moved toward the biggest armchair. "Sorry," said Twining at the last moment and let Fritz have it. He joined Harriet on the sofa instead. Fritz seemed to have been maneuvered out—but George realized that if Twining had captured the armchair, Fritz would have been just as much the loser. There was no beating him at these parlor games.

"I saw Nancy Fitzroy on the Coast," he said.

"How was she?"

"Very well, she's sold the big house, you know."

"It *was* awfully big."

"Yes, for a woman living by herself, it was just too much. She's bought a charming little house instead overlooking the bay. Perfect for her."

To George, this was just the price you had to pay for going round with Twining. He picked up a small green statuette of a cat and was surprised at how heavy it was. That was the hallmark of wealth, he supposed: the statuettes were solid, not hollow.

"Have you seen Pooky?" asked Twining.

"Yes, I bumped into her the other day, as a matter of fact. At the Met. She was looking marvelous."

"Was Fletcher with her?"

"Yes—looking quite wretched, of course."

"Poor Fletcher, how he suffers. *Tone* deaf, poor chap."

"Look," Fritz broke in pleasantly, "do you mind if we get down to, you know, business?"

"Hush, Fritz," said Harriet, "we'll come to that in a moment."

Fritz subsided, and the conversation resumed. Fritz and George couldn't possibly take even a small part in it. But surely it couldn't last for long. Fritz assumed a tolerant, slightly amused expression—Pooky and Fletcher. And Bubbles and Carpenter. And Tania and Philmore and Blessington. The Swedish maid brought them drinks, and then more drinks, and Fritz's smile grew perhaps just a little bit strained. It was, George supposed, like watching your opponent run off a hundred balls at pool. Unless you had practiced for years at Eton, a tolerant smile was probably the hardest expression to sustain.

"Look, dear, it is getting late," said Fritz.

"Quite right," agreed Twining. "We shouldn't go on like this. But it is such a pleasure to talk about friends, isn't it?"

"Yes," said Harriet. "One so seldom gets the chance." They gazed at Fritz, like interrupted lovers. Fritz looked appealingly to Harriet, but George could see that it was no sale. Twining had been sweet-talking her to death with these ridiculous names. She had probably fought like hell for the right to talk about them, and the ability. George tried to think of any name that he and Fritz could contribute, but came up empty. Fritz cleared his throat aggressively.

"Well, what is it, Fritz?"

"*You* know, the magazine."

"Oh yes, that. Fritz informs me that you've bought some of Polly's stocks, Harriet."

"Yes, yes, I have."

"I'm afraid that Polly and I have rather fallen out. But I'm glad she sold them to you and not to some stranger."

Fritz was doing everything now but using hand signals. George had no trouble reading the message. Tell him, dear. Tell him what we're going to do. But Harriet didn't seem to get it at all. She had slept with him all afternoon, but she couldn't read the simplest instructions.

"I thought you were much sicker, Gilbert," she said vaguely. "I didn't think you'd be back so soon."

"Well, here I am, thank God, fitter than I've ever been."

"That's nice."

Fritz looked away. He seemed bemused. He had played the ace and nothing had happened. There was a silence.

"Mr. Twining doesn't think you should write the drama column," he murmured, almost experimentally.

"He doesn't?"

"No, he doesn't."

She looked questioningly at Twining and he met her eye with suitable gravity.

"No, Harriet, I'm afraid you've been rather naughty about that, haven't you? I told you, you know—"

Her eyes were slow, wondering, but not, George suddenly realized, stupid.

"You're no good at that kind of thing, you know,"

Twining said gently, fondly. "I could tell you you were, of course, but you wouldn't really respect me for that, would you? I'm in the magazine business, not the flattery business. You know as well as I do that people with money are seldom told the truth. Many so-called friends encourage them to make fools of themselves—"

"You think I've done that?"

"Frankly, yes."

She frowned at him. Obviously she was proud of her drama column. Fritz must have thought this was real writer's-pride, and had gambled on it, but the hint of calculation in the slow innocent eyes was growing, crowding out the blankness. She wouldn't be here at all if she hadn't some streak of realism and a very large streak of suspiciousness.

"I'm no judge of these things," she said.

"It isn't true," said Fritz, "it isn't true at all." He looked pleadingly at Harriet—stand up for your own column, for pity's sake.

Twining turned to him, with the full force of his amusement. "Come now, Fritz. You don't really mean that. You're a professional. Harriet's a wonderful girl, and we all love her dearly—but a drama critic, dear me, no."

Fritz lowered his eyes. "Who are you, God? What makes you so sure of everything?"

"The barest professional competence, old boy. You know I'm right, of course—that's why you're arguing so feebly. Harriet isn't a fool, you know—far from it. She has the sense to respect professional opinion in any field, if it's honestly given. She knows that it's in my interest to flatter her, just as much as it's in yours; and she knows that I wouldn't be fit to edit a magazine if I did. After all, she is a principal stockholder, you know. She cares about the magazine, bless her—we'd be in the soup by now if she didn't.

And naturally she wants to know that the magazine is in good hands."

Fritz didn't look up. "Christ, Twining, you might be wrong."

George felt that awful instinct to help. "Are you suggesting that only an unpleasant opinion can be an honest one?" he said.

Fritz looked up hopefully. "Thanks, George," he muttered.

"The invisible man returns," said Twining. "That's an interesting point, George. And of course it may also be that I am totally blind, and that Fritz is exercising editorial genius. However—even genius must recognize its limits. I take it, Fritz, that you checked your opinion with Brian and George before taking Harriet's contribution—just to be on the safe side."

"I didn't think that was necessary."

"I see." Twining glanced at Harriet. "In case of two conflicting professional opinions, what does one usually do? Follow the genius, I suppose. However, purely for personal satisfaction, I'm going to ask George here for his opinion. We'll let George's opinion settle the matter. Do you agree to that, Fritz?"

Fritz paused and stared, like a baited animal. "Not necessarily. George is new in the business—"

"Well, we'll ask him anyway. Perhaps a fledgling plus an old duffer can balance one putative genius. Anyhow, I really should like to hear his opinion."

Oh God, thought George, is this why I'm here? Is this why he's kept me around all day—so that I can drive the last nail into Fritz? George tried to make the decision seem difficult, but the horrible thing was that it wasn't.

"I'm afraid I'll have to go along with Mr. Twining on this one, Fritz. What the hell, though—it's only one decision."

Twining smiled. "Thank you, George. I've always tried to keep *The Outsider* democratic. A valuable tradition. Now what about Brian, shall we try him? One duffer, one fledgling, and one, what shall we call Brian?"

Fritz seemed to think about this for a moment; then he suddenly looked tired, as if he didn't want to play any more. "Don't bother with Brian," he said.

"Are you quite sure?"

Fritz nodded.

"Well, what do you think, my dear?"

"You're making too much of this," said Fritz. "It isn't everything."

"Well, you're the one who brought it up, Fritz, not me. As if it was a great bombshell. But we'll talk about something else if you like. We'll talk about your conduct of the magazine in my absence—"

"We talked about that."

"Or we can talk about your qualifications for running a liberal magazine. Your conduct toward the staff—"

"Christ, Twining, you never let up, do you? We already talked about that too."

"Or we can talk about your rather shabby efforts to use Mrs. Wadsworth to gain control of the magazine. Luckily, rich people are accustomed to this kind of thing."

Fritz stood up, as if honor demanded that much at least. "I don't have to take that stuff. Harriet, do you think I used you?"

Harriet gave a small, weary sigh. "I really don't know what to think. I suddenly feel quite exhausted."

"We're keeping you up," said Twining quickly. "I'm so sorry."

She touched his arm and said, "That's all right, Gilbert. It's always such a pleasure to see you."

"Do you think, Harriet, do you really think—" Fritz

stopped, looking to her for one last signal. She patted her hair in a quite repulsive gesture, and Fritz headed for the door. Gilbert kissed Mrs. Wadsworth and George shook hands with her. Fritz stood in the doorway indecisively, ludicrously, as if he couldn't remember what the *Daily News* etiquette column prescribed for this situation. It would look silly if he stormed all the way out, and as between kissing and shaking hands—perhaps even the *Daily News* would be stumped by this one.

"Good night, my dear," said Twining. "We must have lunch together very soon. Perhaps we could arrange a game of bridge with Clarence—"

Out in the hall, in the small space in front of the elevator, Fritz said, "You dirty limey bastard." There was no room for a fight, and anyhow this was just verbal froth. The elevator arrived a moment later. Twining said to no one in particular, "I'm always amused, aren't you, by these chaps who say, 'Call me a liar, will you'—I mean, most of us are at one time or another, yet these chaps—well, you know what I mean." Twining was tired now too, although a minute before he had seemed fresh enough to go on all night, and his words became a little confused. "We'll let George be the judge again. Was that or was that not a fairly objective account of my learned friend's doings?"

"Damned if I know," said George bleakly. Fritz's "doings" hadn't seemed so frightful at the time. Yet as Twining summarized them they seemed deeply villainous.

Fritz didn't say a word to the elevator man, but Twining said, "Good night, Wilbur." And Wilbur said, "Good night Mr. Twining. And have a nice weekend."

On the way to the car Fritz tried to reopen the discussion, but Twining had nothing further to say.

"You played dirty pool up there," said Fritz.

"Possibly."

"I'll ring Harriet tomorrow and explain how it really was."

"Very well."

They passed the church entrance and George was reminded incongruously that tomorrow was Sunday. Twining's day of rest.

"Here we are," said Twining. "You seem to have collected a parking ticket." He detached the green card from the window wiper and put it in his own pocket.

They drove to Fritz's place first. Fritz had taken the outside seat this time, and *that* seemed like the bad seat now. There was no licking it. After a while, Fritz said, "I suppose if you do win this thing, Twining, my days at the magazine are over."

"Suit yourself."

"Magnanimous in victory, aren't we? Supposing you do win, of course."

"I've been called worse things than limey bastard, and by better men. You're a good editor within your limits—any small magazine would be glad to have you."

"Thank you."

"Not at all. The only question is whether you can bear to work for me, after what *I've* called *you* tonight. However, perhaps you can't see anything wrong with what I've called you tonight. 322, 326, I think this is it." George stopped the car, and Fritz got out. He took a couple of steps that looked incongruously like dance steps and then looked back at Twining with a kind of calculating defiance. "Good night, George," he said. "I'll talk to you on Monday, Twining."

"Right you are." The commander stretched across the front seat and George took off the hand brake. "The hotel now, if you don't mind. I don't mind telling you, George— I shall sleep soundly."

XI

1

He did not sleep soundly, although heaven knows he was tired enough. The sweet satisfying sleep of the West Coast had left him the moment he hit New York; that is to say, he had known by the middle of yesterday afternoon that he wouldn't sleep that night; and he had known all day today that he wouldn't sleep this night; and he knew that to-morrow night wouldn't necessarily make up for the other two. His words were jumbled all right, his mind was fuzzy, but he couldn't sleep.

He got out of bed and watched the late Saturday night movie. God, it was stupid. He couldn't, really couldn't, go back to this strenuous life. The excitement had turned to sheer giddy pain by now. And the only cure for that was a pill. One pill tonight, two pills tomorrow night.

No, thank you very much. He believed in the magazine but he had absolutely no intention of giving his life for it. The doctor had said: no stimulants, no depressants, leave your heart alone. One would simply have to work out another solution. One couldn't face another day like today.

Guam was occupied. The kid from Brooklyn died a hero's death. The star survived. The movie ended. Twining got back into bed.

Life had been so gentle in California. Perhaps he could return to that. He had earned his rest. Must work out some sort of arrangement tomorrow. Too tired to do it now. Get some sleep. Sleep? Why, that's a marvelous idea, why hadn't one thought of it sooner? Little jokes.

Breakfast with George. The last interview and the most important. George was the key. He must have learned something today, he's clever and quick, and the lesson was broad enough. A rather hurried apprenticeship, but time running out and he's quick, he has an inner life perhaps— God only knows with Americans . . . Anyhow, he's all I've got.

At five o'clock Twining got up and took a bath. His body looked old and frail at that time of night, the skin pale and slack. He had aged incredibly, but the others hadn't seen it yet. The moment they did, his effectiveness was truly over.

Thank God his restlessness did not entail the smallest grain of lust. He felt as if he had been excused from that. He had done his best, he would not be asked to try again. Tomorrow afternoon he was going out to see Polly, but he wouldn't have to woo her back. Reconciliation was blessedly out of the question. She had sold her shares and that was that. He wondered if she would feel sheepish. "My dear—Harriet Wadsworth?"

The bath made him a little sleepier. The taps stood out

queerly like objects in a dream. If he ran much more hot water in, he might have a stroke, and that would be the end of that. He turned off the water and gazed mesmerically at the tiles. Hotel bathtubs were, mercifully, too small to drown in. Perhaps there was an ordinance of the health department to that effect. He managed a modest doze.

George looked as if he hadn't slept much either. Twining felt the comradeship that comes from sitting up all night with someone. "Ah, George," he said. They straggled into the hotel dining room, which was almost empty, and quiet as a church for Sunday morning. George's collar stuck up aggressively at the back, and it was entirely possible that he hadn't shaved.

Twining yawned and said, "Lord, I'm sleepy." The breakfast menu was almost as enormous as the dinner one. Combinations of sausages and pancakes, eggs and pancakes, sausages and eggs filled the expanse.

George just ordered toast and coffee.

"I suppose you're in a hurry to get back to your wife?"

George nodded.

"How is Matilda, anyway?"

"She's O.K."

"And the little boy?"

"Fine."

"You know, I've never met your wife."

"You must come out some time."

"I'd love to."

That was always the end of that. Twining had never been able to wangle a precise invitation out of George. Nor had the Wrens ever accepted an invitation to his place. George had come alone once, and been unable to make it on two other occasions. It was one of life's minor puzzles.

It appeared that George was one of those people who had

trouble talking before breakfast. Twining approached the problem patiently.

"I've been so busy talking to everyone else," he said, "that I haven't had a chance to talk to *you*, George. How are things in general?"

"Fine." George shifted restlessly as if someone was sitting on the edge of his coat, and looked at his watch. "Look, Mr. Twining, I don't want the 'treatment.' O.K.? It takes too long, for one thing, and I doubt if I'm up to it, for another."

This was odd. "George, are you all right? I'm afraid I don't quite follow you."

"I haven't time for games. I want to get out to Pennsylvania in time for lunch. My wife is out there."

"With her parents?"

"Yeah, and they're fine too."

Twining smiled. "Yes, I suppose that's how it must look to you. As if I'm 'giving everyone the treatment.' I suppose I am, in a way. Still, it isn't as simple as all that, you know. I don't lie awake devising stratagems. I do lie awake, of course—"

George looked at his watch again, and Twining said, "If you're really in that much of a hurry, perhaps we'd better postpone this conversation until next week. I have a number of things to discuss with you, and I'm afraid they may take a little time."

George deliberated a moment. Then he said, "No, let's get it over with. Only no fancy stuff, please, and keeping the main points uppermost. O.K.?"

"Very well. But first, tell me, George—do we have to be *quite* so tense about it? I'm so tired of tense discussions . . ."

"You call this getting to the point?"

"Do try to relax a little, George, I beg you. I almost have

a feeling that you have deliberately steeled yourself to say something—possibly something unpleasant—and that you'll lose your resolve if the conversation takes a friendly turn."

"Maybe that's it."

"It's depressing, if so. I had expected better of you. There is no reason why you shouldn't say whatever is on your mind without striking fierce attitudes—"

"I'm sorry, I didn't go to Cambridge."

Twining sighed. "Perhaps we *had* better postpone it," he said. This was the most tiresome development yet. George was behaving like an absolute child. He couldn't believe his ears.

"What I mean to say is this," said George. "I really don't know any other way to deal with you. If I get into a fencing match with you, I'll wind up on the floor with the others. I've seen you at work, remember? I know that you can talk the ass off anyone in the house."

"Thank you for the pretty words."

"Fritz, Brian—you just talked the poor bastards dizzy, that's all. Your victories are verbal, that's all they are."

"In our profession, we don't necessarily make light of such victories," murmured Twining—but George ignored this.

"It's the goddamn *small* talk that does it, isn't it? The conventional weapons. By the time you get to the point, they've forgotten what the hell you're talking about."

"Excuse me, George, but I seem to have forgotten what the hell *you're* talking about."

"O.K., to sum up. I'm sorry if I seem to be acting suspicious, but after watching the whole staff being goosed methodically . . ."

Twining shook his head sadly. "You Americans always fall back on toughness, don't you? In a moment you'll be asking me to settle this outside."

"It might be an idea."

"The funny thing is, you don't even know what I'm going to say, do you? It might be something rather nice."

George said in a dreamy voice, "You know, I'm suddenly very tired of sitting in restaurants and diners and bars, eating and drinking and talking. Do you ever get that feeling?"

Twining smiled and said, "What is supposed to be the answer to that? Well, I suppose we don't *have* to sit in restaurants. We don't even have to like each other—although I had always supposed we did—"

"I'll think that one over and let you know," George said unexpectedly. "I agree that it's not important."

Twining sighed. "You *are* in a mood today. Anyhow, as I said to Fritz last night, personalities are not fundamentally important. The magazine is what matters. I hope you at least agree with me about that?"

"Not necessarily."

"*George!* You're being tiresome! You wouldn't have written to me if you didn't think the magazine was important. You wouldn't have informed on your colleagues . . ."

"You call it 'informing'? I just wanted to clean up a nasty mess, that's all. I didn't think of it as informing."

"Why not call it informing? You've just said you don't want me to be diplomatic with you. I suppose that does put me at a sort of disadvantage. All right then. I believe you did the right thing, George—I think informing is sometimes justified . . . But it still . . ."

"Christ, this gets worse and worse."

"The trouble with you Americans is that you still expect moral decisions to be simple. You think it is possible to pass through life in total purity, whereas all of us . . ."

"Never mind about 'you Americans.' This is just the kind of bypass I want to keep off, if you don't mind."

"I don't mind at all."

"Just say your piece and I'll be on my way."

"Well, I just wanted to say that, despite the apparent deterioration in our own relations, which I trust is merely temporary, you seem to have become the next logical editor of *The Outsider*." He peered at George. "You look surprised. You may be thinking of your age. But you are actually a year or more older than I was when I became editor in chief of *The Watchman* in England. You have learned every aspect of the game by now, far more than I knew at the same stage. You have a resilient temperament, unlike our poor friend Brian. As for maturity, I think you'll find it comes with practice. And besides, you will have my help."

"Your help?"

"Yes."

George wiped his mouth and said, "I knew there was a catch."

—One never knew for sure with Americans. But surely that was a joke?

2

"You English are extraordinarily subtle and world-weary and accustomed to fine distinctions and moral nuances," said George. "All the same, I doubt if you'll understand what I'm going to say."

"And what are you going to say then?"

"I don't know in the name of God whether you're a good man or a bad one, Twining . . ."

"It's hard to say, isn't it? I think of it as rather a pseudo-question . . ."

"But you're not a good man for some of us to be around. To put it as politely as I can, I don't believe that everyone is improved by your company. I've been thinking about that all night, and that's the conclusion I've come to."

This was rather unexpected. "You don't mean Brian and Fritz, do you? You don't believe I've been a bad influence on *them,* do you?"—how extraordinarily American. "They're grown men, you know, George. I can't take *all* the responsibility for them. I think you'll find . . ."

"I don't know what constitutes a decent relationship between men—well, I see from your smile that that's a pompous, typically American way of putting it—but I do know that I was shocked by what I saw yesterday. After the fun was over, after I got back to Queens, I began to feel a little sick."

"Relationships, relationships. George, you know I don't talk that language."

"I thought to myself—he will probably disclaim all responsibility for those people, but then I thought, (a) who chose them? and (b)—"

"You know I'm a poor judge of Americans, George, I've told you that so often. I daresay you'll prove a better one. If there's anyone you wish to hire, I give you carte blanche: if we can afford him, that is."

"Wait a minute, Twining. I went over that ground between two and half past three this morning. I don't think you're such a bad judge of Americans. I think you're pretty good when you put your mind to it. I think you've got some good people in that office—"

"And I don't know how to handle them? That's entirely possible too."

"No, you know how to handle them all right. All too well. But just look at them a minute. Fritz must have been O.K. once upon a time. I've talked to people who knew Fritz in the old days. What the hell have you done to *him?*"

313

"He's a grown man."

"Sure. And Brian. He was a bright guy too, I'm told. Before you got here. And Wally Funk—I *know* he was bright . . ."

Twining yawned, "And what precisely am I supposed to have done to all these people?"

"That yawn looked like a fake," said George suddenly.

"Come now, George, let's not lapse back into that. Your argument is confusing enough without these childish outcries . . ."

George gripped the table, a naked effort at some sort of self-control. He really is capable of hitting me, thought Twining. Extraordinary people. "Look," George said. "It is possible to manipulate grown men, run them the way you run a child. None of your old world cant about that, please. And the worst thing about it from my point of view is that somehow, with your left hand, you were manipulating me too, so that I was *on your side* yesterday."

"My, my. I am the little Machiavelli, aren't I. George— you don't understand authority at all, do you? What you saw yesterday was the absolute minimum of manipulation . . ."

"I'll have to take your word for it."

"It sounds to me as if you're being a typical utopian liberal about this—running away from power, because it's a little dirty: leaving it to rascals like me."

"Liberal, liberal. Christ, what a stupid word." Twining chuckled encouragingly, but George seemed to be rather carefully avoiding humor, his particular pitfall. "I wouldn't mind having power," he said. "I just don't want to be around you when it arrives."

"You what? What was that?"

"I don't want to be around you."

"What *are* you talking about, George? What am I supposed to have done to *you?*"

314

"I don't know, for godsake. I see it in the others, I don't see it in my*self*. Whatever the hell strain in my character you play on—I don't see it at all. I know I'm being fucked up royally, that's all I know."

"George, you're making this up. This is pure hysteria."

"I see it with Fritz and Brian. It's as easy as a cheap conjuring trick—well, maybe you were doing it slowly for my benefit yesterday, so that I could do it myself when the time came. But when you do it to me—then I can't see it."

Twining shook his head in honest bewilderment. "This is fantastic," he said.

"I've actually regressed since I started working for you, do you know that. I'm like a damn child. I've gotten emotionally incontinent. I laugh over serious things, and then I turn round and start feeling sentimental over Brian Fine's waistline. I even feel sorry for you sometimes. Christ *knows* how you do it."

"I *don't* do it. I don't do anything."

"And one footnote to that, since I seem to be letting down my hair. Even my marriage stinks now, it never used to stink. I see my wife's faults like a god, and then I handle them like a child. Like you and your, *you* know. And I've gotten *facetious* about everything, like a damn schoolboy."

"And that's my fault too, I suppose."

"Well, you're in charge of the school, aren't you? And I know that nobody ever grows up in it. Little Fritz still plays his practical jokes. Brian is the class grind. George Wren sits in the back and giggles."

"I must say, you have an extraordinary imagination, George. I've never heard anything like it."

"Well, I don't especially want to go on talking about it anyway. I'm tired and I want to get out to Pennsylvania."

"Has it occurred to you that this whole thing might be an invention?"

"Oh, sure." George yawned. They had had three cups of coffee each, but it wasn't keeping them awake. "My soul probably isn't worth much, but I want to save what's left of it, if you'll excuse the impossible, philosophically meaningless expression," he said.

"I'm sorry, I just don't know how to think in those terms," said Twining. "It sounds like purest fantasy to me, but, who knows, perhaps on some level of meaning, it has some sort of truth. But what difference does it make? Our job is to put out a magazine. Our mythic relationships have no bearing on that. The truth is that you people simply paralyze yourselves . . ."

"Yeah, I told you you wouldn't see it." George started to rise.

"Wait. Wouldn't see what, for heavensake?"

"That you personally have some responsibility for these lousy people. That the reason they can't put out a magazine without your help is you." He slumped. "I'm sorry, I can't express it."

Twining stood up too, as if they had reached that part of the service. "You slept badly, and you had a lot of wild thoughts."

"Well, *that's* true."

"You still see everything in the colors of nightmare. It isn't really like that. It's just an office, you know. Green paint, secretaries, in-trays and out-trays. Three editors of varying characters and abilities. Your own temperament changing as you grow older. Learning to handle this. Learning to go on working as if it was nothing worse than a bad cold. That's truth, George. That's truth you can use. The rest is bad dreams.

"And even"—he tapped George's lapel—"if what you say is true, and even if it is important, you're now in a position to *change* it—"

"With your help."

"I'm afraid so, yes, George. You will need *some* help. Is that really so terrible?"

"Yes," George said. They stood next to the table, and Twining suggested that they sit down again for a moment, but George declined. He had a stary look, like a man with sunstroke. "I have a feeling," said Twining, as if to make one more appeal to his humorous side, "that you are about to assert your integrity. All Americans reach this stage sooner or later." George's expression did not alter, did not even acknowledge. "You want to make a big gesture, and at the moment the biggest gesture would be simply to renounce the whole thing, to storm out. Storming out, for whatever reason, has moral stature, and Americans cannot resist moral stature . . ."

George suddenly seemed to wake up. "Hey, is that how you do it with me? *Jokes?*" He gave a sudden, startled laugh. "I'll be goddamned," he said.

"George, what *are* you talking about?"

"Listen, Twining, there's no reason why we shouldn't part on good terms. I'm not the man for the job. Let's just leave it at that. You're really an extraordinarily bad judge of Americans, old boy, me included. I'd get to the office too late every day, the blooming place would be closed by the time I arrived."

He shook hands warmly, and then Twining was just standing there, wondering what the blazes had happened. He could make no sense of it at all. An astonishing performance. Perhaps George *was* a little unbalanced. One made all allowances for American psychiatry-mongering, but this was really too much.

He sat down and ordered yet another cup of coffee, although his heart wouldn't like it. He was honestly perplexed. To be told, after all these years of muddling and improvising, that he had been planning and scheming all the time—well, it was all raving nonsense, of course. And rather nasty-minded nonsense at that. It was bad enough having no sense of reality: but these people's sense of *un*reality was so unpleasant. It left a slightly acrid taste in the mouth.

A narrow escape, in a way. George would not have been suitable, would he? Besides being rather a foolish young man, he had not carried off his big scene with much distinction. The tough-guy role didn't suit him very well. It emphasized his essential adolescence. His coat collar had remained sticking up right through the conversation . . .

The fact was that these people were all too desperately self-important. You would suppose they had accomplished something, or had some special talent. It was rather touching. And they made such heavy weather of their psyches. As if anyone cared . . . Thoroughly difficult people altogether.

The situation was now decidedly sticky. He would simply have to devise a new plan. He had made the thoroughly American mistake of banking on George because he was young. So many promising young people over here—but they all turn into Fritz and Brian eventually, don't they? (Fancy blaming me for that. As if you couldn't find that pair in every office in the land.) George has just begun to turn. Into some sort of cheap, deluded middle age.

He made a face at middle-aged America. Felt for a moment grotesquely youthful. He hadn't done too badly this weekend, for a man on his last legs . . . Now as to plans: Fritz would certainly be in on Monday. So would Brian. Fritz had shown some character last night. (He had done better than George at least.) His attitude was, of course, deplorable, but he was, by American standards, a realist of sorts. He might become a good editor out of simple self-interest. One had seen it happen before. And perhaps he had learned some sort of lesson last night—Polly thought well of him, and Polly was a good judge of the simpler sort of personality.

Well, for the moment it was either Fritz, with a weather eye kept on him, or Brian, properly backed up, and with me to lean on if necessary. People of distinction were rare in any organization, one simply had to make do . . . Planning was still exhilarating, it was still the thing he did best—but already his heart was beginning to thump, and he knew that he musn't plan any more for now. The excitement musn't get a grip. Tiresome. He adjusted the tip and stood up. He didn't know what sort of nap he would manage on four cups of coffee, but he'd better try, before taking the train out to Edgemont to see Polly for perhaps the last time.

3

A nap was a bad idea. If manners, consciousness, speech were his element, semiconsciousness and confusion were George's. In the kind of high-strung, rasping doze that followed from too much coffee, George's insane accusations took on a certain plausibility: yes, he had indeed kept George a boy, for reasons that were now quite clear to him: so clear that he didn't bother to put them into words. Of *course,* one had wanted to keep George a boy, it was the only thing to do with George. It wasn't so much that words and reasons were out of his reach as that they were splendidly unnecessary.

He half woke several times, and then wanted words and reasons very much indeed. But all he could remember then was this purring certainty on the point. One needed a boy about the place. A boy wonder. To handle matters as only a boy could. Brian and Fritz were different, they were children by choice. Brian was the fattest lad in the class, the sort who ate too much to deaden the misery of being fat. Fritz was an incurable tease with a dull anxious little core. No need to worry—neither of them would ever grow an inch at Twining's School.

But perhaps George—Twining woke all the way, and all the foul staleness of daytime sleeping in New York descended on him. His head ached in that special queer way. If he hadn't known better, he would have supposed that he had flu. He went into the small bathroom and washed his face.

The morning's conversation had made a deeper impression than he would have supposed. It had dictated the terms of his shallow dreaming—too precisely, of course. He had never seen Brian or Fritz or anyone as schoolboys until George had suggested it.

Where Americans made their mistake (and perhaps he should stop saying that sort of thing, it must be tiresome for Americans: one had grown careless in some of these respects)—anyway, where Americans made their mistake in this psychiatry business was in allowing too much weight and depth to these fantasies. He lectured his own slightly bored reflection in the glass. It was all very well to call dreams the truth, and waking the dream, but dreams themselves were so feckless and unreliable, anything could set them off. Four years ago, he remembered dreaming exactly the opposite—dreaming that he was a schoolboy and that Brian and Fritz had taken down his trousers and were beating him insensible with a cricket bat. That kind of thing was nasty enough to attract certain types, but it was also basically trivial. The mind picked up some chance remark of the day and made a picture of it. Sometimes nice, sometimes not so nice.

The world that mattered was the world of will and intention. And he wasn't going to hold a tedious debate with himself on the point. George could have his few hours of triumph during the night; but people like himself were lords of the daylight. George's theories might (or might not) be amusing, but they left him uncommonly ineffective in real life.

He tried to turn his thoughts now to Polly. One had dispatched the George matter—it lingered in his system because he hadn't quite discharged the last scrap of dream. Washing his face helped, putting on a clean shirt helped. Polly was a simpler soul than George. George had imagination; he was "religious." He also wrote poems that Twining couldn't make head or tail of. Polly was a bright girl, but no poet. He had decided absolutely about Polly several years ago. Her ideas were a guide to what the Big Seven were thinking in that particular year, and that was about all.

Nothing to be alarmed about. Yet, as he began to stroll in the direction of Grand Central, he found himself feeling a mite less confident than usual. He wondered whether he could face another interview with anyone. He was mystified, nagged, disappointed by something. George had said that one was bad for people, and Lord knows there was evidence that at least one hadn't done them much good. One had, for instance, tried to encourage initiative—and look at the result of that; one had tried to establish personal friendships with each of them, and look at that.

It was faintly bothersome. (He couldn't remember having any of these problems at *The Watchman*.) He didn't feel like seeing Polly in this mood. . . . Still, it had to be faced, he supposed.

He went to the upper level and was told to go to the lower level: which restored one's faith slightly in the normality of things. He took the Sunday afternoon train to Rye and found it as empty and solemn as the restaurant had been. The first compartment he tried was too hot, with that rusty railway heat; the second had no heat at all. He settled by the window feeling slightly querulous. Really, something should be done about the Bronx. A perfect disgrace. He was slightly sick with fatigue. The doctor had taken him off smoking, but of course he would start again in a day or two. He would have to go to *The Outsider* every day next week and that would bring it on. He would have to follow up yesterday's work with an efficient performance. For the first time in his life, he wasn't absolutely sure that he could manage it. Even with tobacco.

Fuss fuss fuss. An efficient performance was a form of exercise that might easily be bad for the heart. He didn't want to die, he just wanted to rest. Why the hell had young George let him down? What was the matter with these people? He touched his coat pockets, where the cigarettes and pipe soon would be. Something had happened to him in California; yesterday's performance was from memory, he wouldn't be able to do it again. He couldn't go into that dreadful office and work in that awful clatter and get his collar filthy; he couldn't read galleys or worry about ascendancy. (Couldn't George see that? Couldn't Polly?)

Polly. Polly would be leaving in a day or two. (Marrying? Of course. A big, wholesome, dynamic, well-adjusted, progressive Republican. Considerate, potent and boring.) He would have the house to himself. He would have to get his own breakfast and supper, and that suddenly seemed like an immense imposition; having to keep house at his age. Oh, dear. He felt for a moment fussy, put upon. The mechanics of independence were such a trial; and the cold railway compartment was intolerable.

Of course, he could find a little comforter, one of those girls who came in eagerly from Wellesley and Barnard, looking for jobs and all-round fulfillment—but he really couldn't go through that again, could he? The cycle of hope, and disappointment, the awful scenes of failure, the usual explanations. Trying to salvage with the tongue what had been lost by the body. Altogether too tiresome.

Besides, these American college girls never knew how to cook, or make a bed properly. And that was important. They were athletic, demanding, but had no idea how to dust. They would never do for Captain Twining ret'd. You see, the captain likes his tea brought to him *really hot;* he also likes to stare over the tops of his spectacles at girls and receive a little respect from his juniors—all the things one despised in old men, oh dear oh dear.

He got up and went into the washroom. Railways made one feel so scruffy. Washing the face was more and more the answer. The train water was yellow and smelled of iron, but he dabbed his cheeks with it and felt a bit better. He wasn't as old as all that. Or as loathsome. Fifty-four. The skin on his face was still tolerably firm in the murky looking glass. He didn't really give a damn about his morning tea or other small comforts: that had been a brief intimation of the future, perhaps. Some day he might indeed sink into that beady-eyed helplessness. But not yet. There were vigorous years ahead.

All the same, when Polly saw him through the window of her car and gave him an odd look and said, "Gilbert, you've changed," he knew absolutely what she meant.

She got out of the car and then, rather surprisingly, shook hands with him. "How are you feeling, Gilbert?" "Quite fit. A little tired." She opened the door for him, as if he really was suddenly old and feeble. He had braced himself for something rather harsher, and sat bemused while Polly drove.

He found himself talking of local matters. This was his home as much as anywhere, and he still had a residue of interest in the place. Even on this gray day, the houses and lawns looked trim and pleasant. If Polly wanted to talk about something weightier than that, she gave no sign of it. Her attitude seemed rather neutral. Extraordinary, the way Amercians could turn one off. He supposed that he was now a legal object, a chattel, property, disposable unit: therefore, nothing to get excited about one way or the other. Something one put one's glasses on before discussing.

Has she met her new chap yet? Tend to think not. No sense of love in the air. Polly would make sure one knew, if there was any occasion for it. Love was a Very Important Thing. Second only to supporting your Community Chest. He found himself smiling at her—she was a good, simple soul in her way. If he despised her slightly, it was only out of self-respect. She was the scene of so many failures.

She smiled back, reminding him faintly of those people who pick you up and take you to dinner before the lecture. Polite, noncommittal people. In many ways, his favorite type of American.

They were home in the usual seven minutes. It felt splendid to be in his own living room again. He hoped that Polly would stay for a few days. He made drinks for both of them and then stood with her in the kitchen while she fixed lunch. One felt like getting into old trousers, puttering.

Without any conspicuous transition, he found himself talking now about the last two days, about Brian and Fritz and George. Polly concentrated on her cooking, so that in a sense he was both telling her and not telling her. A rather satisfactory arrangement.

"I must say I was rather surprised to find that you had sold your shares to Harriet Wadsworth. I daresay you had your reasons, yes of course you did, but I should have liked a chance to discuss it. Is this what you're looking for?" He held up a can opener, and she took it mutely. "I think we differ about Fritz. You remember him from the days when he was promising—I wish I could have a guinea for every promising young man I've known who's failed to make the cut-off. As we say in golf. George Wren, for instance." He supposed he was one of the few people who still pronounced it "goff."

"What's wrong with George Wren? He seemed quite bright."

"Yes, I thought so too. But I had a most extraordinary conversation with him this morning—and the upshot of it all is that he seems to be leaving the magazine."

"Oh dear. I'm sorry."

"Are you? Why?"

"Well, you're going to be rather shorthanded, aren't you?"

"Yes—but we'll manage. It's nothing to feel sorry about."

She handed him a plate and asked him to carry it into the dining room.

"You've been having a bad time," she said. "You've been sick, and now you've come back to find that all your associates have turned against you. That's why I'm sorry."

"Well, that's very fair-minded of you, Polly. It's true, I don't seem to be very popular, do I? One never knows why, does one? That's a very pretty dress, by the way. I meant to comment on it."

"Thank you."

He looked around him at the pictures, the wallpaper. He had changed all right; he was looking at things differently. He wanted to talk about the flowers on the table, and about the flowers in California, and so forth. He didn't want to talk about the magazine.

"I feel that we've all let you down, somehow or other. You deserved better treatment."

"Well, *I* would have thought so too. However, I gather

I've been pretty frightful myself, so perhaps I deserved what I got. George gave me a proper talking-to about it. I don't profess to understand." He wanted to talk about the chairs and the likelihood of snow.

"Fritz kept hinting about it, and I finally saw what he was getting at. And I told myself that it would be good for him to have a little responsibility," said Polly. "Of course I suppose I was really trying to get even with you."

"Is that so?"

"Yes, of course. I knew that Fritz was horrible, and that Harriet Wadsworth was horrible. But I had to have a noble reason for betraying you, so I pretended I was doing it for Fritz."

"The things that go on in you people's heads—I shall never understand it."

"What do you mean?"

"Well," he gestured helplessly, "all these motives and countermotives, and real motives and hidden motives . . . you never just *do* anything, do you?"

She waved this aside. "I knew that Fritz hated you, of course, but I had no idea about the others. If I'd understood that the whole crowd was against you, I promise I never would have joined in. I shall always feel guilty about that."

"My dear girl," Twining raised his hands in despair. "Don't feel guilty."

"Why not?"

"It's all so pointless. Feel affection or don't feel affection. Help me or don't help me. Those are real things. They exist. But 'feeling guilty'—I tell you, America should never have allowed all those German professors to enter . . ."

She looked at him directly, personally for a moment, as if she suddenly remembered why she didn't like him. But only for a moment. "I hate to see a man being picked on. I hate to see injustice. I think we all owe you an apology."

"Oh, please . . ."

"I do. I also think you're worth all of us put together, in some ways. You've stuck to your principles, Gilbert . . ."

Oh, God, why did they have to go on like this?

"You have your own kind of integrity, we don't have any kind at all. Well, I know you think this is commencement-day oratory . . ."

"No, do go on, if you like."

"So, all I wanted to say was, I've changed my mind about the divorce. I want to stay with you. If you'll have me."

It was surely the bleakest offer of the year. It was also so preposterous that he wanted to laugh. Polly was capable of intelligence. Even of humor. Couldn't she see how funny this was? Was everything, even marriage, to be a liberal cause?

Plunging below the joke, though, one found things not quite so cheerful. She had noticed that he was an old man, now, with a bad heart. Love, even his kind of love, was no longer an issue. She didn't care about the girl on the West Coast. Old men didn't count in this respect. There was nothing left to be jealous of.

An old man. That was no premonition, on the train. That was the present. The youthful moments would be the exceptions from now on. Polly had seen it right away, and had adjusted herself swiftly. She was now an old gentleman's nurse—he would be seeing more and more of the type from now on, he supposed. He recognized the style perfectly. She wouldn't even get angry with him any more, would she? His worst faults had become harmless crotchets. Fanny-pinching, the poor old dear. She wasn't involved enough to get angry.

At fifty-four, this was all quite patently absurd. One

327

didn't become old at fifty-four. The only thing to do was to fling her offer straight back at her. Laugh at it, and make her laugh at it too. This was absolutely necessary, if one was to survive. Surrender on these terms would be the end of him. He felt his hands trembling slightly and sensed that for once his face was betraying him. A rather alarming development. Still, not too late to reach back for his old manner, compose his face with a supreme effort . . .

He felt something give. Really, what good would it do? There was nothing behind it any more. And it was dishonorable to fake. And even this quick rush of thought was probably a strain on the heart. He must get hold of himself. He was making the American mistake of dramatizing, of mythologizing his own situation. He had been made a perfectly practical offer and it was now up to him to give a practical answer: "Very well, my dear," he heard himself saying lightly, "if you're game, I'm game." His face, he knew for a fact, was creased and tired and glad to have that settled.

He went upstairs shortly afterwards and had a really successful nap.

XII

George thought about Matty most of the way back to Pennsylvania, held her face up against the windshield. It looked pretty good. He hadn't seen it clearly for some time. He had used her as a prop in his play, but he hadn't really seen her. He didn't mind if she was angry at him, because he could fix it this time, and fix it for good. No more makeshift repairs, boy. "Yes, I told him off—well, I don't really remember *what* I told him. Probably a lot of crap. Anyway, it's all over. It's all *over*."

Inside a huge glossy soap bubble sat Twining and Fine and Tyler, against a background of green filing cabinets; and now the bubble began to drift away and get smaller and smaller until it was no bigger than his thumb. George would never have to enter that cruddy office again, never have to deal with those benighted people. The laureate of

The Outsider decided to dash off a brief memorial for the occasion. "Skewered by pinheads, down among the filing cabinets, take a letter, Miss Marplate, take it and stuff it; come hither, Philo, knight of the festering grievance, put your hand just above your heart—and flush it to hell and gone. Next please. Fatstuff Fine, clothed in buckram and old newspapers, product of a cruel and pointless joke, played by society upon itself." It was getting a little too much roll. "Fritz, the right shape for a villain, but woefully lacking in, how you say, star quality. Twining, beloved ringmaster, cracking his crumpet like a bullwhip in a cage full of (actually rather ferocious) mice." Well, needs work.

His high spirits were getting a little hysterical. He had tightened his nerves to concert pitch, and they were still twanging briskly. And driving fast conduced to a certain kind of allegro musing. But the major traffic was already heading back for New York, reminding him that his escape was only partial. There were no happy endings for people who had to earn their livings. Tomorrow he would have to return and start looking for work in another office, with a new set of Twinings and Finings, fresh Tylage, Philage and Sewage, and probably a less noble product at the end of the chain. There really wasn't a hell of a lot to exult in.

Mr. Frobisher would be glad to hear he'd left that radical magazine. A change in one's political and social opinions would follow in due time. George could easily imagine sinking gently into Frobisherism, out of a modest, unexcessive death wish; some day he would sidle up to the old boy and say quietly, "You know, sir, you're quite right, social-ized medicine *does* sap the character. A sound dollar *is* the answer . . . I've been dense about these things." There would be a certain fusty pleasure in agreeing with the old man—a very mild aromatic pleasure, exquisitely nuanced for the connoisseur. Matty, he supposed, wouldn't really care one way or the other, she would just move her little tent to the Right—wherever I goeth, she goeth, intellectually speaking.

This was a clearly signposted route to suicidal depression. The next milestone said, how little your opinions matter anyway, Wren. How little the world cares. You spend years and years perfecting your stance, taking the right attitudes to absolutely everything, and then you find that nobody has been watching. George Wren, prominent liberal; George Wren, rock-ribbed conservative; George Wren, Doesn't Know, Hasn't Decided, Isn't Sure that He Understands the Issues. It's all the same to us, George. Do whatever makes you feel best—the world will hack along somehow, whatever you decide.

It was to escape this very feeling that he had gone to *The Outsider* in the first place. The terrible aridity of working just for George Wren, just for a paycheck for George Wren, and then going home and having generous opinions about everything else. Getting heated about the race question, telling the neighbors they ought to be ashamed—and then back to George Wren Advancement for another eight or nine hours.

If he hadn't left the dining room so abruptly, Twining would probably have made a wry comment or two about this: "Have you considered the alternative, old boy? Perhaps you wouldn't find us quite so disgusting if you tried somewhere else for a bit—somewhere bigger and more enterprising, say. Perhaps the thing that disgusts you is humanity itself . . ."

So that was the road to depression. He decided not to take it. Irony was not absolutely compulsory, even for liberal brain-workers. He wanted to think about his wife, get that straight anyhow, and then see. "Sex, of course, is the great American escape," said Twining, but George didn't have to listen.

He busted the car to 80 along the turnpike, in his hurry to get to Matty and reality, and away from phantoms. He had lost touch with Matty, in the most literal sense, and they no longer thought and felt together. That particular magic could only pass through the flesh.

And face it, when they weren't feeling and thinking as one, their feeling and thinking was pretty second-rate. With the current turned off, she thought about furniture and trips to Bermuda, and he lapsed into liberal cant: his thoughts theoretically the more edifying of the two, but what a cheat *that* was. Ideals without life in them, without bone and blood. When we have been united again physically, we can talk about the future decently again; Matty's tongue will be loosed, mine tightened.

As he turned off the pike, it struck him that of course Matty wouldn't be prepared for any of this. Her mind had not been working on the same lines. She might be a little stiff with him, and this would soon repel him, however hard he struggled. He thought of buying flowers and then thought, God, what a silly suggestion. There was no escaping the frustrating scene in front of him. It was wrong to expect her to perform to order. Matty couldn't change her heart quickly: the best news in the world could not hurry her.

He stopped the car a hundred yards from the house and sat girding himself. The Frobishers would all be together in the glossy, quasi-farmhouse living room. Matty was one of *them* for now. "I've quit." "Oh. You have?" "Yes, I have." "Oh. Well, that's nice. Matilda's young man has quit." Scene shifts to bedroom. "Don't you understand—I've *quit*." "So?" "So." "Hush, you'll wake Peter. I don't see what having quit has to do with it. I don't see . . ."

It turned out that her mind had followed quite a different path. He found her sitting alone in the living room (her parents had gone Sunday-visiting), staring at the fireplace; and when she saw him she jumped up and came over and kissed him. She was sweeter than anything he had imagined, the girlishness of being at home suited her today, and they melted together upstairs as if it had all been decided in advance.

She talked in a rush for once, as if she had prepared it, and he had trouble taking in what she was saying. She said she was sorry she had driven him away with her impossible behavior, that her parents were impossible too, and that listening to her father had really made her appreciate George, that conservatives were awful, but that she had forgotten how awful—"No, I shouldn't say that, I just mean Daddy's friends who came over last night"—and that she guessed that what it was was that she was jealous of George's work and that she had personalized it womanwise onto poor Mr. Twining: it was a prolonged case of early marriage jitters, Queens apartment blues and average-housewife angst, but thank God George had been so patient with her, etc.

He lay there with her head on his chest, breathtaken by this concoction of correct thoughts. He wanted to tell her that she had been right the first time, right to personalize it onto Twining. Her instinct was dead accurate. These things were always personal.

But her attitude was so damn impeccable that he didn't really know what to tell her. Even down to hating conservatives—and then not hating them. Her family sometimes did this to her—made her 200 percent loyal to him. Oh, well—intellectual honesty wasn't the *only* attractive quality in a woman. He began at last to relate to her in a lazy way what happened over the weekend, caressing some sense back into her while he talked. "You were dead right about Twining. His cruelty to Brian the other night was simply beyond reason." Yet, as he recited, Twining didn't seem so bad again, he must be telling it wrong—besides, these moral judgments were giving him a headache; were they really necessary?

Matty's breathing began to feel awfully regular, and it seemed as if he was talking to himself—as he had been all his life. He shifted slightly and she came alert and said, "You mean he offered you *his* job? Editor in chief?"

"That's right."

"And you turned it down?"

"Uh-huh."

"George! Why? It sounds like a marvelous opportunity."

"He'd keep interfering, I know he would. I just don't want anything more to do with that man."

"George"—she lifted her head and looked at him with genuine distress. "That's neurotic!"

He had to laugh. He drew her face toward him and kissed it, still laughing, but with hopeless tenderness. She would never understand.

The Frobishers had taken Peter with them for the afternoon, so the Wrens were free to stroll in the countryside around the farmhouse. You could tell it had been a real farm not long ago—the faintest of farm smells hung over the flat fields, and there was a pond with a duck on it. The last survivor, circling aimlessly.

They walked arm in arm along a dirt road that ran like string through some nearby woods. Matty might have nothing useful to tell him, but she had the considerable wisdom to know it. It was no news to her that her verbal mind was hopelessly undeveloped. It could only say things like, "It's a good job, isn't it, you'll be famous, what are you afraid of?"—hopelessly inadequate to the situation. But her presence was a real help. If he had wanted a word-clever wife, he could have had one. The woods were full of them.

Matty's instincts really were exceptionally good. She knew that there was something wrong with Twining: she had smelled it from miles away. After that, any damn fool could work up a theory about it.

Matter of fact, he realized, Matty was one of the few intelligent people he had ever met who was no good at words. That was an asset to a man who had words enough for two. With a word-woman wife he would have had a whole different theory to contend with by now, a different reading of Twining and the gang, and no way of knowing which was the truth. Matty was a divining-rod.

"You're a witch," he said. "You have these curious powers."

"What are you talking about, darling?"

"You knew that something was wrong at *The Outsider*."

"No, I didn't. I was just jealous."

"Knowing when to be jealous is some sort of instinct."

"I don't know what you mean," she said. "I was just wretched."

"I don't know what you should do next. I feel awfully stupid," she said. "You were so miserable at C.B.S., and now you're miserable at *The Outsider* too."

"My misery was worth more to C.B.S. Of course it was probably better misery."

"Couldn't you just stay at *The Outsider* and not go drinking with Mr. Twining?"

An insanely simple suggestion which solved the whole thing—except that it wouldn't work. "It wasn't just the drinking, Matty. He has a very strong personality and it just louses you up, whatever you do. He has a thousand different ways. It seems to me it isn't right to be influenced that much by anybody, to *think* about anybody that much; I don't know how to put it, do you understand what I'm saying?" He had a way of simplifying things for Matty to the point where he lost the thread himself.

"Yes, of course," she said.

"I'd rather waste forty miserable years doing nothing at C.B.S., being nobody, wasting my talent, selling out, giving up, than have a relationship like that with any man."

Matilda looked as if she might be going to say, "I'm sure you don't mean that." So he said, "By Christ, I mean it, yes, every mothering word of it." Much too violent, as if he was really afraid of something.

And then suddenly he didn't want to talk about it any more. He just wanted to get back to the house with Matty before her parents returned from their parish calls, and to forget the whole damn business.

The Frobishers came back at six, looking a bit distrait. Peter had been crying all the way home, and Mrs. Frobisher had forgotten the various antidotes to this. She was still patting his back nervously as they entered the sunken living room.

"You came back," she said to George.

"Yes."

"Did you get everything done?" asked Mr. Frobisher vaguely. "What you wanted to do, I mean."

"Yes, I"—George almost said "quit" but decided that he couldn't face the explanations, or the talk about the future. Mr. Frobisher might have some suggestions. "Did," he said.

"That's good," said Mr. Frobisher.

They had a quiet supper. Little Peter Wren had taken it out of his grandparents; they chewed morosely, as if to say

336

the weekend will soon be over, that's one good thing. "He knocked over a lampstand," said Mrs. Frobisher.

"I'm so sorry."

"It was Cousin Harry's best china lampstand. He completely smashed it."

"Oh, dear. We'll pay for it."

Mrs. Frobisher sounded a little bitter, as if she was trying to get even for something. It must have been one hell of an afternoon. George felt a certain vague pride in Peter's performance. Cousin Harry would have to whistle for a new lampstand, as far as he was concerned. The old fag shouldn't get so attached to his furniture.

He smiled at Matty and she smiled back at him. He felt pretty great. *The Outsider* was already a bad dream. Tomorrow he would find a normal job, flanked by fellows called Jim and Ed who worried about their bowling scores and how their kids were doing, and who talked about their wives with simulated terror and disgust—no, he would surely be out of that bracket by now: up with the fellows called Scott and Perry who worried about crab grass and inflation—and what the hell, he wouldn't really mind working in a clean building for a change, with elevators that got you there in under five minutes and water coolers that shot the stuff up to a decent height, no more groveling for a little dribble of warm water; no more sitting under blinking fluorescent lights that nobody ever got round to fixing. He hadn't thought much of the superficial changes in his life, but now in the soft-chewing silence, he completed the record.

He didn't give much of a damn what kind of office he worked in, but it was better than thinking about the people again.

"Don't you agree, George?" Mr. Frobisher had begun, in his melancholy way, to talk.

"You know George doesn't agree, Daddy," said Matilda.

"Oh. I see."

The phone in the front hall began to ring. Matilda ran out to get it. Her voice sounded a little surprised, and when she came back, she said, "It's for you, George. It's Mrs. Twining."

"How did she know I was here? Excuse me." George stood up. Twining knew everybody's phone number, of course; and everybody's in-law's phone number. Result of a good intellectual background.

"Yes, what is it?"

Polly Twining's voice seemed unreasonably cold, and older than he remembered it. "Is that you, George?" she said.

"Of course. Yes."

"Gilbert told me where you were staying."

"Oh. He did."

"Yes." Polly paused again. "Gilbert isn't feeling very well this evening. He's very tired."

"That's too bad."

"Yes. I think he did too much yesterday. He's lying down in his room."

"Oh, yes?" There was something indefinably strange about this conversation. "Did he have another attack?"

"No, not exactly. I don't think so. He's just awfully tired, poor dear."

"Yes, well—" It hardly seemed worth a long-distance call, to tell him that Gilbert was lying down.

"He would have talked to you himself. But he understands that you don't wish to speak to him. So he asked me to give you a message."

She paused as if she was looking at an actual written message. "He says that he has thought it over and has decided that going back to *The Outsider* is simply out of

338

the question in his present state. He says he can't face the strain. Therefore he has no alternative"—George had never noticed that Polly had an English accent—"but to make one more appeal to you. He says that you can name your own terms, that he won't interfere in any way . . ."

George stood in the dark hallway rocking slightly on his heels, thinking of the old boy lying upstairs, fanning his tea, croaking out his last wishes. "George doesn't want to talk to me, you know. Can't imagine why. I've always treated him decently. Like a son, you might say." The old agonized Twining, crucified in a pith helmet and tennis shorts. "*Never* understand these people. All seem to hate me."

The idea that Twining might be *funny* was really the last straw. George shrugged to himself in the dark. *Funny.* The poor miserable bastard. "Put him on," said George. "I don't mind talking to him." Stuff Scott and Perry and their crab grass.

It didn't really matter who edited the damn thing, anyway, it always came out the same. At least he could get his poems in—or would he see them differently from his new vantage point? See them as what they probably were, the dying gasps of an overgrown boy? . . .

The next voice he heard was the worst imitation of Twining yet, shrill and rather fussy and not impressive at all.